Evil an

Evil and the cross

Christian thought and the problem of evil

Henri Blocher

APOLLOS (an imprint of Inter-Varsity Press),
38 De Montfort Street, Leicester LE1 7GP, England

Unless otherwise stated, Scripture quotations in this publication are from the Holy Bible
New International Version. Copyright © 1973, 1978, 1984 International Bible Society.
Published in Great Britain by Hodder and Stoughton Ltd.

English translation by David G. Preston
first published 1994 by arrangement with Les Editions Sator,
11, route de Pontoise, 95540 Méry-sur-Oise, France.

British Library Cataloguing-in-Publication Data
A catalogue record for this book is available from the British Library.

ISBN 0–85111–140–8

Set in Linotron Perpetua

Typeset in Great Britain by Parker Typesetting Service, Leicester

Printed in England by Clays Ltd, St Ives plc

Contents

Translator's preface

This study first saw the light of day in 1982 and 1983 as a series of articles in *Hokhma*, a French journal for theological students. These were translated into English and appeared in the Anglican quarterly *Churchman* in four parts in volume 99 (1985).

Professor Blocher then developed these into a book, *Le Mal et la croix*, which was published in 1990. This volume is a translation of the book, with a few amendments and additions for English readers. No attempt has been made to remove material of particular interest to the French-speaking world, or to replace it with equivalent reference to those whom Charles de Gaulle dubbed 'les anglo-saxons'. While it is hoped that this book will prove valuable to theological students, ministers and pastors and other Christian workers, it contains much that the general Christian reader will appreciate. Those who find some of the technical discussion daunting, particularly in parts of chapter 3, are encouraged to persevere in order not to miss the much more accessible material of the last two chapters.

David G. Preston

Introduction

While it is evil that tortures human bodies, it is the *problem* of evil that torments the human mind. It is a 'problem' in the original sense of the word, that of an obstacle thrown across our path, something that blocks our view, for it resists our unremitting efforts to *understand* it. Our intelligence stumbles and becomes irritated or dispirited, or perhaps even tries to avoid the real issue.

It is still true in our own day. At the start of the twentieth century, the French sociologist Georges Sorel invited philosophers to set about the great task of 'reworking the theory of evil'. Our ears still ring with the cry of artists such as Dostoyevsky whose Ivan Karamazov had protested passionately against suffering inflicted on a child: 'I would persist in my indignation, even if I were wrong.' Albert Camus, the intellectual idol of the post-war generation in France, never stopped reflecting 'around' evil, whether it was its meaninglessness, the absurd, in *The Myth of Sisyphus*, evil as a scourge in *The Plague*, or the hell of an accusing conscience in *The Fall*, his most profound work.[1] The originality of the 'New Philosophers' seems to flow from their hyper-awareness of evil in the world, particularly in those totalitarian states designed to ensure human happiness.[2] Nor have intellectuals been the only ones to reflect on evil; everyone comes back to it in his own way, as a problem that is intolerable and insuperable.

Everyone comes back to it, not least believing Christians. For them the problem of evil appears the worst; who has not heard, or even uttered, the protest wrung from grief: 'If there were a God, such things could not happen!' Or even the enraged cry of Mikhail Bakunin: 'If God existed, he would have to be destroyed!' The existence of evil appears to refute the existence of God. The German playwright Georg Büchner (1813–37) eloquently described the problem of evil as 'the rock of atheism'; once the atheist has taken up position on it, he considers himself unassailable. So believers look for a *theodicy*, a 'justification of God'. Jewish thinkers have attacked the task with great zeal, redoubling their efforts in the wake of the Holocaust of the years 1939–45. Nor are Christians evading the issue. Jürgen Moltmann, the most widely read of contemporary ecumenical theologians, inquires: 'But if there were no theodicy question, where would the risk of faith be?'[3] In his view, in the light of Auschwitz and Hiroshima,

Christian thought is authentic only where it is concerned to come to grips with the question of evil.

Our intention is to study the principal solutions to the problem of evil that have been worked out down the ages by those thinkers who have been professing Christians. We shall classify them, selecting the most representative examples. We shall aim to give the distinct solutions as presented by their most typical exponents; but in order to keep this volume within reasonable bounds we shall not consider particular variations or intermediate positions. We shall, however, respect the language and the logic of the authors referred to, taking every care to avoid any kind of distortion. We shall also spare no effort in testing the validity of these proposed solutions. Do they resolve the problem, or do they only appear to do so, by skipping or concealing some of the hard facts? Since they claim to be Christian, do they conform to the standard of Christian truth, the teaching of Holy Scripture? The reader will soon realize that we judge them all in turn to be inadequate. We must not anticipate our conclusion, however, but rather leave the reader to appreciate the rigour of the struggle that Christian thought is engaged in with the problem of evil, and to follow its fluctuating fortunes.

The background to the structures built by the philosophers and theologians of Christendom consists of the apprehension of the 'phenomenon' of evil, the key questions that it immediately raises, and the answers to these questions formulated *outside* the Judeo-Christian tradition. We shall now consider the main characteristics of these.

Evil: the reality behind the word

All languages have a word for evil. What do they include in this term, the antithesis of the good? With what are their judgments concerned? Against what are their opinions a reaction? An 'impressionistic' approach allows us to define the common, basic notion of evil. We ought not to despise the findings of such an approach, however imprecise they might be, for it gives us the sense of evil in its initial and emerging stages; and that is the sense of evil that is nearest to the living experience of human beings, still free from the sophistications perfected by the experts in their commentaries on, and doctrines of, evil. It has a much better chance of not distorting the truth about evil than have the systems that were built subsequently in order to exorcize the full horror of evil.

What do people mean, when in a real-life situation they use the word 'evil'? They are talking about its *unjustifiable reality*. In common parlance, evil is 'something' that occurs in experience and *ought not to*. It has occurred, but it is not what you would expect. Spontaneously and whole-heartedly we say 'No!' to it, like Jackie Kennedy when the assassin's bullet hit her husband by her side in the open car. At that time Claude Terrien commented: 'No, that is *the* cry of human beings in the face of death.' And we could add: in the face of the evil of death, and of the evil of evil.

As unjustifiable reality, evil is something that provokes *indignation*. And that reaction which we all experience allows us to appraise the idea of evil. The shame it brings, which is likewise universal, plays the same role. But other emotions allow a closer definition: evil arouses fear, rebellion, reluctance to accept it, and disgust; after that it is the object of remorse, penitence, confession and forgiveness. Two aspects of evil may be distinguished: evil endured, or misfortune; and evil committed, or malice, malignity and (in the full sense) wickedness. Indignation is particularly concerned with evil one has suffered and shame over the evil one has committed. And it is in fact that very connection which leads us to prefer the distinction of 'evil suffered and evil committed' to that of natural evil, moral evil and metaphysical evil (for example sickness, injustice and the absurdity of death). The former distinction is more firmly rooted. And moreover people blush at the evil of which they are victims, like the child beaten by its drunken father; and they also feel indignation against themselves for the evil they have done. Such is the effect of human complexity, depending on the fact that the individual identifies with the other party (even with his tormentor) and is able to become two in one in *self*-awareness and *self*-reflection. Nevertheless, evil remains that which causes indignation and shame.

The experience of evil in its primitive power is still expressed by the association of allied themes and by clusters of symbols. The unaffected words of daily conversation link evil with ruin, failure, loss, corruption, illness and aggression, as do also those works of art which strike a chord with the general public. Evil is *disorder*, it oppresses and is oppressive; and yet it is utterly empty, for the other figure used of it is *vanity*. All these elements combined might produce the anguished picture of a disordered wasteland swarming with large rats and emitting undefined threats. Everywhere you find the symbol of *night* and of darkness, all cultures endorsing the Latin saying *bona lux*, 'light is good' (meaning the light of life). The symbol of defilement is equally widespread, so much a part of the landscape that one can easily forget that it is metaphorical. It gives rise to a whole network of symbols, realized in purification rituals and reinforced by such memories as Pilate washing his hands and Lady Macbeth rubbing her hands in despair: 'What, will these hands ne'er be clean?' Even today the media speak of the 'laundering' of dirty money by certain financial institutions. The whole range of elementary expressions, without any careful elaboration, confirm what we noticed immediately: evil is 'something' which occurs; it is not merely 'nothing', as we know only too well. That is the 'positive' side of evil. But it leads to destruction, it represents lack with respect to what ought to be, it is failure as far as implicit or explicit norms are concerned. That is the 'negative' side of evil – evil as unjustifiable reality.

The three questions about evil

The first question that arises, once intelligence has got off the ground and left sheer feeling behind, is that of its origin, cause or reason. The ancient Greeks asked why there was evil and where it came from.[4] We could label the question 'logico-speculative', but must not assume it to be the prerogative of intellectuals and philosophers only. It is inseparable from the initial thrust of human thought, springing from the clash between the unjustifiable nature of evil and the need for consistency and meaning that belongs inextricably to the human mind. It is also born of indignation, which transposes it to the realm of theoretical reflection, however rudimentary that reflection might be – in other words, universally.

We should not, however, limit the problems of evil to the question of its origin. As early as the third century, Plotinus (203–270), the last great mind of pagan antiquity, argued for the priority of the question of the essence or 'nature' of evil. St Augustine (354–430), in his passionate response to the Manichaeans who had kept him enslaved for ten years, followed in the footsteps of the great Neoplatonist. He denounced as absurd all efforts to reflect upon the origin of evil as long as one does not know what it is.[5] What is evil? That is the first question, properly speaking. It may be termed 'metaphysical', since it inquires about the existence (or non-existence) of the phenomenon.

The most ancient question, however, seems to us to be of even greater importance. It is forgotten too often: 'How long?' The Assyrian suppliant cries out:

> How long, O my Sovereign,
> Shall my enemies look on me with evil eye . . .
> How long, O my Sovereign,
> Shall the *lillu* [storm-demon] come at me?[6]

The prayers of the Old Testament take up this set wording, as in Psalms 6, 13 and 94 and as in the lament of the prophet Habakkuk at the start of a short book devoted, no less than the drama of Job, to the enigma of evil:

> How long, O LORD, must I call for help,
>   but you do not listen?
> Or cry out to you, 'Violence!'
>   but you do not save?

> Why do you make me look at injustice?
> Why do you tolerate wrong? (Hab. 1:2, 3a)

Finally, the question of the victory of evil, a question that is both existential and religious, deserves to be called the ultimate question, if it is not the first. For a humanity that is overwhelmed by suffering (evil endured) and guilt (evil committed), that is the question that matters.

The three solutions of human reason

The human mind is so constituted that it can no longer remain at rest once the question has been implanted in it. Tirelessly it formulates proposals for an answer, even if that entails submerging the problem, in the absence of a solution, beneath obscure, subtle phraseology in order to mask its failure, as a cuttlefish covers its flight. It is even ready to provide solutions that merely paper over cracks, so gaining an illusory peace for a limited time. Outside the field of biblical revelation, the reason of 'natural' man, *i.e.* humanity without the special grace of redemptive revelation, has produced countless systems. In order to recall their principal directions (or, rather, misdirections), the three academic labels remain the handiest: optimism, pessimism and dualism. We all know the drawbacks of such simplifications, but we also know that they remain indispensable in any account of a subject that is so rich and prolific, and that they help in making an initial approach.

The first path, that of *optimism*, can claim to be of the noblest ancestry and to have been given the accolade of being wisdom itself. Wisdom, writes Etienne Borne in his brilliant essay on this subject, 'places man within a beautiful totality which cannot be other than it is, and the awareness of which has the property of removing the evil from evil, *i.e.* of excising what appeared to be unjustifiable about it'.[7]

Likewise, anyone who accepts evils that befall him as if they were not such, is said to react 'philosophically'. The implication is that rational reflection will judge the evil in such a way that it is stripped of its evil character. For the one who sees sufficiently broadly and sufficiently far, says the optimist, evil does not really exist: all is for the best.

This optimistic denial of the reality of evil takes on an extreme form in the religion of the Vedas, the wellspring of Indian thought, or in its strange American descendant, Mrs Mary Baker Eddy's 'Christian Science'. For the Vedas, all differences are unreal; the final, and only, secret is to be summed up in the words, *Tat tvam asi*, 'Thou art That', *i.e.* 'You are identical with the Absolute'; the diversity of the world and of beings is no more than an optical effect, a device that is deceptive (*maya*, a word connected with 'magic'). For such a system, the difference between good and evil is abolished along with all the others – that between good and evil in particular.

The two greatest rationalists of the Western philosophical tradition, Parmenides of Elea in southern Italy (fifth century BC), and Spinoza (1632–77), born in Amsterdam of Portuguese-Jewish parents, are only a very short distance from that position. For the former, Knowledge finds no room for evil, an irrational notion, in the full, seamless unity of Being. It is only deceptive 'opinion', clinging to appearances (the same Greek word means appearance, resemblance and opinion), that suggests evil, and Parmenides radically devalues opinion. For the latter, good and bad are not 'in things considered in themselves'; they are relative to our 'modes of thought', which we form by making comparisons.[8] Spinoza introduces the activity of the thinking subject, but he uses it in order likewise to reduce the reality of evil.

Modified versions are more common. The Stoics, after three centuries of expansion, dominated the Greco-Roman world at the time of the New Testament (*cf.* Acts 17:18). They provide the example of optimism labouring under great strain, incapable of overlooking evil, yet resolved to do so. For them, the underlying reality, or soul, of the world was divine Reason itself (*Logos*); this Reason is a providential fate which leaves nothing to chance, which links together *all* events, small and great, in its mysterious rationality. Human reason can have only one calling: to adhere to the divine-cosmic Reason and acknowledge its expression in everything that happens. So the wise will be happy inside the bronze bull in which the tyrant Phalaris used to roast his hapless enemies: in that trial they will recognize a good, beneficial link in the divine, universal chain. Certain Stoics, by a Herculean effort of willpower, seem to have achieved that, like the slave Epictetus who was capable of smiling even while his cruel master deliberately broke his leg. A rational optimism was also professed by Plotinus, mentioned earlier, the last great architect of philosophy in the ancient world. He celebrated the harmony in which evil finds its place: evil 'inevitably caught in the shackles of beauty, like a prisoner weighed down with chains of gold'; like every instrument taking part in the concert of the world, 'the malice of human souls has its place in the beauty of the universe; that which for them is contrary to nature, is for the universe in harmony with nature'.[9] Are we then to conclude that the mainspring of all art, of our striving after beauty, is the constant effort to deceive or to exorcize human anguish, as Etienne Borne suggests? 'The unreal light' of myth, 'the white magic of art', he dares to write.[10]

Clearly, optimism does not respect the spontaneous sense of evil which we have set as a benchmark. It suppresses it openly, judging it to be too simplistic. So it lays itself open to the charge of wishful thinking, by evading what it cannot accept. When its denial is one hundred per cent in particular, optimism resembles the anaesthesia produced by excessive pain (unable to tolerate it, the organism accommodates itself in order not to feel it) or the anaesthesia that accompanies certain pathological conditions.

Whereas optimism seeks to resolve the opposition of good and evil in unity, *dualism* by contrast hardens it and gives it a firm metaphysical foundation. The presence of evil is explained by its status as a primary ingredient in being. Reality is constituted and then governed, like two poles, by the two principles of Good and Evil. From all eternity these two have been in conflict: a conflict that can never end in peace but which, after all, makes the world go round, as the opposition of positive and negative poles gives rise to electric current.

Dualists in the pure form are rare. Zoroastrianism, the official religion of Persia from the time of Darius I (*regnit* 522–486 BC), is the most eminent example. It teaches that the Principle of Good, *Ahura Mazda* ('The Wise Lord'), is in eternal conflict with *Angra Mainyu* ('The Hostile Spirit'). The final victory of good is expected, but that is an obvious inconsistency if the two antagonists are equally ultimate. Mani (215–277), a descendant of the Persian royal family, produced a cruder form of this, known as Manichaeism; in this the two Principles have physical existence, and the world arose from the temporary imprisonment of part of the Light within the evil powers of Darkness. Making loud claims about its rationality, Manichaeism proved to be surprisingly successful in its conquests, the Albigenses of the twelfth century being an offshoot. It also had undisputed links with the kaleidoscopic Gnostic movement which threatened to engulf the church in the early centuries. The Gnostics hated matter, making it an intrinsically evil principle, and were dualists.

Mixed versions, in which dualism is mixed with optimism, are common. Plotinus retains a Gnostic element with his notion of evil matter in which human souls have become imprisoned. He is prepared, however, simply to exaggerate a feature that is already present in the thought of Plato (427–347 BC), who was a moderate dualist. What is wrong with the world, according to Plato, arises from the substratum of the tangible world, the *chōra*, the 'receptacle', a kind of wax on which is imperfectly imprinted the image of perfect Ideas. Even Aristotle (384–322 BC), despite great efforts to drive out dualism, and although he takes matter as an abstract principle which he would like to be totally relative, admits that matter is odd in its resistance to form – hence the monsters and accidents found in the sublunary world.[11] In modern times, partial dualism is found lurking in the systems of evolutionists in particular. They account for evil by the inertia of a mass that Evolution is thrusting forwards; this inertia is a basic fact which stands over against the progressive tendency. Charles Werner of Geneva, the philosopher-historian who has specialized in the problem of evil, ends up in this kind of position: evil comes from the dissociation in the human mind between desire (matter) and intelligence; the submission of desire to intelligence requires a long process of evolution. This need and the present degree of dissociation constitute, in the face of the divine, a second Principle, which is the cause of evil.[12]

Dualism appears to sharpen and aggravate one's spontaneous sense of evil. That is its instant attraction. But on closer inspection it becomes apparent that instead it corrupts and weakens the message of human experience. Not only does it pass over the aspects of the void and lack within evil and of the corruption of a prior goodness; it also has the effect of averting our indignation and dissolving our shame. Dualism takes evil as one of the pillars that upholds the order of what is; so one's indignation will be no longer directed against evil, but against what is – or, rather, against nothing at all, because what is more stupid and pointless than being indignant against what is? How can you feel shame about *Angra Mainyu*? The opposition between good and evil is transferred to the realm of metaphysics, which alters the nature of that opposition and thrusts evil back into normality. The Dutch theologian, G. C. Berkouwer, was right on target when he wrote: 'Dualism is only a cosmic excuse in metaphysical garb.'[13]

Pessimism generalizes evil. All that is real is basically evil. There is no need to delude oneself by going any further to find the explanation for misfortune and unhappiness. Listen to the mournful chant of the Buddha, in his famous Benares sermon:

> Birth is attended with pain, decay is painful, disease is painful, death is painful. Union with the unpleasant is painful, painful is separation from the pleasant; and any craving unsatisfied, that, too, is painful . . .[14]

Let us strive to loose all attachments and join ultimate reality, the Void.

Pessimists give the impression of being paradoxical figures, at least in the West, where they have been growing more numerous over the last two centuries. One of the strangest, Arthur Schopenhauer (1788–1860), went so far as to declare that the Will that constitutes the basis of reality is itself evil. He it was who made the breakthrough for contemporary irrationalism. The solution offered by pessimism is presented to us as the philosophy of the absurd expounded by Camus, and as the (almost) consistent atheism of the writings of Sartre. As admirable as it is useless, the courage of Camus's Sisyphus could not possibly have any meaning in a world that has none, which is nothing but dark, pitiful disorder. Sartre's major work of philosophy, *Being and Nothingness*,[15] appears to envisage only failure for that 'pointless passion' that is mankind. (Later Sartre came to believe in Revolution, and then once more had to change his tune.) More recent writers, in particular Michel Foucault, who affirm the death of man, following the death of God, seem to revel in living on the borders of nihilism, but their deliberate subversion of language and their praise for falsehood and lies do not make it any easier to interpret their arguments! The 'new philosophers' tend to confuse the world, every kind of 'mastery' and, in a way, all law, with evil; but they escape from pessimism by appealing to the transcendant Intention. This Intention reveals itself in horror and shows its character by its absence from the world.[16]

Pessimism goes a step further than the spontaneous sense of evil; it is generally agreed that it takes the reality of evil seriously. But is that really so? It is significant that the Void of Buddhism bears a very close resemblance to the Absolute of the Vedas; extreme pessimism coincides with extreme optimism. The Buddha, in fact, wished to reform and purify the old religion of India, not to contradict it. One of its most knowledgeable experts, Ananda Coomaraswamy of the University of Harvard, wrote:

> The more superficially one studies Buddhism, the more it seems to differ from the Brahmanism in which it originated; the more profound our study, the more difficult it becomes to distinguish Buddhism from Brahmanism, or to say in what respects, if any, Buddhism is really unorthodox.[17]

At this point one begins to suspect that, paradoxically, pessimism is not so distant from the denial of evil. And could we take literally Camus's conclusion, 'We must imagine Sisyphus as happy'?[18] Happy, endlessly and for no purpose rolling his wretched boulder up the hill, only to see it roll down the other side straight away? Yes, why not? After all, in the absurd no comparison is possible. And to that add pessimism's abandonment of the human perception of evil. It forgets that one property of evil is to mingle with and corrupt the good. Even the 'new philosophers' overlook the fact that evil is second: it is disorder, decline, the perversion of a norm that had already been set, the violation and corruption of a prior law. By making everything evil, pessimism cuts the nerve of protest. Protest has been made irrelevant. The pessimists of today are genuinely inclined towards indignation, over-much in fact; but they abolish any basis for it, and their zeal becomes, as they say, meaningless.

The proposed shape of our study

There is no need to proceed any further with our criticism of non-Christian views. It is generally accepted that the biblical testimony supports none of the three approaches already described. It maintains the truth of distinction, particularly that between the world and a God who judges the world, and thus it excludes systems that are optimistic, pantheistic or inclined towards pantheism; it asserts original unity and resists the temptation to make the devil a second god; it confesses a God who is good, the very God who is denied by pessimism. If we have argued that the three 'solutions' fail to do justice to the human experience of evil, the decisive argument against them is the witness of divine revelation. For this revelation has been able to bear witness of itself to us with the authority of Truth itself.

Against the background provided by this brief sketch, it is the 'Christian' doctrines – those that at least aim to take account of the Hebrew and Christian Scriptures – that we now wish to examine, before constructing our own synthesis of what Scripture affirms. We shall group the suggested solutions around three key themes: the vision of an all-inclusive order, the passion for liberty, and dialectical solutions of one kind or another. The 'solutions' produced in Christendom are not unrelated to the 'solutions' or pseudo-solutions fashioned by the 'natural' man. Straight away we shall observe the affinities of the first group (chapter 1) with pagan optimism; and there is no need to burrow very far back in history in order to find the lines of communication.

The second group (chapter 2) shares with dualism the idea of a causality that is independent of God, although the absolutization of liberty is a new feature. The third (chapter 3) corresponds to pessimism on one point, that of the presence of an original negativity, but at the same time it is connected with both optimism and dualism. These affinities may make us cautious and even suspicious, but they do not allow us to condemn this group for combining these disparate elements, as if it were guilty of complicity. It could be that the Christian ingredient combined with optimism or dualism might correct that very point that made their pagan options unacceptable. These close resemblances permit us neither to recommend nor to absolve; they help us to see the context of these proposals, but the critical task is not one whit diminished.

Weighing the arguments for and against is not the end. Our criticism must prepare the ground for building. Our final two chapters will attempt to construct an answer, using the data of Scripture. First we shall take its principal teaching on evil; then we shall address the immense 'residual' difficulty, that of the persistence of evil after the coming of Christ. From the cross there will spring light sufficient to illuminate even the darkest night.

1

The solution by universal order

To the angry or anguished question, 'Why?', asked by human beings confronted with evil, Christian thinkers had to find an answer. The one most often put forward, at least in ancient times and in the great periods in the history of the church, is closely related to optimism. Moreover it reflects the influence of philosophies that we have classified under the heading 'optimism', such as Stoicism and the Neoplatonism of Plotinus. The strategy consists of erasing or blurring the most scandalous aspects of evil, and choosing a perspective which appears to diminish the anomaly. It is rather as if the existence of evil and the goodness of God are the two lips of a wound that have to be brought together, and you must find as many clips as possible – the clips being in this case the rational considerations that suggest harmony. The Church Fathers who developed this 'solution' wished to do so with regard for Holy Scripture, certain elements of which they made use of. In this way they calmed human hearts and they justified God in permitting evil – that same God whom they traditionally confessed as all-good and all-powerful.

This line of argument, which is well respected in the church because of its antiquity and the calibre of its proponents, bears two characteristic features. They are to be found in the majority of forms and variants, if not in all. It backs reason in its power to construct and to classify, and in its power to comprehend, to grasp its objects together and link them one to the other. Evil as a phenomenon or as an event is included in universal order and contributes to it in its own way. Furthermore the explanation of the origin and the function of evil rests on an interpretation of the nature of evil that roots it in finitude. Every creature is finite, it does not possess being in all its fulness; therefore there may be detected in it a lack of being, the mark of non-being. It has been drawn forth from non-being, or from 'nothing' (created *ex nihilo*), whose print remains upon it indelibly. It is from that that the possibility of evil arises, in the eyes of the thinkers whom we are considering together in this opening chapter.

But is the solution, in whatever form, one that satisfies us? Is it clear and coherent? Does it do justice to the message of human experience? Above all, does it agree with divine revelation? We shall try to appraise it in the three examples that we take; first and very briefly Leibniz, who has already received more than sufficient critical attention from vast numbers of writers; secondly and less hurriedly Teilhard de Chardin; and finally the major example, that of Thomism.

The best of all possible worlds

In the history of Western Christianity, the very word 'theodicy', the justification of God, calls to mind Gottfried Leibniz. This version of the solution by universal order has largely benefited, or suffered, from the publicity given to it by Voltaire. Leibniz' proposition, 'All is for the best in the best of all possible worlds', recurs throughout Voltaire's *Candide* (1759) as a sardonic refrain commenting on the terrible Lisbon earthquake and other such disasters.

The greatest mind of his time, Leibniz (1646–1716) returned several times to the problem of evil. The mathematician who invented differential calculus before Newton, physicist, lawyer, diplomat, historian, theologian as well as philosopher, he was 'somewhat like the ancients', said Fontenelle; 'capable of controlling as many as eight horses harnessed in a single team'. A Lutheran and a forerunner of the ecumenical movement, he applied all the resources of his prolific and brilliant mind to the supreme problem. The *a priori* concept that he sought to defend was that God is sovereign and wise. From this he drew the proposition that Voltaire took up with such irony: if we are not to suspect the Lord of committing blunders or anything else unworthy of himself, we must suppose that for everything that happens there is a *sufficient reason* in the harmony that he pre-established. (Leibniz was strongly attached to the general validity of the principle of 'the sufficient reason': nothing exists or is true without an adequate cause or reason.) God was able to choose and had to choose the best in order to be the perfect God that we worship; therefore that is what he did; this world could be nothing other than the best of all possible worlds.

This overarching conviction of the rationality of the world and of God, and therefore of evil, is an essential part of his whole analysis. Evil is not a thing, it is *the absence of being* something. Blindness is the absence of sight, injustice is the absence of justice, lies or error are the absence of truth. Evil is therefore inevitable in the case of finite beings, who lack being. The harmonious hierarchy of creatures, explains Leibniz, requires their inequality; they are necessarily more or less distant from perfection, more or less imperfect, and so defective, affected by evil. Evil is the price we have to pay for this good. It cannot be attributed to God as if he were its author, because evil is the same kind of case as the inertia of bodies (a discovery in physics made by Leibniz) when the current of the river carries them along: 'The current is the cause of the movement of the boat, but not of its being delayed.' It 'contributes to the beauty of everything', just like a felicitous discord in music, or those 'apparent irregularities in mathematical series which contribute to the law'.[1]

Who today is liable to be tempted to accept the theodicy of Leibniz? As we approach the end of a century awash with human blood, we are too aware of the horror of evil not to give our support to Voltaire. 'In the face of Leibniz' talk of dissonance linked with consonance, we are much less disposed to enjoy the harmony of the piece when we consider that the dissonance is called Büchenwald (*sic*) or cancer or the death of a child.'[2] The optimism which claimed to be Christian appears to us 'puerile or cynical: Auschwitz with a happy ending'.[3] We do not have to indulge in sentimentality or even give way to a proper emotional response in order to observe the contrast between this and the biblical reaction to evil. Can we proceed to apply the principle of a 'sufficient reason' to God's sovereign rule, and deduce from his goodness what he was obliged to do? If we think we can take God's freedom under our wing in the name of a preconceived idea of his moral perfection, then we are treating the mystery of God astonishingly lightly. Such a procedure must be exposed for what it is. The attitude of believers in both Old and New Testaments is to feel themselves as dust and ashes before him, to bow beneath his mighty arm and to adore him whose ways are inscrutable. Last but not least, psychology has taught us to be suspicious of ringing affirmations and intemperate zeal; our unconscious mechanisms of compensation and overcompensation can go unnoticed and conceal secret faults. Was Leibniz really so sure, deep down, of a God who is sovereignly good? Beneath his overeagerness to prove universal harmony, ought we to detect repressed doubt? Georges Friedmann's perspicacity is as devastating as it is convincing: 'Leibnizian optimism is in reality one of the first forms of the modern philosophies of anguish and despair.'[4]

A few authors, nevertheless, are returning to Leibniz. One is the Catholic philosopher Claude Tresmontant, who teaches at the Sorbonne. Having for a long time fought a courageous battle against the separation of faith and reason, he has been very kind to the *Theodicy*, not holding the author's rationalism against him, or expressing the criticisms that we have summarized. The one omission in Leibniz is 'the *genetic* perspective', that is to say evolutionist; Leibniz never got beyond the creationism of his own time and the Lutheran rejection of the notion of divinization. Now, 'the problem of evil can only be properly discussed from the starting-point' of the idea of human co-operation with divinization, implying an evolutionary progress and also that 'man will become more and more autonomous'.[5] Tresmontant attributes such views to Jesus and to the Bible, though we have looked for them in the texts without success.

When he was a young man, Claude Tresmontant was very strongly influenced by Teilhard de Chardin in person. It was while Teilhard was in Paris, after the end of the Second World War, until he began his exile in New York in 1951. Tresmontant's evolutionary comments on Leibniz provide a convenient transition to the second great version of the solution to the problem of evil through universal order, that of Teilhard de Chardin.

Evil as the waste product of evolution

Pierre Teilhard de Chardin (1881–1955), who was both a palaeontologist and a Jesuit priest, blended in the crucible of his mysticism the contribution of his scientific work and his hope of a cosmic Christ, just as he fused his intense love for the modern world with his Catholic piety. His vision does not belong to any one discipline as strictly defined; it is neither theological nor philosophical, nor yet scientific, but rather meta-scientific. One way or another it fails to fit into any recognized category. But in spite of this handicap, it spread like wildfire in the Catholic Church after 1955, when his death cancelled the ban on publishing his writings, which his superiors had enforced to the very end. The Second Vatican Council has been called 'Teilhardian'. And even if such a claim is excessive, his prodigious under-taking influenced the direction that its thought followed: for he sought to demonstrate convergence – 'all that ascends is converging' – and to involve everything in the synthesis, 'to Christify Evolution'. In the last text that Teilhard completed before he died, *The Christic*, he goes as far as to say: 'It is Christ, in very truth, who saves, – but should we not immediately add that at the same time it is Christ who is saved by Evolution?'[6] The mention of salvation indicates that the problem of evil cannot avoid the attentions of the unified vision.

The least surprising synthesis for the uninitiated is that of Evolution and Creation. (The capitals are Teilhard's – he uses them all the time.) Others before him had identified the two, of course; for a Christian evolutionist it goes without saying. The originality of Teilhard's thought emerges when he asserts the equivalence of Evolution and the Incarnation. This is a 'pro-digious biological operation'; in Christ, God becomes an 'element' that is partially immersed in material things in order to 'create, to fulfil and to purify the world', and thus assume 'the control and leadership of what we now call evolution'.[7] Redemption is not a distinct work done by the Incarnate One, but a dimension of the unique operation Evolution–Creation–Incarnation. Teilhard declares quite unequivocally:

> Christianity, well aware of the conquests made by modern thought, at last realizes the fact that its three fundamental personalist Mysteries are in reality only the three faces of one and the same process (Christogenesis), considered either in its

driving principle (Creation), or its unifying mechanism (Incarnation), or else in its upward endeavour (Redemption): which thrusts us right into the midst of Evolution.[8]

We could also add the equation of the Incarnation with the divinization of life – which is the great theme of *Le Milieu Divin*, his major mystical work[9] – and even the transubstantiation of the universe, according to the vision of the world as the Eucharistic Host, the Mass which grows ever larger until it absorbs the whole cosmos. 'It is the eucharistic mystery itself', he wrote in 1955, 'which extends to infinity in a real universal "transubstantiation".'[10] In order to make the link between all these concepts, that of the unification of the multiple plays the decisive role: 'Plurality and Unity: that is the sole problem to which basically all Physics, all Philosophy and all religion come back.'[11]

What about evil, a phenomenon that is only too human? To the three mysteries already considered, Teilhard adds the Fall: 'All four become co-extensive with the duration and the totality of the World. They are, in a sense, the sides (really distinct, but physically linked) of one and the same divine operation.'[12] Though this might seem to us very surprising, original sin is in fact 'the reverse side of all creation', and it 'tends to merge with the very mechanism of the Creation'.[13] Dare one talk in terms of necessity? This intrepid Jesuit does not hesitate, and his position has the merit of being crystal clear: 'Evil appears necessarily . . . not by accident (which would not much matter) but through the very structure of the system.' It is 'a *rigorously inevitable* accompaniment of the Creation. "*Necesse est ut adveniant scandala*": "Occasions for stumbling are bound to come" (Mt. 18:7, NRSV).'[14] 'It is apparent that the old idea of Fate that ruled even over the gods is not utterly false.' Evil inevitably arising along with creation is 'the truth that is expressed in an indistinct manner in all myths in which the ideas of birth and evil are linked together'.[15] In the various passages in question, Teilhard links pain and misconduct or sin; and also it is the very essence of his method to merge together the physical and the moral. In his *Letters to Léontine Zanta* he writes with enthusiasm: 'Step by step, everything is transformed, morality merges with the physical.'[16] Distinctions are not essential but are relative to the different stages of Evolution.

How does Teilhard conceive the necessity of evil? Sometimes he calls it 'statistical'.[17] But he gives a more precise explanation of it when he speaks of the resistance that the multiple makes to the unifying grip of God. 'We have a tendency to imagine the power of God as supremely at ease in the face of "Non-being". That is mistaken.' 'The general laws of Development (regulating the gradual appearance of the [created] being from an un-organized multiple)' are 'modalities which impose themselves rigorously on divine action'.[18] Creatable Non-being is identified with the pure multiple, springing up at the diametrical opposite of God, by the one fact of God 'trinitizing' himself. Creating, that is to say unifying the multiple in ever more complex arrangements, cannot be done, even in God's case, without pain, wastage and by-products.[19] Evil clings to us by reason of the multiple from which we have emerged and which still marks us. It will disappear only with the perfect unification of the '*Plērōma*'.

Teilhard's theoretical solution brings us the consolation of understanding. But the vision is not satisfied with that. For Teilhard, the distressing wastage is salvaged. By a remarkable reversal, it changes into factors of divinization: this is the great thesis on the 'passivities of diminishment', physical and moral suffering, according to which God avenges himself 'by making evil itself serve a higher good of His faithful'.[20] Evil becomes a kind of auxiliary motor of the progress that has given rise to it. It acts as a goad to prevent us from getting stuck at the present stage of Evolution, to detach us from a world that is still imperfect, and to project us and throw us out of our own centre into God.[21] An 'uprooting' is necessary in order for one 'to be unified within oneself, or to unite oneself with others', and beyond the uprooting from 'the inertia which tends to keep them trapped in one position', in order to grow further, men and women must abandon themselves to 'the death-struggle' of a total transformation.[22] The final part of *Comment je vois* gives a good summary of the reversal of the negative:

> The sufferings of failure and diminution (the sufferings them-selves!), transformed into a factor of a unitive projection out of our own centre . . . cease to appear as a wastage from the Creation in order to become a wonder of spiritual energetics, a positive factor of super-evolution: the supreme and true solution to the Problem of Evil.[23]

Optimism will be complete and perfect if we can foresee the continuation of the process. Often Teilhard appears to be assured of it: 'Under the tension of personalization which exercises its pressure on them, the ele-ments push forward in an infallible direction.' In spite of hesitant groping, the mass effect is that 'the process tends to render itself infallible'.[24] However, Teilhard certainly notices that, for the moment, the machine appears to be working 'in reverse'.[25] He brands large modern cities as 'heartless, faceless Molochs'.[26] Now and again he goes so far as to envisage failure. Yet his optimism, which could be said to be as ascetic as his own face, regains the upper hand. Since Christ is to be found at the end of the process, as the Omega, and since it is his power of attraction which moves the whole of Evolution, the universe cannot abort, nor can humanity take strike action.[27] The present difficulties are the cross-currents of a crisis of growth, the 'critical crossing of the Equator' (of a symbolic globe) of the wave of hominization; this wave is passing 'from Expansion to Compression'.[28] But the tide of Life, of the Spirit, does not stop rising. Optimism seems to feed on the energy of despair when in the darkest hour of the last war, in 1942, he speaks of the war as a phenomenon that gives 'a positive sign', because it is universal, and he hopes for the synthesis, by convergence, of the three great currents of democracy, communism and Nazi-fascism.[29] We must at least acknowledge the courage of Teilhard's supporters when they publish texts like that.

Criticism of Teilhard's thought should really cover his whole system. It should, for example, question the assumption of homogeneity which he formulates so lucidly at the beginning of *The Phenomenon of Man*. The different points referred to in the *Monitum* of the Holy Office, dated 30 June 1962, a warning against his 'grave errors' (explained in the *Osservatore Romano* of 1 July), each merit examination. But is there any need to labour the obvious? In the end, everything depends on the weight you give to the authority of the Bible. Teilhard revealed his mind so frankly that any reader can compare the declarations of Holy Scripture with those of the Jesuit visionary. That is our purpose in compiling the quotations and references above. Busy readers have often been unaware of the clearest expressions which best set out Teilhard's 'originality', and allow one to measure the distance between his position and Christian orthodoxy.

As for evil, we must take fully into account the price Teilhard pays in order to be able to claim: 'The famous problem *does not exist* any more!'[30] The idea of a multiple that resists the Creator is diametrically opposed to the whole tenor of Genesis which is dedicated to celebrating the exclusive sovereignty of the LORD who creates by his Word alone – 'He says, and the event occurs.' If the biblical narratives allude to myths, it is in order to demythologize them, in a radical, monotheistic sense. Teilhard quite openly takes the opposite path. Concerning necessity, he frankly admits its pagan connections. He goes as far as to restore the position of Fate over the gods! This interpretation of the origin of evil can do no more than provide a perfect excuse for the sinner. Only one scriptural text is called upon to support the position, Christ's utterance about the inevitability of occasions for stumbling (Mt. 18:7), but Teilhard does not attempt any exegesis of it. If the inevitability of which Jesus speaks is not merely that of the fulfilment of the Scriptures, or that of the manifestation of latent sin, but is a reference to the plan of God, even then it is not a reference to creation and to its coming to grips with the multiple. Jesus immediately emphasizes the sinner's responsibility, which vanishes in the face of Teilhard's interpretation of that inevitability. The idea of the salvaging of evil then leads Teilhard to a doctrine of redemption that is far removed from the gospel; in it, ascetic effort, particularly on a collective level, replaces the Lamb of God who took the place of sinners to wipe out their debt once for all. One shudders at the thought of this complete indulgence for certain forms of evil. The indignation of the prophets is smothered, the meaning of the cross is overturned, God's judgment and grace are both distorted beyond recognition. No wonder Teilhardism drew such strong criticisms from the very heart of Catholicism. On the question of evil it has even less to offer a despairing humanity than on any other point.

The enthusiasm for his writings has waned by now. It would be generally agreed that the terms in which he spoke of evil were rash. It is worth noting, however, the current interest in a theology which is admittedly less venturesome, and which is represented by another Jesuit, Gustave Martelet. It believes it can lay claim to the authority of Irenaeus, over against Augustine, in order to 'defuse mankind's original offence' and it bears the imprint of evolutionary philosophy and of Teilhard.[31] Taking as its starting point the idea that the Incarnation did not take place firstly to respond to evil, but that it commands creation itself, it minimizes sin. Sin, principally to be thought of as weakness, is linked to 'phyletic hereditary principles that are still infra-human', and is not to be thought of as the cause of death. Over against the virtual unanimity of the Church Fathers, Martelet suggests: 'In order to become himself, man *must* experience his own otherness with regard to God and, on account of his finitude, cross the chasm of his death.'[32] Unlike Teilhard, Martelet is too good a biblical scholar not to be aware that his views part company with Holy Scripture: 'The narrative of the Fall is directed, via sin, at biological death,' he recognizes, but he continues at once: 'Catholic *exegesis* has taken time to stand back the necessary distance from such an assertion; but now that's been done,' and he adopts the contrary position to that of the Bible. Further on he launches a strong attack against the 'pernicious' teaching that is based on Romans 5 and Genesis 3, and against 'exegetical fundamentalism'.[33] With great aplomb the skilful exegete assures us: 'The world of which God is willing to be in charge for us is, from the point of view of nature and of liberty, the best that he can see.' Leibniz *redivivus*![34]

Evil, the 'bite of non-being'

With the Thomist doctrine of evil we are no longer confronting the grandiose, vulnerable dream of an isolated figure. It is the great work of a powerful, lasting community of thinkers, tested in the fires of controversy, finely chiselled by the long passage of time, and it deserves to be approached with respect, even awe. Thomas Aquinas (1224–74), from whom the system of doctrine takes its name, simply built on foundations laid down long before, by Augustine in particular and even Origen. Likewise the Thomists of our own day do not limit themselves to slavish repetition; despite the constraints imposed by their allegiance, their originality is none the less apparent and fruitful. The decline of the influence of Thomism since 1950, which came as something of a shock after several generations of dominance within Catholicism, must not be taken to mean that its representatives have next to nothing to say; and we must also remember that Thomism is to be found outside Rome, in Anglican and other Protestant circles. In spite of internal differences, the school remains philosophically very homogeneous, and it provides by far the most solid and refined version of the solution to the problem of evil by universal order.

Its chief insight remains that which Augustine used against the Manichaeans: evil is *nothing*, not principle, or substance, or entity. It is rigorously relative to good; it is privation, defect, *privatio boni*. Several Fathers of the church, from the days of Origen (*c.* 185–254), pioneered this line of thought.[35] Etienne Gilson, the great authority on medieval thought, speaks eloquently of 'a fundamental unreality, determined and, so to speak, hemmed in on all sides by the good that limits it'.[36] Such an understanding not only avoids dualism, it also makes clear that evil cannot proceed from God, or exist apart from creatures that are good as such.

But we must guard against misunderstandings. Privation is not just any kind of absence. There is evil in the lack, only if good was its proper due. Aquinas draws a clear distinction between privation, which he takes in this sense, and pure negation (man has not the agility of a goat or the strength of a lion), which in no wise deserves to be called bad.[37] It is not something bad for me if I do not have a third eye like Siva, for that is only the negation of a good that is not due to me, it is alien to my nature. But if I am deprived of one of my two eyes, that is entirely different. Leibniz overlooked this crucial distinction, and thus he confused finitude, and the inequalities that are necessary among creatures, with evil. He slandered the order of creation before apologizing for it; but being limited within the integrity of its own nature inflicts no evil on a creature.[38] And again, there are at least some Thomists who argue that the anti-dualist analysis by no means leads to the minimizing of evil; as privation, evil exists in things: 'the paradox of evil is the *terrible reality of its privative existence*'.[39] There is categorically no watering down of the evil of lying by defining it as the privation of truth, or of the evil of blindness by recalling that it is the privation of sight.

Where, however, does the privation come from? The origin of evil is to be found in the 'bite of non-being' which leaves its mark on every creature. The phrase comes from Jacques Maritain, the most influential of the French Thomists when Thomism was at its height.[40] Every finite being, coming from non-being, retains a kind of affinity with non-being; he is mutable, corruptible, fallible. The tendency towards non-being 'is inseparable from the very root of its being', writes Charles Journet, the theologian from Fribourg who was very close to Maritain and in due course was made a cardinal.[41] Thomists are closely agreed at this point: 'God cannot . . . create any person naturally impeccable, any more than he can make a circle square.'[42] According to A. D. Sertillanges, one of the most eminent French Thomists in the early decades of the twentieth century, this analysis of nature and of the causes of evil rests

> on a doctrine of ontological emanation whose influence affects the whole Thomist system. In it, evil is presented in the last analysis as a consequence of the descent of being into the multiple, and consequently into the imperfect, starting from the One and Sovereign. He realises being in its full state, without any imperfection at all; but, going out from him, being necessarily sinks to a lower state, and, along with being, so also does good, which is in reality identical to it. The multiplicity of natures that are limited, and consequently fallible, has its compensation in the unity of order, and it is in view of that order that evil is permitted. Thereby evil finds a foothold in good . . .[43]

This vision carries us into a Neoplatonist atmosphere. Aquinas was heavily influenced by this philosophy which was filtered through Augustine and very widely diffused by the writings of Pseudo-Dionysius, on which Aquinas reflected at great length. It comes extremely close to attributing evil to finitude as such, and to Plotinus' justification of evil through the beauty of the Whole. But Sertillanges used the word 'fallible' and that sets off a new train of thought.

Has evil been adequately explained? Using the words 'fallibility' and 'corruptibility' is not the same as saying 'fault' and 'corruption'. Thomists have one further step to take. Aquinas did so with his eyes wide open, appealing to a principle that to him was unquestionable: 'The perfection of the universe requires that there should be some [beings] which can fail in goodness, and thence it follows that sometimes they do fail'.[44] In this Thomists follow him,[45] and Sertillanges explains that the ability in question (the creature *is able to* sin) would otherwise not be 'real and objective'; 'the ability being supposed, in a system of nature that is in a constant state of flux, where the *wheel of fortune* carries everything along, it is inevitable that one day or another the ability will trigger off the deed, and that the lottery number that has been really picked will come up'.[46]

Thomas Aquinas deals with natural evil and moral evil together.

Justifying the presence of things evil by the good things that result from them, he gives these three illustrations:

> . . . for fire would not be generated if air was not corrupted, nor would the life of a lion be preserved unless the ass were killed. Neither would avenging justice nor the patience of a sufferer be praised if there were no injustice.[47]

If Gilson recognizes that with reasonable beings 'the problem becomes more complex', he considers that the 'principles we have already will be sufficient to prepare the way for a solution'.[48] That is the decision, fraught with consequences, that seems to have been taken by the early Thomists, in harmony with the spirit of their system.

But Maritain and Journet bring in some bold innovations. They both explore the difference between natural evil and moral evil. Maritain, who was chosen by Pope Paul VI to represent the laity at the opening ceremony of the Second Vatican Council, warned that 'if you were to read carelessly, you could confuse the position of Saint Thomas with that of Leibniz . . . a rationalist corruption of Christian truth'. The mechanism of the world will not console the mother who is weeping for her dead child, he argues forcefully.[49] When you consider persons, each one of whom is a complete whole, a universe, 'the existence of evil in things gives rise in the individual being to a sense of incongruity for which nothing can bring consolation. *Et noluit consolari*' ('she refuses to be comforted', Je. 31:15; Mt. 2:18). It is 'an anomaly beyond all comprehension'.[50]

Journet is equally categorical: 'The evil of sin, on the other hand [as against natural evil], in itself is inseparably connected to nothing good and acts only to destroy the work of God'; if it is permitted, 'this cannot be taken to mean that it is accepted, consented to and tolerated, in other words indirectly willed, as the reverse side of some good looked for by God'.[51] It is true that Journet admits the idea of evil as the reverse side of good (*Felix culpa*, he reminds us, as it is sung in the Roman liturgy, 'O blessed fault which won for us such a Redeemer!'), 'but to believe sin to have been willed for the sake of the redemption would be to fall into the blasphemy of the Hegelian view'.[52] It is clearly understood, in all this, along with Aquinas, that the evil of punishment is not such an evil, since it re-establishes order, and that natural evil is, for mankind, wholly penal: if he suffers and dies physically, it is on account of his own fault, it is the consequence and the wages of original sin and actual sins.[53]

The new tones of these Neo-Thomists, Maritain and Journet, do not sit comfortably, in our view, with propositions defended at the same time by these writers. According to them, God permits (without wishing) the evil of sin, because from it he will draw good; is that not a 'consolation' which is supposed to dissolve 'the incomprehensible'? Maritain explains that 'the sin of Adam was permitted for the sake of the redemptive Incarnation', and he does not retreat before the formula: 'Sin, – evil, – is the ransom of glory'.[54] Recalling the illustration given by Aquinas of the death of the donkey that is useful to the lion, Journet writes: 'The same answer will apply, but transferred to a much more mysterious plane, to the permission of the evil of sin.'[55] The Augustinian-Thomist axiom according to which God permits evil because he brings good out of it 'is valid still, but in a transposed sense, proportionately the same but essentially different, when the passage is made from the evil of nature to the evil of sin'.[56] How is this proportion conceivable, if it is blasphemous to imagine the evil of *persons*, as opposed to the evil of donkeys devoured by lions, to be willed as the reverse side of the good? 'The order of freedom and morality is a particular order made to return, by one path or another, into the universal order.'[57] But to include the order of liberty in an order that is more comprehensive, is that not to backtrack on the refusal to consider the person as part of a complete whole? Making the declaration more palatable with words such as 'transferred', 'mysterious' and 'by one path or another' reveals embarrassment rather than assurance through clarification: the structure of the argument is not affected by these powerless attenuations.

Jacques Maritain is also fond of a text of Thomas Aquinas which in his opinion has received too little attention.[58] It concerns 'the cause from which it results that a free action is bad': 'a particularly difficult problem'; 'the solution that he (Aquinas) puts forward is one of the most original discoveries in all his philosophy'.[59] The quest is for the antecedent of evil that is not already itself evil, and which explains the emergence of evil. Whoever finds that will indeed understand evil! But is it not impossible? No, says Maritain: Thomas Aquinas found it. It is necessary that the source of moral evil be in the will, and yet not be itself the offence ('which would be a vicious circle').[60] The solution is simple in its subtlety: because he has not looked at his rule, the carpenter cuts his wood askew; likewise, because the human will does not look at the rule (the law of God), and pays no attention to it, being free to do so or not ('it is there that the essence of liberty rests'),[61] it commits the offence when it proceeds to the act by choice.

Watch carefully the steps in the argument. The lack of attention, the non-consideration of the rule *is not an offence* and *is not an evil*, 'because the soul is not obliged, nor is it always able, to pay attention to the rule *in actu*.'[62] It is certainly a negation, but not of a good that is due, so that the creaturely non-being shows itself to be indeed the cause of the evil; the initiative is one of not acting, of not looking at the rule, 'it is not yet sin, but the root of sin ... it is a pure absence, a pure non-existence, but which is the very root of the evil action'.[63] Aquinas and Maritain do not share precisely the same concerns when they develop this argument: if we read the former carefully, we shall see that he is combating dualism in particular, wishing to avoid, while tracing back from evil to an evil cause, arriving at a *principle* of evil. Maritain emphasizes that in this way evil arises from the creature alone, God in no way being its cause.[64] This difference, however, does not make Maritain unfaithful to his master, and takes away none of the interest of the analysis – providing, of course, that the analysis is correct.

Further than that, one can recognize in both Maritain and Journet fragments of the second kind of theodicy which we shall be examining further on, when Maritain excludes a divine plan which might be 'a scenario written in advance', and when Journet hurls his accusations at Calvin.[65] But these elements are hardly characteristic of the Thomist doctrine of evil which resolves the problem by universal order and the efficacy of non-being.

Evaluation

Let us pay tribute to the labours of the Church Fathers. Their analysis of evil in negative terms, as a deprivation of good, constitutes a lasting gain. By driving away all confusion of evil with a substance or form such as exists in created substances or forms, they have put us in their debt for this act of liberation. It throws into sharp relief the absolute dependence of everything with respect to God who is very good; it denounces evil as a parasite and a perversion. It is in agreement with the experience of real life and more particularly with Holy Scripture: biblical language interprets evil with the help of terms that suggest emptiness and non-existence (there are four in a single verse, Zc. 10:2),[66] and the vocabulary of the New Testament is clearly marked in Greek with a prefix of deprivation, *a-*, which comes across in the English equivalents sometimes as a prefix: *adikos* – *un*just, or *un*righteous; sometimes as a suffix: *anomos* – law*less*; *asebēs* – god*less*. In company with the Thomists we subscribe to these lines from Augustine:

These things are yours: they are good, for you that are good are their Maker;
Nothing of us is in them except for our sin, who, in scorning
The order you set, give our hearts not to you, but instead to your
    creatures.[67]

The danger that accompanies this invaluable insight is that of under-estimating evil: if it is *nothing*, evil no longer seems to weigh very heavily. This trap can, however, be avoided. When one recognizes with Journet the paradox of the positive aspect of this negative, and its 'terrible reality', then one can keep in tune with the horror of evil preached in Scripture, by discerning that the positive aspect of evil settles fraudulently and like a parasite on the good creation of God. With this, evangelical theologians find themselves in agreement.[68]

Let us nevertheless admit to a small measure of dissatisfaction. If Journet moves us by the vigour of his denunciation of the negative reality, does he also take adequate stock of its perverse strength? In line with the Thomist tradition he maintains that the sinner always wants something *good* (but a relative good that diverts him from his final end).[69] Does not evil conceal in its depths a derangement that is far more malevolent? In the suicidal bitterness of his hatred of God, does the sinner desire something good? If he does want something good, might that not be a pretext for concealing from himself the depraved frenzy to destroy, and the thankless rejection of the infinitely good God, precisely because he is good? Georges Florovsky, the Orthodox theologian of the Institut Saint-Serge in Paris and then of Harvard, described vividly the antinomic virulence of evil:

> This illegitimate force is by no means a bloodless phantom. It is really a force, a violent energy . . . Evil is a void of non-being, yet a void that exists, which engulfs beings and devours them. Evil is a powerlessness that never creates, but its energy for destruction is enormous. Evil never climbs, it always goes downwards. But the degradation of being that it causes is terrible. Nevertheless there is an illusory grandeur even in that humiliation in depths of evil. There is at times something brilliant in sin and in evil.[70]

Does Thomism allow itself the means to say that much? Even in order to distinguish mere negation from evil privation, a crucial distinction, has the criterion of 'nature' the cutting edge that is desirable? Does it follow that nature or essence (inherited from Platonism?) should serve as a norm? Who can discern beyond all possible doubt what requirements it would involve? How can I know with absolute certainty that a third eye would not be the perfection of my humanity, or, contrariwise, that one single eye would not determine a one-eyed-nature without privation? 'Privation' is a correct word; but in order to distinguish the evil of non-being, the concept calls for a degree of strengthening. Thomism presents evil as 'quasi-non-being'; but as 'quasi-being', evil remains somewhat in the shadows.

Another strong point in the Thomist position is the real consolation it brings in proclaiming the overthrow of evil by redemption. God makes evil serve his glory and the salvation of mankind, including sins (*etiam peccata!*). It is beyond doubt that divine wisdom includes the perverse doings of free creatures within his purposes, and in a way produces good from evil. 'God writes straight on crooked lines.' But can we go further than that? Is the permission of evil justified by the wise, universal order that encompasses it?

First of all we must draw a clearer and more definite distinction between the evil that is called 'natural' and that of sin with its consequences. There is absolutely no question that the cycle of natural phenomena is a cause for wonderment, and justifies the perpetual destruction that it implies. But where is the evil in that? By what measure would you define it? With all due respect to Thomas Aquinas, it is a misuse of language to label as *evil* the union of the oxygen in the air with carbon. Likewise, in the case of the cell, death means life. Even in the case of the donkey devoured by the lion, the term 'evil' is questionable: we confuse it with evil only in terms of an anthropomorphic projection on to the victim and of an imaginary identification (which may have its own reasons!). Of the carnivores in Paradise, Paul Claudel says with good sense: 'Their perfection being to eat sheep, and that of the sheep to be eaten by lions, neither side lets the other down.'[71] There is no evil, properly speaking, except for persons: Maritain and Journet both felt that intuitively, but did not carry that insight to its conclusion. And the evil of punishment ought to be even more clearly distinguished: in so far as it is a satisfaction of justice and a restitution of order, we are talking about something good; in so far as it flows from sin, it is an evil, or rather an effect of evil, for evil properly speaking is the will that is at enmity against God.

> This precisely is the Christian position, that there is this infinite distinction between evil and evil, as they are confusingly named; this precisely is the Christian characteristic, to talk of temporal sufferings ever more and more frank-heartedly, more triumphantly, more joyfully, because, Christianly regarded, sin, and sin only, is destruction.[72]

As for spiritual and moral evil, it is one thing to say that God is capable of bringing forth good from it once it is there; it is quite another to conclude that God permitted it *with a view to* that good. One passes from the sense of wonderment before the News of the utterly unexpected, victorious wisdom of God, to the possession of a 'reason' which makes us *understand* the decree of God. Never does Scripture take that step across what is a qualitative chasm. No biblical text, interpreted strictly, states that God *changes evil into good*. In Genesis 50:20 Joseph declares literally: 'You had thought evil, God thought it for good.' If sin is really, as Maritain says, 'the ransom of glory', can one exonerate God from a share in the guilt? He is not the author of evil, but he is the author of the law that makes evil the ransom of good or its 'reverse'. Is he not thus tied in with evil? Whether a ransom, or the reverse, these images are not far removed from the notion of a *means*: when an agent permits (sovereignly) one thing *in order that* it serve his purposes, what difference is there between that and the use of means? And is the agent not responsible for the means that he acquires? There is no need to follow the more sensational elements of the media by picturing the most horrific forms of evil, in order to bring home the utter repugnance caused by the suggestion of a God who uses these as his means. The scandal of personal evil totally explodes the justification of evil by universal order.

As for the explanation that evil arises from created non-being, its pagan connections are so obvious that it is astonishing that Christians should advocate it with such assurance. Sertillanges goes so far as to admit without any sign of concern: 'Our author would concede the point to Plotinus that being itself is the source of evil, if it is taken to mean common being' (combined with power).[73] The non-being which is something, the substantialized non-being which, before the creation, enters the composition of creatures, is nothing other than the *mē on* of the Greeks. That was how they spoke of 'what is not' – with a weak, relative negation: what is, in fact, a little bit! The non-being *mē on* is close to the notions of matter and of (real) potentiality.[74]

The argument about fallibility which of necessity entails failure illustrates perfectly the ambiguities in the notion of the *possible*, linked to that of relative non-being, as in Greek thought: when the Thomists call man fallible, they do not mean simply that he is not infallible-like-God, they are talking about a 'real possibility', as we have seen. It is all about a tendency at work in man at the outset, like a germ of evil present from the very creation. The notion of possibility serves here to slander the good creation of God. And, since the words 'necessary', and even 'fated', appear from the pens of Thomists, how could the sinner fail to think that he was excused for his transgressions? Either it is God, being responsible for the whole of being and for all the laws of being, that must be held responsible for this necessity, or else it is a higher law (some kind of Fate, as in Teilhard) which thrusts itself upon God. And, of course, Sertillanges also mentioned 'the wheel of fortune', the super-God of Chance.

Jacques Maritain's attempt to dig up the discovery of Thomas Aquinas to explain the origin of a bad action is all part of the same attempt to make evil spring forth from the natural creation as such. He seeks to establish a *continuity*, instead of the discontinuity of the shameful scandal. He thinks he has found the antecedent, the producer of evil, something which is not itself evil: a *legitimate* creaturely fact, *i.e.* failure to observe the will of God, engenders sin. So evil is rooted in being, and we can understand how it arose. But in fact the discontinuity remains total, a gaping hole when viewed in the light of Holy Scripture.

The demonstration can be criticized from the two hasty joins that it implies. Let us suppose that it is indeed legitimate, within a given time, not to take the divine rule into account: that in no way explains the sin of *beginning to act* without taking account of that rule. In that one step there are monstrous ingratitude, criminal disobedience and abominable arrogance on the part of the creature who owes everything to his Creator and who *must* consider his will at the very outset of any action. Once again there is a qualitative abyss between a prior disregard that was permitted and disregard *when God has commanded the contrary*. And are we able to concede the legitimacy of this disregard which Maritain treats as the initial stage? It is disconcerting that the agent he describes appears to be, as it were, suspended in a moral vacuum. Have we forgotten that the first and great commandment is to love the Lord with *all* one's heart, with *all* one's soul, with *all* one's mind, and with *all* one's strength? Does that not mean a *permanent* directing of the will and the mind towards the will of God? If that stops for a single moment, that is *anomia*: violation of the law, sin. True, what we call a 'directing' is not an endless conscious concentration and meditation on the various commandments; but Maritain, firstly, does not describe the 'consideration' of which he speaks (which he said is not demanded), and then he takes up a position at such a level of metaphysical analysis that our objection finds its target. From the heart of total love (which is the minimal obligation on every creature), no continuity can lead to sin. Evil arises as some alien factor which has neither reason nor excuse. In the image of Gregory of Nyssa, it is 'a grass that was not sown, that has neither germ nor root',[75] and as such is wholly blameworthy and condemned.

In spite of the rich and subtle content of the Thomist doctrine of evil, we are obliged to conclude that it fails in its claim to explain the origin and the point of evil. In the last analysis it leads to making an excuse for evil by a false necessity, and to painting over its horror by considering it, to our own horror, as a means of accomplishing the purposes of God, permitted *in order to* serve in that way. As is the case with the optimism of the Stoics, of Plotinus and of Spinoza, its tendency is to eliminate the evil from evil. That we most categorically reject. This disorder does not enter into order, which would then proceed to justify it. The Thomist provides a valuable contribution by clearly revealing the privative reality of evil; but the painful enigma of this prolific phenomenon, without germ or root in the created order persists. Let us then turn our ear away from the illusory peace terms offered by human reason. Rather, let us listen to the 'voice of truth', the voice of Job, according to Philippe Nemo, which

> says that evil is not something of the world that has being, something that has being in the world, co-ordinated to the world in one single Order. It says that the horror of evil is to be evil, casting the human soul into the battle against the monster.[76]

2

The solution by autonomous freedom

It was the Greeks who thought of political freedom; but only the biblical message prompted the awareness of *human* freedom, of its dramatic greatness at the crossroads of people's destinies and of its essential distinctiveness over against the world. That is how the idea of the prominence of the person came about, and the Church Fathers were all the more inclined to emphasize free will because they were combating the astrological fatalism of the occult religions of the late Roman Empire. The doctrine of the good creation of God who is himself absolutely good also left no room for the pagan idea of the evil of matter. Although the Fathers did not make as clean a break with this unbiblical notion as they should have done, it was to the will that they first attributed evil. Their judgment has remained part of the church's theological heritage throughout its history, and came to be even more highly prized at the time of the Renaissance: from that time to our own day there has been a sharper appreciation of liberty and its value. So arose a variety of conditions favouring a second doctrine that was supposed to resolve the greatest of all problems, that of evil.

The painful question asked by the human mind and by the faith of Christians when confronted by evil can be given a better answer, many thinkers consider, in accordance with Holy Scripture, than that offered by Augustine and Thomas Aquinas. We shall take them together under this second head, although they are admittedly quite a varied company. They reject the excuse provided by the idea of the necessity of evil within universal order. They avoid confusing evil with a metaphysical ingredient of reality. Their strategy consists of clearing God of any suspicion of complicity with evil by isolating the point of origin of evil, that is to say, freedom, by designating it as absolutely the first cause of all the horrifying disorder, and by portraying God as having nothing whatever to do with the event from any point of view and in any respect. In the eyes of its advocates this so-called solution can be proud of its distinctively Christian origin; it is free from the pagan affinities or contamination which taint the alleged solutions of the first group. It has a strong appeal to the modern mind, which shares its faith in the independence, or strict autonomy, of the human will. Christian apologists today turn to it gladly, as they feel that it will give satisfaction to large numbers of our contemporaries.

This explanation of the problem of evil through freedom is presented in a very wide variety of forms, some highly speculative, others commonplace and popular. In the majority of cases it is *analytical* reasoning that can be seen at work: a reasoning that looks for distinction at critical junctures, and seeks to trap its opponent by the implacable force of its dilemmas. It loves sharp, clear alternatives. It goes for a 'hard' kind of logic, one of inescapable connections, that is able to link together the various 'proofs' on which its arguments rest. Among these 'obvious truths', arrived at intuitively and tinged with affectivity, there are three that recur all across the spectrum. Evil is considered as a *possibility* that is inherent in freedom: it would make no sense to call a creature free if it were not *a priori* possible for it to do evil. Secondly, the *free* choice of a personal agent, human or angelic, could not (for defenders of this solution) be *determined in advance* by God. It goes without saying that, if my choice is free, no-one, not even God, has made a decision about it ahead of me. Lastly, since freedom is held as an extremely high, if not the highest, *value*, being essential to any relationship of love, it was good for God to 'take the risk' of creating free agents. God had to do so, if he wished to be loved, for that is not possible except where there is freedom. God is not responsible if the free creatures choose badly. At first sight it seems that this doctrine pays greater respect to the perfect goodness of God and of his works, than does the explanation of evil by universal order, and thereby also offers a clearer view of 'the evil of evil'. But the question arises, what becomes of the sovereignty of God?

First we shall set out certain versions of this view which are far removed from biblical orthodoxy; then other versions that are closer; and then those which deliberately place themselves under the authority of Holy Scripture. Next we shall consider a solution of combined ancestry and of striking originality which make it difficult to classify neatly: it is that proposed by John Hick in his classic work, *Evil and the God of Love*. It brings to mind Teilhard de Chardin (and more particularly Gustave Martelet) from our first group, while also offering certain Hegelian overtones which anticipate chapter 3; but it is still the dimension of human freedom that is the key element. Our critical analysis will bring the chapter to a close.

'Meonic' freedom: Nikolai Berdyaev

The loftiest and most fiery form is unquestionably found in the writings of Nikolai Berdyaev (1874–1948). This Russian philosopher, freed from Marxist influence, an émigré first in Berlin and then in Paris, called himself 'a Christian theosophist',[1] following in the trail of Jakob Boehme, his spiritual ancestor and the thinker he most admired. In his study of him published in 1950, Matthieu Spinka dubbed him 'the captive of freedom', meaning that he was a captive by reason of his passion for, and devotion to, freedom. Without the slightest hint of hesitation he proclaims:

> Freedom is the only answer to the problem of justifying God. The problem of evil is the problem of liberty. Without an understanding of liberty we cannot grasp the irrational fact of the existence of evil in a divine world.[2]

Berdyaev is certainly not representative of the group that we wish to study. His style makes it difficult to determine his precise position: he wrote in the way a prophet speaks, like a single outpouring of a mind in ferment. Depending on which of his books they read, people might classify him at varying distances from biblical Christianity, and sometimes so remote from it that the comparison loses all point. His work merits attention, however; in it you can see the tendencies of the other thinkers we shall study magnified several times over. The sheer scale of his vision will help us detect points of significance and their consequences which are less obvious in more measured writers.

'*The irrational fact* . . . of evil', writes Berdyaev. He proceeds to attack the 'Euclidean' mentality, and qualifies the freedom that he extols:

> There is in the very origin of the world an irrational freedom which is grounded in the void, in that abyss from which the dark stream of life issues forth and in which every sort of possibility is latent. . . . It is the source of evil as well as of good.[3]

This freedom is, then, 'the source of evil'; for him, 'the source of evil is not in God, nor in a being existing positively side by side with Him, but in the unfathomable irrationality of freedom, in pure possibility, in the forces concealed within that dark void which precedes all positive determination of being.'[4] At times Berdyaev calls it 'meonic', because it issues forth from non-being, from the paradoxical *mē on* of the Greeks that we have already mentioned – 'that which is not', but in a merely relative negation, a substantial non-being, material and potential.[5] This fearless thinker glories in his antinomies, which serve simply to illumine further the irrationality of the freedom that he so loves: 'I confess an almost manichean dualism. So be it. "The world" is evil.' And he immediately continues, 'And I also confess an almost pantheistic monism. The world is divine in its very nature. Man is, by his nature, divine.'[6] You can see there would be little point in quarrelling with him about the odd word here or there!

Over liberty, even God himself cannot lay claim to any control. 'God is All-powerful in relation to being but not in relation to nothingness and to freedom; and that is why evil exists.'[7] As Journet points out, Berdyaev never wearies of repeating that the fundamental error is 'to regard God as the Creator of Liberty'.[8] Our eulogist of the void knows perfectly well who his opponents are: in his view, confronted with Pelagian rationalism, 'St. Augustine denied freedom' and later 'St. Thomas Aquinas also completely rejected freedom'.[9] It is not only these two Doctors of the Church, it is the whole of the church's traditional teaching on the sovereignty of God that he is rejecting. And from his rejection of this doctrine he draws this consequence: 'Divine life is a tragedy.'[10] The will of God, in fact, runs up against an adverse causality which is absolutely independent of him, so that God can know failure.

Although he was wont to look into abysses, Berdyaev resists the dizzying attraction of despair. He *knows* the final outcome of the tragedy, and perceives that unconquerable liberty, the source of both evil and good, is essential to the Meaning of the world. 'Without darkness there is no light. Good is revealed and triumphs through the ordeal of evil.'[11] 'The fall of the first man, Adam, had positive meaning and justification, as a moment in the revelation of creativity, preparing for the appearance of the Absolute Man.'[12] The dramatic story carries us over from primitive, ambivalent freedom to the divine freedom (of man deified by Christ), the freedom for which 'in the final sense of the word, there is no evil' and which opposes 'Diabolic freedom'.[13] Thus, in spite of the antinomies that affect even these propositions, Berdyaev explains evil through freedom.

Hardly God at all: Wilfred Monod

If we strip Berdyaev's solution of the esoteric trappings of its Slavic theosophy, we are not so far from the views of a French Protestant pastor, Wilfred Monod (1867–1943), a leading proponent of the 'social gospel'. Given to high-flown oratory, he presented an initial sketch of his views at a conference in 1904, before developing them fully in his book *Le Problème du bien* (*The Problem of Good*) in 1934. Charles Werner ventured to call it 'undoubtedly the most powerful effort made on behalf of theodicy since Leibniz'.[14] It is certainly one of the most lengthy; its three volumes run to 2,839 pages altogether, with inevitable repetitions, a wealth of information on prehistory and the natural sciences, anecdotes, extracts from sermons, from letters and from his own personal diary and poems, the whole mixed in with theological and philosophical reflections.

Wilfred Monod launches an impassioned attack on the traditional ideas of providence and prayer. He mentions 'the predestinarian God' of the apostle Paul among 'the false, immoral "revelations"' which need to be cut out of the Bible; he denounces 'the metaphysical tsarism, the eternal sultanate, the infinite absolutism of this all-powerful character'; he believes he can trace its sociological origins back to the days of absolute monarchy.[15] But he is not satisfied just to appeal to an undetermined freedom of the creature: 'Since the creature is the work of the Creator, to attribute sin to free will is to clear God perhaps of direct blame, but not of indirect blame.'[16] Nor is he satisfied even with the surrender of divine omnipotence: in answer to Franz Leenhardt who went that far, Monod asked: 'Why not go further? Why not attribute our world to a mere Demiurge?'[17] He even took the step of separating the creation from the 'Father' who is worthy of our adoration. The Father is no longer the cause of existence, but a moral magnetic pole, represented by the ideal of the Kingdom, the City of righteousness ('It can also be called "God"'):

> I refuse to worship a God who is said to be the Cause that is responsible for reality. That Cause is an X, a factor whose origin is completely beyond my knowledge: and I give the name 'God' to that Effort which can be seen on all sides striving to transform reality; that Effort is intelligent, moral, sorrowful, continually frustrated, but advancing more and more positively every day.[18]

The cause X is the Demiurge which is grappling with the devil. God is 'God *in fieri*, God in the process of becoming, the "God who is coming"'; to affirm him is to affirm that 'history has a goal'.[19]

With such a God, 'the problem of evil does not exist': it has been *invented* from the starting-point of a God who is utterly unacceptable; and the message of the powerlessness of God at Golgotha, the demonstration of the love that suffers, that implores and that puts itself at the mercy of the beloved, can ring out in its paradoxical simplicity:

> What distinguishes the Christian God from all others, even from the God of the Israelites, is that he is a God who is vulnerable. To those who worship him he no longer appears pre-eminently as a redoubtable potentate seated in the heights of heaven, impass- ible, his serene brow encircled with a diadem incorporating myriads of tiers of ice-cold constellations. Our God is distin- guished not by a Crown glittering with the lights of heaven, but by a crown of thorns. Where will you seek the Father's throne? Not on the summit of a Conqueror's triumphal arch, but on the Cross.[20]

The law of redemptive suffering is *general*, for Christ is 'the motive force that drives humanity onwards', 'God being the motive force of the world'; moreover, 'God did not become *a* man, God became *man*' (which is radically different).[21] Consequently, prayer, 'the decisive and definitive manifestation of the human soul ... a vital release of its highest energies', is to be understood as a method of working together with God. It hears *and answers*

God: 'All can pray, all can hear and answer God calling them, all can foster this humble, glorious ambition: *to become someone in the spiritual realm*.'[22] Monod, however, understands things sufficiently clearly to ask himself once: 'Shall we still pray if "God" were to lose his attributes of metaphysical absoluteness?' as he obviously does in this theodicy.[23]

Is Wilfred Monod likely to be reread, after his books have gathered fifty years of dust? Recently his catechism was republished. But, apart from the over-mythological point about the demiurge, what is particularly striking is his affinity with one of the more recent trends in theology in North America.

Process theology

Among the followers of the mathematician and philosopher A. N. Whitehead (1861–1947), there is nothing that resembles the lyrical eloquence of Monod; instead, we encounter metaphysical speculation and painstaking logic. The divine immanence in the world, in nature as it evolves, is the key concept of process theology, quite different from the social Messiah of Monod. But the relationship of God to evil is more or less similar.

According to his 'consequent' nature at least, God is limited, emergent, advancing with the universe, and can influence the agents of historical change only by persuasion. André Gounelle very aptly compares him with an orchestral conductor who does not achieve everything he wishes with the orchestra, having to put up with their shortcomings.[24] For Whitehead himself, God as the antecedent ground of reality must be 'non-temporal' and even 'above change', but he is only one of the factors in the cosmic Process, distinct from the creative Power. He does not exist by and through himself; to him we owe the order in the world, its 'aesthetic consistency', and its worth, but he does not determine everything, for in that case he would be the source of evil. He is not infinite, and 'he gains his depth of actuality by his harmony of valuation'.[25] 'The nature of God is the complete conceptual realization of the realm of ideal forms. The kingdom of heaven is God.'[26]

His disciples are sometimes less difficult to interpret. The theologian Daniel Day Williams, putting forward the view that God reveals himself through human love, attributes to God limitation due to the freedom of others. Hence God knows suffering and exposes himself to risks.[27] David R. Griffin, in a study of evil written specifically from the standpoint of process theology, makes the following statement as a kind of theorem:

> Any actual world will, by metaphysical necessity, be composed of beings with some power of self-determination, even vis-à-vis

God, so that it is logically impossible for God unilaterally to prevent all evil.[28]

Without such independence there could be no reality properly speaking: that is the axiom on which Griffin bases his certainty. The whole school thinks roughly like him. Thus Peter Hamilton excludes the resurrection of Christ because the empty tomb and the bodily appearances would have operated as a constraint on 'the disciples' free will', whereas 'neither human free will nor the normal processes of nature are subjected to, or interrupted by, divine compulsion'.[29]

Faced with evil, God has his powerlessness as his excuse. He aims, intends, seeks, works and 'tries his best' to overcome evil: rather than blame, he deserves sympathy, even pity.[30] Since it was divine persuasion that first brought the cosmos out of chaos, however, one wonders whether God is not guilty (perhaps through lack of foresight) of giving the initial impulse to the emergence of such a world. Whitehead believed in the 'transmutation of evil into good' in the Process, an 'actual evil' becoming 'a stepping stone in the all-embracing ideals of God'; 'God has in his nature the knowledge of evil, of pain, and of degradation, but it is there as overcome with what is good.'[31] John Cobb and David Griffin analyse good as enjoyment, and evil as that which prevents the occurrence of enjoyment: either discord or triviality, the latter being evil *per se* only when it is unnecessary. In the light of these concepts, they are able to conclude:

> To have left the finite realm in chaos, when it could have been stimulated to become a world, would have been to acquiesce in unnecessary triviality. To be loving or moral, God's aim must be to overcome unnecessary triviality while avoiding as much discord as possible.[32]

Apparently God stands justified because the sum of enjoyment obtained by intensification through the Process is greater than the amount of suffering caused, or, at least, in the absence of any definite forecast, the game was in fact worth the candle.

The powerless God in our midst: Dietrich Bonhoeffer

On the European side of the Atlantic it is Bonhoeffer's reflection on 'the powerlessness of God in the world' in his outline of 'religionless Christianity' which seems to take up the paradox of Wilfred Monod and give it a new impetus and direction. The emphasis moves away from Golgotha to Gethsemane; the style is more cautious, less given to flights of fancy, more virile. But Bonhoeffer scarcely makes any attempt to explain evil. His *Letters and Papers from Prison* are widely known, and do not require detailed consideration here.

We shall simply recall the double motivation behind the new propositions which the theologian sketched out in his cell at Tegel Prison in Berlin. He himself called the outline for his book 'very crude and sketchy'[33] and clearly considered it open to debate.

Spiritually, Bonhoeffer reacts against heathen religion, against the paganization of Christian devotion. Maudlin and utterly self-interested, the religion that so sickens him seeks to exploit God, whereas Jesus summons us to *follow him*. Over against the religiosity of that natural humanity, quaking with fear but always calculating, that seeks a God who is all-powerful, a *Deus ex machina* to protect them and come to their rescue, the gospel summons us to deny self. The Son of God, powerless and suffering, asks his disciples to watch and pray with him in the hour of his agony. It is in this first sense that Bonhoeffer envisages a religionless Christianity, by which one may live, 'even if there were no God'; in which the gift of oneself comes before petition, and whole-hearted commitment to others takes precedence over concern for one's own salvation.

Theologically, things are rather more subtle. One can understand Bonhoeffer, when he preaches the weak, impotent God of religionless Christianity, as a Barthian Lutheran, or *vice versa*. His roots and his religious upbringing were Lutheran, but he also underwent the powerful influence of 'the great Karl', as he affectionately refers to Barth in his letters. He combined key elements from both sides. Luther tended to oppose the law, which condemns us and strikes terror into us, to the gospel which brings us comfort and peace. The law, which has already been discovered by natural theology, as reason has interpreted the experience of human beings in the world, corresponds to the 'naked' God, God in his pure, absolute divinity; the gospel reveals the God clothed with human flesh, who has in his mercy accommodated himself to us, and brings us pardon. The gospel breaks out like a revolution: faith knocks sideways the despairing certainty of reason, and the God who has become man overturns the vision of the God who is 'naked' in his absoluteness. But, of course, the two terms remain inseparable: the gospel draws its meaning from the overturned law, there would be no grace without prior condemnation. For his part, Karl Barth threw himself into his colossal undertaking of 'Christological concentration': *everything* must be understood within the unique Event of the Word incarnate, dead and risen; there is no relationship between God and humanity which does not pass through him. Among the corollaries are the anathema cast on natural theology which has been rejected because it would provide a knowledge of God that was independent of the Incarnate One, and also the reinterpretation of the law not as distinct from the gospel, but simply as 'the form of the gospel'. In the writings of Barth, who came from the Reformed Church, enough of the Calvinistic sense of the Majesty of God survived for God to remain Lord in the Christ event – despite the paradoxes of the divine humiliation.

It is at this point that Bonhoeffer the Lutheran follows a different track. Clearly influenced by Barth's Christological concentration, he nevertheless does not abandon the antithesis of law and gospel, that of the 'naked' God and of the God revealed in human flesh. The 'naked' God, who is absolute, is the omnipotent God of traditional religion and metaphysics; Christological concentration implies not only that his redoubtable image is overturned in grace, but also that it is no longer possible to speak of him, since he may be spoken of only in Christ. This is the source of 'religionless' Christianity.

The link between the two poles of the Lutheran antithesis does not thereby disappear, for all that it becomes concealed. If Christ and the gospel are of such great interest to Bonhoeffer, it is indeed because they bring the end or the abrogation of the law. He is no longer able to say so, but it is what he still thinks. That is why his religionless Christianity is not irreligion. It is also why he speaks of re-establishing a 'discipline of the arcane': just as Christians in the third century used to preserve the secrecy of their most sacred mysteries in their discourse with pagans, Christians in the twentieth century would in public display a religionless Christianity, but among themselves, in secret, they would continue to believe in God.

Bonhoeffer's intention, therefore, is not to establish the autonomy of human freedom, or to make it the mainspring of apologetics. Nevertheless, his witness, his terminology and his renown have been taken over by a theological school that is secular and libertarian. Here is how a thinker like Dorothee Sölle concludes her reflection on the identity of God in the world:

> If, for the nineteenth century, suffering was still the 'rock of atheism', nothing is so eloquent of God in our own century as his defeat in the world. . . . God is helpless and needs help. . . . He made himself dependent upon us. . . . From now on, it is high time for us to do something for him.[34]

The ethical vision: Immanuel Kant

The Protestant philosopher Paul Ricœur, an acknowledged expert in the field, says that the 'essence of the moral vision of the world and of evil' is 'the mutual "explanation" of evil in terms of freedom and of freedom in terms of evil': 'evil is an invention of freedom', and freedom 'is revealed in its profundity' as 'capable of digression, deviation, subversion, error'.[35] He quite rightly sees an example of this ethical vision of the world, with the 'idea of a freedom entirely responsible to and continually at the disposal of itself', in the extension of the Old Testament developed by the rabbinic theology of the Pharisees.[36] We know that they taught a doctrine of two tendencies implanted by the Creator: the tendency towards good (*yēṣer ḥaṭṭôb*) and the tendency towards evil (*yēṣer hārā'*), between which free will must constantly choose. This doctrine is carried to its fullest development, beyond Augustine and Pelagius, by Immanuel Kant, perhaps the most influential philosopher of modern times. His work marks the watershed between the age of 'pre-critical' thought and the thought of a world come of age.[37] Brought up in a pietist family, Kant retained sufficient of its mark and was sufficiently concerned to defend Christian 'belief' for us to include him in this part of our survey, among the thinkers of Christendom.

Kant spells out clearly the *locus* of evil. In spite of the preponderance in his thought of the antinomy of reason and sense-experience and that of law and nature, Kant sees quite clearly that the operation of the senses is not evil in itself. *Evil arises from freedom.* Where and how does what we denounce as evil reveal itself? When free will follows its own interest rather than its Duty, and when it thus vitiates the hierarchy of its motives. This subversion of the order which submits personal interest or natural motives to the moral law is the one thing that deserves our indignation. As for freedom, that continues to be thought of as 'the absolute spontaneity of free will'. When it chooses wrongly, it certainly seems to reveal itself as *Willkür*, 'the power of contrary inclinations', comments Ricœur;[38] in other words, we are not far from evil as an inherent potentiality of freedom as such.

The theory of 'radical evil' which, along with the preceding analysis, is developed in the first part of *Religion Within the Limits of Reason Alone* (1793), however, takes us in a new direction. Kant finds in the whole human race an inclination towards evil which runs counter to its ultimate purpose of good. I am created for good, as is shown by the grip that the moral imperative has on my conscience; and yet I have a tendency towards evil. My freedom has developed the bad habit of turning away from Duty and preferring its own pleasure and advantage. It is freedom that chooses this misdirection, which entails slavery for it. How can that come about? Kant dismisses as mythology or superstition the explanation given in Genesis of a fall at the beginning of history; he refuses to countenance such an event within time. The origin of radical evil is *inexplicable*, indeed even *inscrutable*.

Radical evil leaves a slight hint of mystery hanging over the explanation of evil by freedom. It is nevertheless not an ill-digested piece of residual theology, or, as Goethe complained, a dogmatic spatter with which Kant 'soiled' his philosophical coat.[39] Goethe, who admired Kant as the philosopher of the Enlightenment and as a rationalist, was irritated by this admission of a failure on the part of reason, and detected a whiff of the abhorrent doctrine of original sin. Radical evil certainly occupies a vital place in Kant's thought. Duty, the keystone of the whole huge edifice, presupposes both a rational and free will that is going to submit to it (the Subject), and also that its object is not yet realized: if what a person must do were already there, the call of Duty would be pointless. This 'not yet', this delay which moral conduct has to catch up with, this disjunction between what is given in experience and what is required, amounts to a resistance; this resistance, since it belongs to the moral order, is necessarily located in freedom. And yet Kant is not all that radical on the subject of radical evil! He remains convinced that free will is capable of overcoming the evil tendency, and that the individual can turn away from evil by his own resources. Kant has not really got away from 'the moral vision of the world and of evil' in which autonomous freedom explains the introduction of evil.

If you look around for original thinkers on the subject of evil, Kant's successors are not very easy to spot. The work of Jean Nabert comes to mind, but the author has not given it a Christian focus.[40] Etienne Borne, whose brilliant essay puts many others in the shade, would belong to the Kantian school by his criticism of all-embracing systems of thought and morality, by the way he stands on the personalist Cogito in order to 'break out of Totality', and by the sense of a necessity which calls faith to go beyond all knowledge, the faith that 'reason is right'.[41] But evil, according to Borne, is much more the evil of death rather than that of wrong conduct, much more metaphysical evil rather than flouting the moral imperative. He inevitably inclines towards the tragic side of life when he allows a final conflict of moral values, with good divided against itself. That is why he extols passion and not virtue.

The dizzying anxiety of freedom: Søren Kierkegaard

The father of existentialism, as he is called, that strange witness to the gospel of suffering who confronted the established Lutheran Church in the kingdom of Denmark, must be considered at this point. Kierkegaard is, after all, the thinker and writer *par excellence* on both sin and choice, the one who refined the Kantian disjunction between knowledge and faith to the point of creating the sharpest possible antithesis between them. He was also transfixed by the demands of *duty*. It is true that at times he allows the ethical demand to be suspended, everyday duties to be set aside, as in the case of Abraham on Mount Moriah when the ban on killing one's child was suspended (Gn. 22). But Kierkegaard calls this a 'teleological' suspension. It operates to the advantage of the higher order, by passing to the religious level. It is another duty which is giving the orders, 'an absolute duty towards

God'[42] which relativizes ordinary rules. Thus Kierkegaard does not deny his Kantian connection, and one might suppose that he maintains or strengthens his explanation of evil by freedom, according to 'the moral vision of the world'.

We should, however, not draw any hasty conclusions. The interpretation of the relation between evil and freedom in Kierkegaard's writings is in our view extremely finely balanced. To begin with, the psychology of *The Concept of Dread*, by exposing in the dizzying anxiety of freedom 'the real possibility of sin',[43] appears to go totally in the direction of the explanation of evil by autonomous human freedom. Dealing later with despair, which is sin, the only 'sickness unto death', he expresses himself in similar terms. Writing under the pseudonym 'Anti-Climacus', the Christian alias among the half-dozen he adopted, Kierkegaard refers to his profound, ironical conception of the human spirit as a 'relation', and says:

> Whence then comes despair? From the relation wherein the synthesis [*i.e.* man] relates itself to itself, in that God who made man a relationship lets this go as it were out of His hand, that is, in the fact that the relation relates itself to itself. And herein, in the fact that the relation is spirit, is the self, consists the responsibility under which all despair lies . . .[44]

A self which escapes from the hand of God seems an instance of independence, possessing in itself the potential for evil. It is undeniable that such a proposition figures in Kierkegaard's development of his material.

Kierkegaard's indefatigable insistence on the 'qualitative leap' when sin is posited, however, shows that things are not so simple. The qualitative leap indicates *discontinuity* between being and evil. Qualitatively, sin is *other* than the created order; it does not follow on from the creation in a continuous line, rather it arises from a break with it. Kierkegaard was well aware of the trap into which so many writers fall, the superficial explanation of the origin of evil through freedom in terms of a choice either of good or of evil:

> Sin presupposes itself, just as freedom does, and cannot be explained, any more than freedom can, by any antecedent. To let freedom commence as a *liberum arbitrium* (which nowhere is to be found, as Leibnitz says), which is quite as free to choose the good as the evil, is to make every explanation radically impossible.[45]

In this passage he attacks the idea that sin might be necessary as the realization of the possibility of free will. If so many people find it a plausible explanation, that 'is due to the fact that lack of thought seems to many men the most natural thing', despite Chrysippus, Cicero and Leibniz, with whom Kierkegaard associates himself in denouncing it as 'a fruitless argument', 'hollow reasoning' and *sophisma pigrum* or 'lazy thinking'.[46]

It is only *after* the qualitative leap, once sin has been posited, that the nothing of dread appears as 'the presupposition in which the individual goes beyond himself',[47] for Kierkegaard comes back nevertheless to the idea of something antecedent, preparing the way for sin, and that is located in the very state of the creation. It is to be found retrospectively, one might say, without there being any right to take the path of logic in the opposite direction. Thus Kierkegaard links together assertions which scarcely seem reconcilable without recourse to great mental gymnastics. On the one hand, with regard to freedom itself, 'the formula which describes the condition of the self when despair is completely eradicated' gives no suggestion at all of any autonomy, gap or fault in created freedom which could foreshadow sin: 'by relating itself to its own self and by willing to be itself, the self is grounded transparently in the Power which posited it'.[48] On the other hand, Kierkegaard continues to treat the possibility of evil as a sort of prior reality, and to make the nothing of dread a kind of correlative of freedom. Without clarifying all the argument of this tormented thinker, we must keep hold of the fact that it is certainly not his intention to glorify the independence of the human will, or to dispel the enigma of the emergence of evil.

God's withdrawal

Among those who argue for the solution by freedom, there are many who would like to reconcile the autonomy of free will with the omnipotence of God. They are to be found in particular in or near orthodox circles, and it is not hard to guess why. The mediatory idea seems brilliant: it is that of God's voluntary withdrawal, his divine self-limitation. God *could* determine everything that happens, but he *does not do so*: he freely withdraws in order for his creature simply to be, and in particular for his creature to be free.

The Cabbala with its liking for paradox came close to this line of thought with what it called *zimzoum*. In the middle of the twentieth century, the neo-orthodox theologian Emil Brunner drew on the idea of kenosis, stating plainly:

> The maximum of the divine self-limitation is equally the maximum of actual 'over-againstness' – the free position of that being who is 'over against' God, and is therefore able to answer the Word of the Creator in freedom. . . . Now we begin to see what a large measure of self-limitation He has imposed upon Himself, and how far He has emptied Himself, in order to realize

this aim, to achieve it, indeed, in a creature which has misused its creaturely freedom to such an extent as to defy God.[49]

The Frenchman François Laplantine abandoned neo-Calvinism, from which he had drawn heavily, to conclude in typical fashion:

> God does not create robots, puppets or marionettes, but free human beings, free even to resist him, to say No to him, and to hang him on a cross. And that is what happened. Because the God of Jesus Christ is not a despot, an absolute monarch, a sovereign with limitless powers. The God of Jesus Christ withdraws from his creation, and forgoes the immediate completion of mankind and the world in order to allow human freedom to unfurl and create history. This incomplete state of the world is the cause of evil.[50]

These are not isolated examples. This kind of language is to be found in many writers of recent times. Among eminent apologists in conservative Protestant circles, two of the best known turn discreetly to the same idea.

C. S. Lewis gives a vivid yet delicate portrayal of the sheer delight experienced by Paradisal man in his filial self-surrender to his Creator. But even in that state Lewis finds the possibility of sin: 'The mere existence of a self – the mere fact that we call it "me" – includes, from the first, the danger of self-idolatry.' He calls this 'the "weak spot" in the very nature of creation, the risk which God apparently thinks worth taking'.[51]

Francis Schaeffer, whose popular presentation of an apologetic for the latter half of the twentieth century has left its mark on a whole generation of young American Christians, presents as the solution to the problem of evil the argument that God 'created man as a non-determined person'. He is a being 'who could choose to obey the commandment of God and love Him, or revolt against Him'.[52] At this point Schaeffer is attacking the secular determinisms, whether biochemical or psychological, which if true would destroy freedom and responsibility. But he also excludes the determination of the human will on the part of God, as found in the Bible by Augustine and all who belong to his tradition; and that is why Schaeffer's apologetic presents the choice of Adam, a free and radically non-determined person, as the key to a rational solution to the problem of evil.

Like C. S. Lewis, Stephen T. Davis speaks of the 'risk' that God took knowingly, when he created this world. In his article on process theology which we referred to earlier, he is critical of the whole basis of that movement, and yet can accept the concept of God taking a risk. He is ready to admit 'that God *potentially* controls all events', but criticizes process theologian David R. Griffin for attributing to 'traditional theists the much stronger view that God *actually* controls all events'. The position taken by Davis is 'that he has limited his causal power precisely to allow for human freedom'.[53]

This reconciliation of the omnipotence (or lordship) of God with the existence of evil, primarily of moral evil, since physical evil is merely a consequence of it, appears to us to be widely held. It is at the centre of quite a vigorous debate being carried on among philosophers who belong to the 'analytical' movement, that of 'logical empiricism', the successor to the logical positivism of the 1930s and 1940s, and which is still so influential in Britain and America. One of its most noted exponents is Professor Alvin Plantinga, whose ecclesiastical links are with one of the Reformed bodies in North America. He has in recent years emerged as a defender of free will as the clue to bringing about the required reconciliation.[54]

In this category of the solution by freedom we would also put Jean-Michel Garrigues's original work, *Dieu sans idée du mal* ('God without the idea of evil'), which is attractive both for its devotional warmth and for its love of the Bible. Its author, who is both a theologian and a monk, reveals the temperament and outlook of a traditionalist, but adds to that a notion of freedom that is clearly influenced by modern humanism. Garrigues takes up the vision of history as a process of divinization that is inevitably gradual and arduous, a view which he traces back to Irenaeus in the second century. His position is close to that of Gustave Martelet, though it is more cautious; he does not make a greater effort to account for the supposed *inevitability* of that slow progress. Where he breaks new ground is in the relation of God to human freedom (although he clearly understands that the possibility of sinning is not an *essential* condition of freedom). For him, 'God is the omnipotent Father because he does not foresee the unforeseeable, and the unforeseeable is the freedom of his child', and 'all our acts are known to him only in the very act in which we perform them', in the *present*, to the point that God 'has no memory' either. If 'God does not foresee evil', if he 'is blind to evil because he is Being', how could the Son of God have been known in advance, from before the foundation of the world, as the Lamb whose blood redeems us (1 Pet. 1:19f.)? In great difficulty, Garrigues argues that it was only after the fall that God's gracious plan took the form of the sacrificed Lamb. Before the world's foundation he had the form of a Lamb, that is to say the vulnerability of love, but he is not sacrificed until sin makes its appearance (Rev. 13:8) – which is obviously diametrically opposed to the biblical symbolism, and the specific reference to the blood in 1 Peter 1:19. Simply in this matter of God's foreseeing human actions, the very different stance of Holy Scripture is quite clear in a passage such as Acts 4:27f.: 'Herod and Pontius Pilate met together with the Gentiles and the people of

Israel ... They did what your power and will had decided beforehand should happen.' The love that is reckless, impassioned, blind, and passive beneath what are for him the 'staggering' blows struck by evil, to which Garrigues returns time and again, is more indebted to the Romantic movement, and to certain of its mystical roots, than to divine revelation.[55]

The constraints of soul-making: John Hick

An elegant style and admirable clarity have helped secure an unusually wide audience for the theologian John Hick, once of Edinburgh and Oxford, and now of California. In recent decades his *Evil and the God of Love* has proved to be one of the most influential attempts at a theodicy in the English-speaking world. Even if the author has somewhat changed direction since then, by turning his attention to Eastern religions, his brilliant synthesis retains its distinct authority. We must now begin a rather lengthy detour in order to consider its significance and validity.

Although he is an innovator and recasts his material, John Hick ranks among those who explain the problem of evil in terms of human freedom. He carefully examines the objections that Anthony Flew and J. L. Mackie make to the free-will defence, and refuses to accept their conclusions.[56] Created persons need a 'degree of genuine freedom and independence over against their Maker',[57] the terms 'freedom' and 'independence' constituting a hendiadys. In his view, 'there is a necessary connection between personality and moral freedom such that the idea of the creation of personal beings who are not free to choose wrongly as well as to choose rightly is self-contradictory', and the only alternative would mean that man is 'a mere puppet'.[58] A world deprived of such a symmetrical, double-edged freedom, and therefore deprived of the genuine possibility of evil, would be 'a poor second-best':[59] thus Hick does not break free from the line of thinking that is common to all who base their theodicy on freedom. Later, reacting to Dostoyevsky's powerful denunciation of deliberate human cruelty, he comments: 'If human beings were not free to be cruel, they would never *be* cruel, but they would also not be free ...'; human fulfilment, 'the realization of which requires man's freedom, can render worthwhile the whole process of interacting human lives ... which includes on the way the fearful misuse of freedom in acts of wickedness and cruelty'.[60] The writer is so committed to this concept of liberty that he consciously opposes Holy Scripture: Hick, a perspicacious reader of the apostle John, deplores the fact that 'in the Fourth Gospel the notion of a free response to Christ upon which men's eternal destinies depend is obscured and indeed undermined' by the doctrine of predestination.[61]

He is not content, however, simply to put forward free will as the substance of his argument; he sees the inadequacy of a theodicy built on this foundation alone.[62] It is the conflict with universalism that embarrasses him first of all. In his view, 'if there are finally wasted lives and finally unredeemed sufferings, either God is not perfect in love or He is not sovereign in rule over His creation'; 'no other acceptable possibility of Christian theodicy offers itself'.[63] But universalism, *i.e.* the universal salvation of mankind, surely contradicts the impossibility of predicting the choices made by free will? In terms of strict logic, that is so: 'it is logically possible that some, or even all, men will in their freedom eternally reject God and eternally exclude themselves from His presence'.[64] At this point he looks to get round the difficulty by moving from the logical standpoint to the 'factual' standpoint: by considering 'the actual forces at work', God's ceaseless working, he thinks he may thereby reach 'a practical certainty': 'It seems morally (although still not logically) impossible that the infinite resourcefulness of infinite love working in unlimited time should be eternally frustrated.'[65] A gap appears here between John Hick and the pure libertarian position. This gap becomes wider when he shows how closely he is attached to divine sovereignty or omnipotence. He is well aware what a disaster it would be for the Christian heritage to abandon it. In his opinion, Leibniz' thesis 'is sub-Christian in the restriction that it sets upon the divine sovereignty';[66] it is 'an inescapable conclusion that the *ultimate* responsibility for the existence of sinful creatures and of the evils which they both cause and suffer, rests upon God Himself. For monotheistic faith there is no one else to share that final responsibility.'[67] John Hick goes so far as to classify the free-will defence with the type of theodicy which he *repudiates* – 'The main motivating interest in the Augustinian tradition is to relieve the Creator of responsibility for the existence of evil by placing that responsibility upon dependent beings who have wilfully misused their God-given freedom'[68] – whereas the Irenaean type of theodicy, which Hick favours, safeguards the omnipotence of God.[69]

The universalist hope and his concern for the kingdom of God drive Hick to review his notion of freedom and to mitigate his notion of independence. The effect of emphasizing the unforeseeable and the undetermined is to reduce freedom to the absurdity of chance. Hick refuses 'to equate freedom with randomness of behaviour'.[70] In order for free action to retain meaning, to be *his* action, it must express the character of the agent.[71] Indeed, man was created with a 'Godward bias' and achieves fulfilment only in the love of God.[72] So Hick accepts a certain determination. But he does not go all the way. He does not break with the tradition of autonomous freedom. He gropes towards a quantitative solution: 'a genuine though limited autonomy';[73] free action 'is largely, but not fully, prefigured in the previous state of the agent'.[74] Thus his adherence to the 'libertarian' family is balanced by his sense of frustration, which acts as a goad to drive him to look elsewhere.

The main element in the discovery that Hick makes during this quest is summed up in a beautiful phrase from the poet John Keats, in a letter written in April 1819: 'The vale of Soul-making'.[75] Instead of 'vale of tears', this is what the world must be called, in order to understand the presence in it of evils committed and suffered by human beings: God includes them in his plan as the means of the moral and spiritual education of his creatures, whom he wishes to make his sons and daughters. Commenting on Leibniz' best of all possible worlds, Hick asks the penetrating question, 'Best for what end, and best for whom?'[76] He gives us his own answer: 'the world is a "vale of soul-making", designed as an environment in which finite persons may develop the more valuable qualities of moral personality'.[77] Three other quotations will show clearly the direction of his argument:

> . . . our theodicy must find the meaning of evil in the part that it is made to play in the eventual outworking of that purpose; and must find the justification of the whole process in the magnitude of the good to which it leads.

> My general conclusion, then, is that this world, with all its unjust and apparently wasted suffering, may nevertheless be what the Irenaean strand of Christian thought affirms it is, namely a divinely created sphere of soul-making.

> . . . God has ordained a world which contains evil – real evil – as a means to the creation of the infinite good of a Kingdom of Heaven within which His creatures will have come as perfected persons to love and serve Him, through a process in which their own free insight and response have been an essential element.[78]

This vision allows Hick to welcome with sympathy the language of Fr Joseph Rickaby who postulates 'a necessity of sin somewhere', and adds confidently, 'this world is the next world a-building'.[79]

John Hick looks for support both to modern evolutionism and to the authority of Irenaeus. Instead of giving so much prominence to the fall as an event and crushing mankind beneath original sin, it is necessary to recognize that man was created incomplete, as 'only the raw material for a further and more difficult stage of God's creative work'.[80] In order to add to the mere 'image' of God the spiritual 'likeness', a long schooling is required in which evil plays its part. This 'cannot be performed by omnipotent power as such', because of human freedom; human beings are called to become children of God, 'but they cannot be created ready-made as this'.[81]

In order to delimit the constraints on the process of soul-making, and in order to provide a precise explanation of moral evil, Hick introduces the notion of *epistemic distance*, which he considers of the highest importance. It would be unthinkable that man, in the divine presence and conscious of that presence, should have sinned; in order for him *to have been able to sin* (a possibility proved effective by his fall), there had to be a *distance* between the Creator and the creature.[82] That is certainly what was required by the freedom of the human response: a distance that was sufficient for man not to be overwhelmed, engulfed or vaporized; such a distance could not, of course, be spatial, but 'epistemic', that is to say, in the area of knowledge. 'The world must be to man, to some extent at least, *etsi deus non daretur*, "as if there were no God"'. God must be a hidden deity, veiled by His creation.'[83] Thus faith will discover God's presence *freely* through ambiguous signs.[84] It is 'virtually inevitable' that humanity would not reach it straight away; that is why 'the creation of man in his own relatively autonomous world, in which the awareness of God is not forced upon him but in which he is cognitively free in relation to his Maker, is what mythological language calls the fall of man'.[85] 'Man as he emerged from the evolutionary process already existed in the state of epistemic distance from God and of total involvement in the life of nature that constitutes his "fallenness".'[86] And so the paradox may be boldly articulated: 'Man can be truly *for* God only if he is morally independent of Him, and he can be thus independent only by being first *against* Him.'[87] *Quod erat demonstrandum*: sin being interpreted as the prerequisite of love. That is what is at stake in the concept of 'epistemic distance', a notion that seems to have originated from Austin Farrer, who, having conceived the idea, immediately rejected it.[88]

The explanation of evil by the constraints of soul-making does not conceal the price to be paid by those who wish to adopt it – or, at least, part of that price. Despite his desire to assume the heritage of the church, John Hick has the temerity, in the name of a 'revelation' which does not coincide with Holy Scripture, to repudiate the teaching of the apostle Paul on sin: 'the Christian revelation . . . does not offer any specific theory as to its origin – not even that sponsored by the Church's first theologian, St. Paul'.[89] And again: 'the cosmic picture, sketched by St. Paul and completed by St. Augustine . . . is a product of the religious imagination'; as for us, 'we can no longer share the assumption, upon which traditional Christian theodicy has been built, that the creation–fall myth is basically authentic history'.[90] Hick's interpretation of the Eden 'myth', with the serpent a morally neutral figure, 'the first scientist',[91] cannot be sustained in our opinion; we have argued elsewhere in favour of another reading.[92] His use of the Bible is that of liberal Protestantism, with its insistence on the mythological character of scriptural language.[93] In the construction of a theodicy, Irenaeus has more weight than the apostle Paul! John Hick honestly admits, however, that 'within Irenaeus' own writings there are cross-currents and alternative suggestions';[94] and that in the patristic age the thesis that he is defending knew only 'relatively inchoate beginnings'.[95] The truth is, that it is to Schleiermacher (1768–1834), the father of German liberal theology, that we owe it.[96] (For this reason, as well as for others, we are not keen on Hick's binary classification of theodicies, as either Augustinian or Irenaean.)

The assurance that he can provide a more rational solution to the problem of evil does not prevent Hick from coming up against insurmountable difficulties, and sometimes admitting it. Does the logic of soul-making not exclude a state of perfection? 'If only challenges and obstacles and sufferings can evoke the highest moral qualities within us, will not these evils still be necessary in heaven? . . . This again is an exceedingly difficult question to meet.'[97] His attempt at a reply is valiant, but does not carry conviction; he goes as far as to put forward the hypothesis that there continue to be 'problems and pains in heaven'.[98] More serious still, 'Need the world contain the more extreme and crushing evils which it in fact contains?'[99] There are many evils whose 'effect seems to be sheerly dysteleological and destructive'.[100] Of the horrors recalled by the name of Auschwitz alone, 'no condemnation can be strong enough, no revulsion adequate', and in no sense can they have been willed by God.[101] But, in that case, what remains of the major thesis? John Hick abandons the attempt to explain: 'The only appeal left is to mystery';[102] 'the mystery of dysteleological suffering is a real mystery, impenetrable to the rationalizing human mind'.[103] Beyond the mention of an inevitable paradox, neither does Hick seem to resolve the difficulty that he articulates so very well: 'if moral evil is thus a "virtually inevitable" outcome of God's creative work, how can it be truly hateful to Him, truly at enmity with Him, truly at variance with His purposes and inimical to all good?'[104] These questions then recede into the background, however, and scarcely appear to count when the final affirmation rings out: 'nothing will finally have been sheerly and irredeemably evil'.[105]

Evaluation

Before coming to the explanatory function allotted to freedom, the common denominator of the theodicies that we are examining, we shall first evaluate the original and complementary ideas put forward by John Hick. So we shall be following parliamentary procedure, voting on the amendment before voting on the motion itself.

Quite apart from the erudition and penetration of *Evil and the God of Love*, we can gladly welcome several valuable features. The critique of Leibniz is most acute, as is that of Neoplatonism as found in the Augustinian tradition, with its aesthetic justification of evil, the role of the principle of plenitude (all possibilities of being must be 'filled', hence inequalities and imperfections), and the ambiguities of the concept of non-being (*mē on*). On the positive side, the educative value of suffering, failure and adversity throws real light on their integration in the overall plan of God. The lament of the poet:

> Each man is an apprentice, bound to pain;
> And none can know himself that has not suffered,

can be accepted, provided that there is no suggestion that here we find the ultimate and primary *why* of evil.[106] We also appreciate that, in this book, John Hick holds fast to monotheism and does not seek to compromise the sovereignty of God.

It is at this point, however, that the rub is felt. In spite of his monotheistic stance, the impossibility of God's creating persons that are morally perfect turns out to be well and truly a limitation on him. The principle which demands a frail beginning, and that mankind should first of all assert itself *against* God before learning to choose *for* him constitutes an *a priori* metaphysical necessity, with which God is on a collision course, and with which he has to come to terms.

Does not Austin Farrer's example point towards the path of wisdom, when he dismisses the idea of epistemic distance, after being the first one to present it in outline? This notion is far from being essential or inevitable. True, Holy Scripture shows the Lord entrusting to mankind's care an estate of his own, situated 'at a distance' from heaven where God dwells in glory; and this is in order that man may live genuinely as the 'image of God', and know God in the relationship of the covenant, one with the other. But it does not follow that God has hidden himself, to the extent of leaving only ambiguous signs and rendering the fall 'virtually inevitable'. Even after the disruption brought about by sin, the revelation of God in his works remains sufficiently striking as *to render inexcusable* the unbeliever or the idolater (Rom. 1 – 2). Never does the Bible give any hint that mankind's catastrophic aberrations might be explained by an epistemic distance intended by God as something necessary to the authenticity of our moral life. When it recalls the distance between heaven and earth (Ec. 5:1), it is in order to humble the arrogance and the presumption of humans as created beings, and that pride which is exposed also by their agnosticism, since it brings them to disparage the things revealed for us and our children (Dt. 29:29). John Hick's idea seems to come from an anthropomorphic vision of God, forgetting our total dependence on the One from whom, through whom and to whom are all things (Rom. 11:36), in whose light alone can we see light (Ps. 36:9). It would also pose problems in Christology, in so far as the perfect communion of the incarnate Son with the Father, from earliest childhood, is scarcely compatible with 'epistemic distance'.[107]

It is disturbing that Hick does not distinguish between partial ignorance, which could be caused by God's self-concealment, and the wicked error, the lie professed and then put into practice, of those who worship the creature rather than the Creator. When he develops the theme of human degeneracy, there is no echo of the indignation that the prophets manifested against idols. And then, when he does recognize an impenetrable mystery (which would call in question his whole theodicy, were he to pause and really take account of it), it is with regard to unjust suffering, rather than sins against God. Neither does he shudder with horror, as do the biblical writers, at unbelief, rebellion, or spiritual infidelity and prostitution. We find rather that his theodicy tends, if not to justify evil (which at times he dares to say), at least to minimize it and excuse it. The refrain that echoes throughout the book is that of the *felix culpa*, which is not to be found in Holy Scripture.[108]

In so far as John Hick magnifies the educative purpose of God in the on-going work of soul-making, he veers away from the central libertarian argument. It is time now to turn our attention to that.

Let us make quite clear then, without further ado, that in our view all efforts to solve the problem of evil by means of appealing to the nature of freedom are a failure. Our critique, however, will first of all highlight the strong points of the proposals that we have examined.

The majority of them include a denunciation of the metaphysical inter-pretations of evil. They refuse to make evil something inevitable. The antithesis between Good and Evil is maintained without recourse to dis-sonance in the name of harmony. So the truth about evil as something inexcusable and unjustifiable is respected. If moral evil is the creature's unjust, ungrateful, senseless *response* to the Creator, and if freedom is, on the part of the creature, the power to respond – and these are premises that we endorse – then the conclusion must be drawn that evil comes through created freedom. Scripture links it primarily with the will and with the heart as the faculty of choice. The prophets in particular point their accusing finger at human freedom:

> I called but you did not answer,
> I spoke but you did not listen.
> You did evil in my sight
> and chose what displeases me.
> (Isaiah 65:12, *cf.* 66:4)

Zechariah sums up his accusations in the same terms (Zc. 7:11f.). Jesus himself vigorously supports their position: he weeps over the evil *will* of Jerusalem

(Mt. 23:37) and in particular he teaches that moral evil comes *exclusively* from the heart (Mt. 15:10–20). By launching an attack on the idea that uncleanness comes from *things* as such, Christ rejects the explanation of evil by an original element in the nature of things, in other words by an ingredient in what exists. It is freedom that he blames.

In the biblical perspective it is sin that is the great evil. It is the foremost evil and the very essence of evil: it is the *worst* evil, its heinousness is not to be minimized at all, and it is the *prime* evil from which flow all other kinds of evil and misery. It is the voluntary break with God which makes the human race liable to suffer physical evils, and makes it vulnerable in this world (Gn. 3:16–19; Rom. 5:12). Of course, this proposition appears exaggerated or strained to some: was it not God who created viruses and volcanoes? Did not the law of the jungle shed blood for thousands of centuries before the human race appeared on the scene? These objections are not insuperable. In his original, sinless and flawless state, mankind was bursting with health, so that viruses and other pathogens, which are all the more dangerous when an organism is weakened, caused him no harm whatsoever. He no doubt had intuitive wisdom and such finely tuned premonitory senses – far sharper than those of the most amazing of today's animals – that volcanic eruptions were incapable of causing him any danger. As for the manifestations of violence in the animal kingdom which shocked Wilfred Monod so profoundly, it is debatable whether they can be considered as *evil*. On what basis, and by what measure could we make such a judgment? Our imagination projects into the life and suffering of animals that are near to us. But at what point do you stop? Peter Geach, a Catholic philosopher who held the Chair of Logic at the University of Leeds, makes the point sensibly enough:

> Someone who tried to sympathize with a shark or octupus or herring would be erring by excess as Dr Moreau erred by defect; their life is too alien to ours for sympathy to be anything but folly or affectation.[109]

The idea that before mankind's creation Satan might have caused the transformation of peaceful, loving animals into parasites and predators, or even that the fall in Eden was its cause, finds no support in the Scriptures; the speeches in the book of Job (38:39ff.; 39:29f.; 40:25ff.) and Psalm 104 (vv. 21 and 27f.) reveal in the behaviour of the carnivores the wisdom of God the *Creator*. This wisdom gives us a sense of wonder indeed, when science unfolds the intricate ordering and complex control of various ecosystems.[110] Pain undergoes a radical change of category, depending whether there is or is not a reflecting consciousness that is able to relate sensations and experiences to a personal centre ('I'). Where there is to be found a similar consciousness, suffering certainly seems evil – that is, in human beings; but you cannot draw the hasty conclusion that it is the same in the case of animals. The apostle Paul teaches that the precept in Deuteronomy, 'Do not muzzle an ox while it is treading out the grain', forbids cruelty to animals that are close to people, not for the sake of the oxen, but for the sake of mankind. By virtue of anthropomorphic projection, the treatment handed out to animals close to us reflects and influences the conduct of human beings one towards another (1 Cor. 9:9f.). So the concentration on the evil of *sin* that we find in the majority of versions of the free-will defence is in accord with Holy Scripture.[111]

In short, despite the apparent contradiction of a few passages, we accept as biblical the proposition that God is never the *author* of evil, that he does not directly cause it, nor does he bring it forth from himself. Evil is defined by its opposition to God and its utter dissimilarity to him; God shows no compliance whatsoever with evil. When set against ancient or modern pagan ideas, the 'ethical vision' of evil and related doctrines display invaluable clarity.

Our applause goes no further than that. To point to freedom as the area where guilt lies is correct; but to imagine that evil is thereby *explained* is to fall into confusion. Let us start by the effort to safeguard God's omnipotence with the help of the idea of God's self-limitation. We might point out that God has to withdraw from an exceedingly vast area if he really wishes to allow free will to operate without him! The whole history of the world is constantly being switched from one direction to another by the choices made by freedom. As Pascal put it, had Cleopatra's nose been shorter, the whole face of the world would have changed; so, had she opted for plastic surgery . . . . Her pretty little face had such a hold over the mighty general, Mark Antony, that the fate of the Roman Empire hung in the balance; in the end his rival, Octavian, won the battle and the imperial crown. At certain moments individual choices of apparent insignificance can decide the fate of the universe. Either God does not interfere and no longer has control over anything very much; or else God contrives to limit the consequences of human choice, and so is not really playing the game and is reducing the drama of freedom to a superficial effect of no importance. There are very few theologians supporting this view who take proper account of the vast extent of the withdrawal that it requires.

Furthermore, have they the right to speak of a free *self*-limitation on the part of God? The whole logic of their argument shows that God *could not* determine freedom (as they conceive it); God could, of course, constrain or suppress freedom, but he could not determine the act as such, *even if he wished to*. There is thus a kind of law which God must accept, a necessity which *obliges him* to limit himself. Alvin Plantinga spells out the position unambiguously: 'God can create free creatures, but He can't *cause* or *determine* them to do only what is right. . . . To create creatures capable of *moral good*, therefore, He must create creatures capable of moral evil.'[112] We have seen much the same sort of thing from the pen of John Hick. Might that law be simply the expression of the divine nature, like the impossibility of God lying, or making square circles? No-one has demonstrated that. Besides, it is significant that the terms used are those of withdrawal and self-limitation, whereas these words do not come to mind when confronted by the absurdity of square circles. So it is no surprise that the most consistent thinkers in this group are also the least orthodox, those who quite simply abandon divine omnipotence. God has to reckon *from the outset* with a factor that is independent of him.

The deceptive clarity of the idea of limitation, like the conviction that God would make a puppet out of a man whom he determined in his choices, derives from the most basic feature of the autonomous free-will defence, namely *anthropomorphism* – or perhaps we should say 'cosmomorphism'. The relation of the Creator to his creatures is represented as combinations of earthly forces. A creature has to withdraw for another to take its place (being metaphysically exterior to each other); an earthly force, whether physical or psychological, which determines my choice is destroying my freedom; and *God's action is imagined in terms of such a model!* What is meant by 'God' is completely forgotten. What has become of his infinite presence which penetrates every creature and which is the only thing that protects it from instantly dissolving into nothing (Ps. 104:29)? Have we forgotten that in him every creature lives and moves and has its being, according to every aspect of that being (Acts 17:28, *cf.* v. 25)? Have we forgotten that the lordship of God is the very meaning of his Name, to which he cannot be unfaithful? We have also forgotten that with the Absolute we must think absolutely; independence with respect to him is *absolute* independence, that is to say that by definition it means a rival *divinity* – and the postulation of several divinities sinks into incoherence. In these ways do we forget what is meant by 'God'. The term is used, but the logical process is bereft of *thought*. Instead, there is a small god doing his best, but who incurs the reproach made by Paul Tillich when he called for the God beyond this inadequate deity, transcending him, and worthy of the Name of God.

Berdyaev alone is brazen enough to indicate the *mythologies* which inspire him. His is a glorious defeat, although it patently entails the collapse of reason: it is a *defeat* because of its obvious submission to pagan thought, but it is *glorious* because Berdyaev is aware of the extreme significance of attributing autonomy to human free will. He at least does not share the incredible myopia of those who take that attribution as if it were something that followed naturally and without any difficulties for the monotheistic believer!

How can anyone at the end of the twentieth century who belongs to a church that lays claim to the heritage of the Reformation with its historic stand on the authority of Holy Scripture seriously revive such a lame theory as that of a *demiurge*, that is to say a kind of second-class god, a heavenly subaltern fashioning a very imperfect world? Secondly, the biblical vocabulary used by process theology might mislead the unwary reader; but a rigorous study demonstrates that the 'God' it talks about is merely the cosmic process itself, viewed from a certain angle, because its absolute pole is simply its utter all-embracing *relativity*; he cannot 'take initiatives on behalf of any or all of his creatures, precisely because they are not his creatures. On the contrary, he is theirs'; he is incapable of *ex nihilo* creation and of final resurrection.[113] Such is the pathetic idol of some intellectuals! As for the analytical philosophers, who stylistically are the exact opposite of Berdyaev, their arguments leave us curiously unsatisfied. They handle propositions about God as if they were simply to do with an ordinary object, without seeking to get beyond the mere word and into its meaning. It is almost as if they were following the advice of Thomas Hobbes to swallow religious truths whole, like apothecary's pills. If we do not allow ourselves to be dazzled by the logical or logistic performance of a writer such as Plantinga, we end up with a sense of a mass of unrelated units of meaning, which leaves no place for 'the blessed and only Ruler, the King of kings and Lord of lords' (1 Tim. 6:15).[114]

The criticism of anthropomorphism rests on the biblical meaning of God: 'The King eternal, immortal, invisible, the only God' (1 Tim. 1:17), 'Sovereign Lord' (*despotēs*, Acts 4:24; *cf.* Jude 4; Rev. 6:10), *Pantokratōr*, which means 'Lord of limitless power' (found nine times in the book of Revelation), not to mention the name 'Lord'. Of course, these titles do not carry the pejorative slant that Laplantine gives them, any more than they justify the image of people as robots or puppets. We must take care not to confuse what comes across in a writer's presentation of his material, and what has actually been demonstrated.

But there is not only the overall position of Scripture to consider, there are also specific points which oblige us to reject the solution by autonomous freedom. That, of course, is where the decisive criterion is to be found. Nowhere does Scripture suggest that God suspends the exercise of his sovereign power in respect of the slightest occurrence in the world. He 'who works out everything in conformity with the purpose of his will' (Eph. 1:11), not only 'works . . . both to will and to act' (Phil. 2:13) in those who obey him, but goes so far as to include in his plan even the wicked acts of those who transgress his preceptive will. The texts declare so in a general way and portray it in a variety of specific cases; the attacks *of which he is the target* depend nevertheless in the last analysis on his decretive will, that is to say they figure in his plan.[115] Nowhere does Scripture suggest that human choice is independent, that it has sprung from 'absolute spontaneity' (*cf.* Pr. 21:1), nor that such independence is the condition of responsibility (*cf.* Rom. 1:18 – 2:16). Nowhere does Scripture explain the emergence of evil by its presence as a potential factor within freedom in the beginning. Nowhere does it teach that the possibility of evil was the inescapable ransom required by creation in order for humanity to enjoy freedom. Nowhere is there any hint of a 'risk' taken by God.

Modern thinkers allow themselves to be drawn towards the paradox of 'the powerlessness of God', no doubt because they like the glamour of paradoxes. We must also recognize the contribution made by the devaluation of authority, and the widespread resentment against power as such. The best of them are moved by a devotional motive: is not Golgotha marked by powerlessness, and Gethsemane by the voluntary humiliation, the kenosis that is the subject of the hymn in Philippians 2? They are not wary enough, however, of old heresies that lie in wait along that particular path. In Christology itself kenoticism (the idea that, in order to become man, the Son emptied himself or stripped himself of his divine nature) is a dead end; the humiliation of the Son in 'the days of [his] life on earth' did not abolish his role as the one who upholds the universe (Heb. 5:7; 1:3), or his role as *comprehensor*, the 'possessor', to be distinguished from the 'pilgrim' Christ, *viator*, at that time.[116] And above all – as far as this study is concerned – confusing the Persons tips us into the abyss of modalism, the fatal error of Sabellius, who reduced Father, Son and Holy Spirit to the status of *modes* of manifestation of a divinity that was fundamentally undifferentiated. The very particular powerlessness of the Second Person in his incarnation is not, if we make the proper distinction, the powerlessness of the divine nature. If the Son did not make use of his divine omnipotence in the life that he led simultaneously as a true man, if he suffered and died as a man in order to complete the expiatory sacrifice that had to be made, that is never said of the Father. In Gethsemane the Son renounced the spontaneous human desire to avoid death, in order to carry out the plan of the Father, who could immediately have sent him thousands upon thousands of angels. To think of the cross as the powerlessness of God is to commit a short-circuit which is a gigantic misconception; in the preaching of the apostles it is rather the triumph of God by means of the sublime manœuvre of his inscrutable wisdom, in realizing the plan that was decreed 'from before the foundation of the world'. And we must add that we see in it not the efficacy of paradox, but the shedding of blood for the remission of sins.

Why does the 'solution by autonomous freedom' enjoy such great popularity? Because it springs up in well-prepared soil: its idea of freedom constitutes the great presupposition of *humanism*, the ideological consensus that is still operative today. The heirs of humanism today, however aware they are or are not of their ancestry, can have their doubts about freedom *sometimes*: might a human being not be entirely conditioned, governed by mechanisms of which he is unaware? But they are sure that, if freedom exists, it must have independence and be non-determined. Their thought goes no further than that, when they locate the origin of evil in the power of freedom. On the subject of freedom, however, there is no hiding the conflict with Scripture – and with experience! The glorification of free will comes up against all the attestations of the *bondage of the will*, to borrow Luther's phrase in his reply to Erasmus, the 'prince of the humanists'. The great scholar from Rotterdam enjoys that title in the sixteenth-century sense, as the most erudite man of his day; but he was also a precursor of humanism in the modern sense, that is the view of the world in which man considers himself the key to it. From the prophet Jeremiah to the apostle Paul, the exposure of the enslavement of sinful human nature and of the slavery of the flesh accompanies the denunciation of the will as evil. 'Everyone who sins is a slave to sin,' said Christ (Jn. 8:34). In that situation, the hypothesis of a free will conceived as independence, even before sin, becomes improbable. Kant wanted to take account of 'radical evil'; however, as Laplantine has clearly discerned, Kant did not fathom the full depth of evil and of its wickedness.[117] He observed the inclination towards evil, but not the slavery it exercises; he underestimated the malevolence of the will that is evil; because of his humanism, he was unable to identify with the radical stance of the Bible.

Refuted by Scripture, the explanations of evil brought together in the second group of our classification would reveal further inadequacies if subjected to a closer analysis. They are incapable of maintaining their opposition to metaphysical solutions all the way. (Berdyaev's work would again serve as an enlarging mirror for the whole family.) It is true to say that for them freedom includes, both essentially and from the very beginning, the 'real possibility' of evil. This phrase of Kierkegaard is precisely the right one, because this possibility is not a pure abstraction, the logical negation of good (an unreal possibility), but it spells out a real possibility of real freedom. Now that is a metaphysical fact, and thereby evil receives an ontological status (that of *mē on*) in the created order. Evil is so strongly implied by freedom, that one must speak about evil in order to define freedom – and that is no mere trifle! And straight away there is evil incorporated, by implication, into the very ingredients of being. So either you accept dualism, or else you admit that God created the real possibility of evil, and God can no longer be excused for its presence. That way you are back in the situation we dealt with in the last chapter. Evil has its seed and its root in the very creation: how difficult that makes it still to say, 'God saw *all* that he had made, and it was very good' (Gn. 1:31).

Those who support the explanation by freedom sense the difficulty, and so they look around for an excuse. So we find ourselves sliding towards the excuse that has already been smoothed and polished by the rationalist systems of the first group: God was right to create potential evil *because of the good for which it was the cost*. Freedom is such a glorious thing![118] You end up with a 'rational' justification of evil, by postulating that evil had to be really possible in order for humanity to be free. Do they not think that in this way they have removed the scandal, and have emptied evil of its evil?

It is salutary to emphasize that evil has its origin in freedom; but every theory which magnifies that truth until it becomes an explanation and a solution to the problem is just a conjuring trick.

3

The solution by dialectical reasoning

The third approach adopted in Christendom in order to provide a rational account of evil is further removed than the other two from familiar ways of thinking. Disconcerting and obscure by reason of its excessive brilliance and depth, it carries no popular appeal, despite its diluted presence in all forms of modern culture. Intellectuals who enjoy philosophical speculation are easily drawn to it; with their quick, agile minds they are far too well aware of the aggressive power of evil to accept the 'sensible' arguments of the Thomists, and too clear in their own minds about the factors that restrict freedom, and about the emptiness of the claim to absolute autonomy, to be satisfied with the 'ethical' or autonomist solution. For them the dialectical approach is the way forward.

The word 'dialectical' can, admittedly, mean almost anything. Once it simply meant the art of conducting a reasoned argument. For Plato it meant the way of advancing towards the realm of Ideas by dialogue. But as early as Aristotle we find it used in a more technical sense, to indicate propositions that are 'arguable', *i.e.* of lesser certainty. For modern philosophy since Hegel, the dialectic has become a manner of thinking which, as it advances, includes rather than excludes the antithesis of contradictory concepts. Antithesis is no longer seen as a barrier, as in ancient logic, but as a valuable means of moving forward. The acceptance of both Yes and No in tension annuls the 'bourgeois' complacency of traditional truths, which are denounced as dated and 'abstract'. Even when the dialectical method breaks free from its strict Hegelian discipline of nearly two centuries, it describes a line of thought that is always on the move, or being resumed, in a constant movement back and forth, supposedly in order to follow as faithfully as possible the shape and pattern of *life*.

The thinkers in this third category probably differ among themselves even more than the advocates of the solutions we have already discussed. Using reason in a very free and speculative manner, and enjoying the delights of paradox, they have two principal affirmations in common. First, they consider that *evil has been present from the very origin of the world*, as a unified power which opposes Good. This evil is often called non-being or nothingness – this is *mē on* once again – but it is given actual reality, either *in* God or *with* God. In the Augustinian and Thomist tradition, non-being is not evil itself, and is limited to causing fallibility in every creature, which will subsequently falter. Even in Berdyaev, the abyss of non-being begets an ambivalent freedom; in this instance non-being is directly the negative. Is this development, then, pessimistic? Far from it; the reversal of for and against, or rather from against to for, allows the most optimistic outcome.

This brings us to the second key proposition: *evil*, or at least the *confrontation* that it implies, *plays a positive role*; the negative is 'fruitful', because it must be denied in its turn, and thus reality is set in *motion*, and being escapes from the deadness of a fixed condition and experiences progress. This emphasis on the dynamism which springs from contradiction makes this line of thought 'dialectical'. When the representatives of other philosophical or theological groupings welcome dissonance as a factor that serves harmony, and consider the ability to do evil as the ransom required to permit the highest values, they have still not moved into dialectics (in the modern sense). By means of dialectics, one may, apparently, take stark realism a very long way, without watering down the power of the aggression of evil, and then follow that by making hope spring forth from it – as in the Christian gospel.

We shall distinguish three versions of this solution, according to the predominant theme of each. The descendants of Germanic mysticism remain fascinated by the depths of the abyss, feeling at home in the language of the philosophy of religion, *Religionsphilosophie*. The second group is the Hegelian tradition, the most dialectical of all dialectics, centring on the kenosis and the death of Christ, from where the Trinity is given a new interpretation. Thirdly there is Karl Barth who has his own distinctive position, being much more concerned to stand in the dogmatic mainstream of the church, and seeking in his dialectic to glorify the free grace of God in Jesus Christ.

The dialectics of the abyss: Jakob Boehme

The precursor, one might even say the father, of modern dialectics has been given the sobriquet of '*philosophus teutonicus*', even though his modest calling was that of a shoemaker. Jakob Boehme (1575–1624) was the one who made the breakthrough, with a welter of rough-hewn metaphors. Before him, in antiquity, Heraclitus and Empedocles had meditated on the inter-play and effects of antithetical elements, thinking, however, that in these they were discovering the secret of balance, not of progress. Stimulated perhaps by a few remnants from the Gnostic tradition, the brilliant theo-sophist received his revelation at his workshop in Görlitz: one Sunday morning his gaze came to rest on a tin plate on the wall and, as it shone with 'Jovian brilliance' against the dark background of the shop, Boehme sud-denly realized that light is alive only by contrast with darkness.[1] The No is necessary to the Yes, the No thrusts the Yes to the fore. Dialectics were in the process of being born! Boehme's first book was most suitably entitled *Aurora*.

Boehme built on his intuition by exploring the depths of his inner self: 'Heaven and earth, and all living creatures, and God himself lie deep down within man.'[2] There he discovered the seething mass of contrary forces, which existed in the beginning, in the primeval *Ungrund*, the bottomless abyss. Consequently he was bold enough to write:

> All things exist by Yes and by No, whether they are divine, diabolic, terrestrial, or whatever you will. The 'One', in so far as it is Yes, is power and love, is the truth of God and God in person. But it could not be recognized as such without the No, and without the No there would be neither joy nor greatness nor awareness.[3]

'Thus', comments Ernst Bloch, 'there is an evil, diabolic element deep in the being of God; the other face of the divine is the demonic.'[4] And Boehme justifies the antithesis, even for God, by its fruitfulness: 'The one always opposes the other, not with hostile intent, but in order that it may stir into motion and appear.'[5] Humanity, identified with Christ, turns the work of Lucifer into good; in this way justification is provided for acts of disloyalty and rebellion, for the sin committed in Paradise and for that of Babel.[6] Here is how Ernst Bloch describes where this finally leads:

> So everything leads to a form of pantheism which carries within itself the confrontation postulated by the dialectic, a confrontation that is transposed into the divine centre of nature (*centrum naturae*) until the time when the divine nature is abolished in the process of the seven dynamic forces – fire being the first metamorphosis, mankind the second and the quintessence of the seven cosmic forces – and with it the suffering of the world, desire with all its qualities (*Quallitäten*). Thus in the end there is reconciliation, the return to the 'One', the suppression of all discord.[7]

The hope of perfect reconciliation is often to be found in the company of dialectical faith.

Non-being overcome: Paul Tillich

The German Romantics greatly enjoyed plunging into the obscurity of Boehme's *Ungrund*, in particular Schelling (1775–1854), Hegel's brilliant younger contemporary, who had two philosophical careers – before and after Hegel's great heyday. In 1911, a little more than half a century after his death, a doctoral thesis on Schelling was presented by a young Lutheran scholar called Paul Tillich. In our view, Tillich (1886–1965) is the greatest twentieth-century thinker in the tradition of Boehme and his dialectics of the abyss. Since the mid-60s his influence has grown throughout Europe, among Catholics as well as Protestants, making him a key figure in our study.

Paul Tillich's major works were written in English and published in the USA, since he had been unable to stay in Germany during the rise of Nazism. Being-itself, he writes on more than one occasion, is the ground and abyss of all beings.[8] No doubt the formula came to him first in German, as he linked the terms *Grund* and *Abgrund*, or even more like Boehme, *Urgrund* and *Ungrund* ('primeval ground/foundation' and, literally, 'groundlessness/bottomlessness'). Being-itself is the ground of what is, but also transcends, and therefore denies, what is finite. A finite being, such as that tree, or you, or I, participates in *being*-itself, because it *is*; in this way, it has being-itself as its ground. But a finite being *is not* being *itself*; it is only that tree, or that individual, and nothing else; therefore it is denied by being-itself, which reveals itself with respect to it as the abyss.

This can be expressed another way: for Tillich, 'being is essentially related to non-being'; 'There can be no world unless there is a dialectical participation of non-being in being.'[9] What does he mean? For him, to be finite is a mixture of being and non-being: the presence of non-being corresponds to the fact that finite being *is not* being-itself (it is thus negated by being-itself, 'abysmally'), and this non-being is conceived as a dynamic reality. Non-being is close to the *mē on* of the Greeks which we have already mentioned. Wheras it is related to matter in Thomism, and is identified with freedom in Berdyaev, in Tillich it takes on a more aggressive sense.[10] Since this non-being combines with being in all finite beings which constitute the world, it cannot be detached from them; an essential link binds them together.

If the situation obtains in the world, it is true *within* being-itself. Tillich, in fact, rejects everything supernatural, everything that is 'another world', every divinity with a separate existence. Being-itself, that 'faith' calls God, is not *a* being, enjoying a distinct existence (Tillich loved shocking the laity by telling them that God 'does not exist'), but is the 'power of being' within all beings, and nowhere else. As a result, the relationship of conflict between being and non-being in the world must be said to be *in him*: 'being "embraces" itself and non-being. Being has non-being "within" itself as that which is eternally present and eternally overcome in the process of the divine life.'[11] So God 'is the eternal process in which separation is posited and is overcome by reunion',[12] in which 'the demonic, anti-divine principle, which nevertheless participates in the power of the divine'[13] must be overcome.

This German-American philosopher-theologian was in no sense suffering from mythomania, nor was he even a visionary. His language with its mythological overtones is easily interpreted. Tillich is consistent in his rejection of supernaturalism: if God is not a being above the world, and if the negative makes itself felt within the world, God must be represented as at grips with that negative. And in this way he utilizes his choice of the notion of power in order to explain the meaning of being – the ontology that he works out is an ontology of *power*: being is the power to be, which suggests a resistance to be overcome;[14] 'We could not even think of "being" without a double negation: being must be thought of as the negation of the negation of being.'[15] And that shows clearly the priority that a sense of a conflict of forces enjoys in his thought. The 'ontological shock' which, according to him, plays the part of a kind of philosophical conversion is our conscious perception of the threat and the onslaught of non-being, to which the counter-attack is made by being within us.

In the wide array of analyses made by Tillich, the most striking is that concerning the import of ontology in the conscious life of human beings. With its rich cultural dimension, it puts substantial flesh on the bones of the system. 'Non-being produces an awareness of anxiety, and this anxiety has three forms, as has non-being: the anxiety of fate and death, the anxiety of emptiness and meaninglessness, and the anxiety of guilt and condemnation.'[16] Pagan antiquity was particularly aware of the first; the Reformation was impelled by the third; the modern age quite obviously suffers from the overwhelming anxiety of the absence of meaning. Tillich distinguishes two levels, that of essence and that of existence, although they cannot be separated in time (only for the purpose of analysis). This threefold anxiety, he argues, belongs to finitude as such, according to its essence. But with the passage to existence, it becomes *alienation*.[17] The human, in order to 'ek-sist', breaks away from the ground or foundation, and thus becomes alienated; alienation also presents three aspects, those of unbelief, of *hubris* or inordinate pride, and of concupiscence or inordinate desire. Estrangement is thus 'unavoidably connected' with self-actualization as *finite freedom*; 'This is the point at which the doctrine of creation and the doctrine of the fall join'; 'fully developed creatureliness is fallen creatureliness'; because of non-being, the existential break with being, mediated by freedom, is dependent on destiny.[18] The dialectic explains therefore what we call evil.

Being reluctant to make predictions about any kind of Utopia, Paul Tillich does not promise total Reconciliation as triumphantly as his colleagues usually do. He proclaims the New Being who overcomes alienation, he makes use of the symbol of the Kingdom of God, but he does not look for a golden age within history, nor for anything beyond history: his business rather is to summon us here and now to exercise *the courage to be*. In spite of the absurd, sin and death, let us believe that victory will be found on the side of meaning, acceptance and life! Thus, through the dialectic, evil is overturned into good, though the expression of that remains half-veiled. It is nevertheless discernible once one appreciates the value that Tillich ascribes to the affirmation of courage (which would not occur without the conflict), and becomes clearer when one considers the *Model* of the courage to be, the effort of being-itself 'eternally conquering its own non-being'.[19] Indeed, 'Non-being makes God a living God. Without the No he has to overcome in himself and in his creature, the divine Yes to himself would be lifeless'.[20] With Tillich too we end up with a justification of the negative by the good that its presence causes; evil works for the affirmation of life.

The dialectics of the cross: Hegel

Paul Tillich ties the courage to be, the victory over alienation, to Christian symbols: to 'the continuous self-surrender of Jesus who is Jesus to Jesus who is the Christ', in the gospel image, that is to say to his self-abnegation for the sake of God; and to justification by faith, which must be understood as 'the accepting of the acceptance without somebody or something that accepts', in the night of doubt and of meaninglessness.[21] But in Tillich's thought the link is clearly very loose.[22] The second dialectical approach is more closely wedded to the themes of the biblical message. It finds its inspiration in the cross.

Hegel! His name is massive, overwhelming. He is *'our* Plato', declared François Châtelet, the one who determines modern thought in the same way that Plato determined philosophy itself.[23] We recoil before the 'terrifying' task of giving an account of the Hegelian system. But no-one can fail to see that the role of evil lies at its very heart. All who have studied him will recall the sickening pointlessness from which, according to Hegel, we are saved by 'the seriousness, the pain, the patience and the work of the Negation'.[24] The Spirit is always denying, and *thus* realizes itself: it opposes itself as Idea by positing the finite, then by denying that negation it reconciles itself to itself, becoming infinite *for itself*, until it reaches the fulness of the concrete Universal. 'The source and origin of human reality', says Kojève by way of summary, 'is *Non-being* or the power of *Negativity*, which realizes itself and manifests itself only by the transformation of the given identity of *being* into the creative *contradiction* of the "dialectical" or historical process of *becoming*'. Hegel goes so far as to speak of the 'magical force' of the prolonged visit of the Spirit to the sphere of influence of the Negative.[25]

The Negative includes what is commonly meant by evil. In the first place, it includes suffering and death: 'Hegel's "dialectical" or anthropological philosophy is, in the final analysis, *a philosophy of death*.'[26] It also includes violence and war: the continued recognition of persons requires conflict and bloodshed, in which life must be put at risk; war

> preserves the moral (*sittliche*) health of the peoples . . . just as the motion of the winds preserves the waters of a lake from becoming stagnant . . . for what is [like Man] negative-or-negating by its very nature (which is Action), must remain negative-or-negating and must not become something fixed-and-stable (*Festes*).[27]

All these human passions that make a mockery of law and morality are, unknown to the participants and by the cunning of Reason, the instruments of progress.[28] Hegel is able to distinguish 'evil' from negativity in general; it is the obstinate individuality of the natural will choosing itself, rather than the universal; but this very evil is necessary, an inevitable historico-logical stage, and, if it 'must not be', it is in the sense that it must be overtaken and left far behind.[29]

Not that Hegel abandoned himself to a superficial optimism – not for him some kind of milk-and-water religion of human goodness! 'No pessimist has painted as grim a picture of history as that presented by Hegel [but] . . . having cleared the ground of all moral philosophy and all eudemonism . . . [he] accepts everything with his unshakeable faith in the rationality of the event.'[30] Since the injury inflicted by evil is ontologically inevitable, since it is the condition of the growth of the Spirit, and since it will heal without leaving any scar, Hegel, who understands everything, also forgives everything:

> In this way he pronounces the absolute 'yes' of the reconciliation of the spirit with itself, in the very action of history, which is henceforth understood absolutely because it is pardoned absolutely. That is the principle of the Hegelian theodicy in action.[31]

Because of the negativity that actuates the life of the Absolute, which embraces everything, there is a theodicy. Kostas Papaioannou says most pertinently: 'the "calvary" of history is to be at one and the same time theogony, theophany and theodicy'.[32] By the last of these terms Hegel defines the work that he proposes: 'Theodicy consists of making the presence of evil intelligible as it stands over against the absolute power of Reason;' and he emphasizes: 'Evil in the universe, including moral evil, must be comprehended and the thinking mind must be reconciled with the negative.'[33]

It was no doubt by a number of different paths that this idiosyncratically 'Lutheran' philosopher reached his justification of God and of the world (the world being a stage in the process of God). His reading of Fichte could have suggested to him the positive necessity of the negative: the Self realizes itself by opposing itself. His acute appreciation of the transitoriness and decay of all things, together with the Romantic intertwinement of life and death, led Hegel to discern in the negative the secret of all life; as also, and even more forcefully, did the experience of the anxiety of the human spirit, and the sense of uprooting implied by free action. It could be shown, we believe, that the supression of every higher judicial authority calls for a dialectical view of reality, that is to say one that integrates contradiction in the unfolding Process, or Becoming. If God is dead, according to one of the meanings of that formula that was dear to Hegel, if there is no longer a transcendence that is outside the Process of becoming and that is therefore capable of judging it, then there is no longer a tribunal to condemn this and absolve that. Everything is true – and truths too are mortal. Hegel was also moved by the nobility of military courage; he discerned the spiritual advance involved in overcoming fear, and in the clear decision to expose oneself to the ultimate danger and to confront death. At a more profound level, he explains the new interpretation of work as self-realization: his dialectic is an absolutization of work, 'whose god knows no sabbath';[34] if there is joy only through the trouble one has taken and the toil one has endured, then the negative is necessary – better still, it is justified. The initial inspiration of the former theology student at the seminary of Tübingen, however, certainly seems to have been *Christian*, closely connected with the gospel: it was the *concept* veiled by its religious *representation* which he wished to extract, Christianity raising religion to its supreme point.[35] The *alienation* that is necessary in order that the Spirit may have access to the concrete and may realize itself is the philosophical rendering of the kenosis of Philippians 2. The role of the negative brings about a 'speculative Good Friday': where then, other than in the gospel, does the most horrific *crime* give birth to the widest *reconciliation*, the reconciliation that is brought into being at the level of community by the *Spirit*? There is no momentary imprecision when Hegel speaks of history as the *Calvary* of the Absolute. One could not imagine any more glorious theodicy: the *whole* of the tragic side of reality is recovered, its sign is reversed, and all proceeds from the cross.

The cross within God: Jürgen Moltmann

The most fruitful development of the Hegelian tradition in our own day comes from the ecumenically renowned Reformed dogmatician, Jürgen

Moltmann, of Tübingen. The great abundance of references to Hegel in his major works is evidence of his extensive reading of the great philosopher. It is true that he often seems to have read him through neo-Marxist spectacles, provided by Ernst Bloch and the theoreticians of the Frankfurt school, Adorno and Horkheimer. He has also gained much from the writings of others, such as certain Jewish thinkers and also the physician from Basle, Adrienne von Speyr. His recourse to potentialities in history, to latencies and tendencies, gives his thought a tinge of vitalism; his idea of non-being mixed with being in the first creation contains echoes of ancient Greek thought; he too speaks of 'the struggle between being and non-being', and links it to creation *ex nihilo*.[36] But primarily and supremely it is to Hegel that he is indebted. Extolling a *Realdialektik*, he has himself declared his intention to 'bring the notion of paradox, connected with Kierkegaard, to the much more extensive dialectic of Hegel and of Marx'.[37]

On the subject of evil, Moltmann's Hegelian ancestry comes clearly to light. In his first major work, *Theology of Hope*, he borrows the phrase 'cross of the present', or 'cross of reality', to universalize the meaning of the sufferings of Christ.[38] Rather than having value as a unique and distinct event, the agony of Calvary finds its meaning as the epitome of the suffering inherent in the human condition, or at any rate in the condition of those who are oppressed. Furthermore, Moltmann is able to write as if this were a fundamental law: 'In exile one seeks home. In alienation one seeks identity. Love is revealed in hatred and peace in conflict.'[39]

In *The Crucified God*, Moltmann develops with great eloquence – in our view Moltmann is above all an orator – his new dialectical theology, of which the Crucified One is the 'criterion'. Developing his theme from Jesus' cry on the cross, 'My God, my God, why have you forsaken me?' (Mk. 15:34), Moltmann asserts: 'The abandonment on the cross which separated the Son from the Father is something which takes place within God himself; it is *stasis* within God – "God against God" – particularly if we are to maintain that Jesus bore witness to and lived out the truth of God.' Insisting on the *enmity*, he discerns 'an enmity manifested and overcome in God himself', the consequence of which in theological politics is the suppression of enmity. If God is love, that is because there is 'an inner opposition to God', 'God overcomes himself'; 'God's being is in suffering and the suffering is in God's being itself, because God is love.'[40]

The theme of kenosis moves Moltmann, like the deeply moving reflections of the Jews on the shekina glory, humbled and trudging along in the dust.[41] The shekina is the Presence and glory of the LORD, Yahweh, who dwells amongst his people (from the word *šākan*, to live, to dwell), the actual word not appearing in the Bible. What could be more Hegelian than this description of the theology of the cross?

> [Because] it sees nothingness itself done away with in the being
> of God, who in the death of Jesus has revealed himself and
> constituted himself in nothingness, it changes the general
> impression of the transitoriness of all things into the prospect of
> the hope and liberation of all things.[42]

And Moltmann quotes with approval the preface of Hegel's *Phenomenology of Mind* on 'the magic power' of a period of time spent in the presence of the negative.[43] Such a theology must reject the traditional distinction between '"God in himself" and the "God for us"': hence Moltmann calls for a 'complete reshaping' of trinitarian theology in which 'the nature of God would have to be the human history of Christ and not a divine "nature" separate from man'.[44] The Trinity issues forth from the cross, as in Hegel; it is particularly important not to think 'as though the Trinity were already present in itself, in the divine nature'.[45]

> In that case, what sense does it make to talk of 'God'? I think
> that the unity of the dialectical history of Father and Son and
> Spirit in the cross of Golgotha, full of tension as it is, can be
> described so to speak retrospectively as 'God'.[46]

We have moved beyond theism by means of the negation: 'A trinitarian theology of the cross perceives God in the negative element and therefore the negative element in God, in this dialectical way, is panentheistic.' This negative embraces the most horrific evil: 'Even Auschwitz is taken up into the grief of the Father, the surrender of the Son and the power of the Spirit.'[47]

In this way, Moltmann stands shoulder to shoulder with Hegel: 'We participate in the trinitarian process of God's history.'[48]

In his more recent writings, he has been adding a little water to his dialectical wine. He has not repeated the most daring phrases from *The Crucified God*. He can speak of an 'inner-trinitarian' order from the beginning, and of a distinction which remains between the 'immanent' Trinity, which is eternal in God, and the 'economic' Trinity, in revelation, in the history of the world.[49] He shows more concern for the plurality of the divine persons, and for the 'social' model which is a suitable expression of their union. But he has not retracted his earlier propositions. He still places the cross within the being of God, and seeks to fuse metaphysics and history; he is most unhappy with the classical duality of the immanent and the economic; he calls into question the contingency of the creation, which does, after all, mark the frontier between the Creator and the created order.[50] There are also other features that would show that Moltmann remains under the influence of Hegel.

Nevertheless, there emerge clear differences between Hegel and Moltmann concerning evil and its role, and they are important. In spite of the role of the negative in the constitution of the divine Trinity, Moltmann avoids attributing fruitfulness and value directly to it; evil is rather the opportunity for love, which in Moltmann's terms is scarcely to be thought of without sacrifice, grief and death. He shows more sensitivity to the scandal of innocent suffering; his passion for the problem of theodicy was born of the experience of the great collective tragedies of our time.[51] He emphasizes political evil, which for our generation takes the place of cosmological evil in the forefront of human concern.[52] He is, however, also fully aware of its other forms, such as neurosis, metaphysical meaninglessness, and *death* for which no consolation is to be found in the thought of a happy posterity.[53] He has no desire to remain with the Good Friday of theory and speculation, but to move on to the Good Friday of *history*; in other words, he does not want to reduce the death of Jesus in his thought simply to the symbol of universal suffering, but to retain something unique and decisive in the concrete event, which was revolutionary in its effect on the world.[54] In the end he rejects Hegel's panlogism, and it is in this sense that he considers there is no dialectical consolation to be found for Maidanek and Hiroshima.[55] He goes as far as to formulate precisely the proposition that we are hoping to establish: 'The person who believes will not rest content with any slickly explanatory answer to the theodicy question. And he will also resist any attempts to soften the question down.'[56] It is not the necessity of cosmic Reason that soothes the anguished heart, but the proclamation of a God who becomes himself by taking evil upon himself through love; and he who alone is able to overcome evil gives us hope.

Like the opposing twins, Esau and Jacob, struggling against one another in Rebecca's womb, there are two distinct persons in this theologian's heart: one is the Hegelian delighting in dialectical about-turns and speculative games with concepts; the other is the man of profound compassion, of passionate indignation with injustice and suffering, particularly when they have a political source. In so far as Moltmann diverges from Hegel, he has no very distinct theodicy to offer. Because he continues to depend so often on Hegelian patterns, even in the overall scheme of his doctrine; because his statements suggest that the negative is so integrated that life, love and the Trinity are determined by it; because evil is sometimes related to 'non-being' by virtue of the conditions of the act of creation; and because he clearly ends up with universal salvation, from a perspective in which the End takes preference over the origin, when the Trinity is unified, the world is unified, and the whole is made one with God;[57] we consider that there is nevertheless a theodicy in Moltmann's work, whose solution is related to that of Hegel: blurred, cracked and truncated it may be, but it is still recognizable.

The dialectics of grace: Karl Barth

Karl Barth (1886–1968) would have frowned to find himself in the company given him in this chapter. He scarcely appreciated Paul Tillich, and their respective followers in the United States have not got on well together. As for Hegel, it was Barth who described the Hegelian system as the greatest attempt (*Versuch*) but also the greatest temptation (*Versuchung*) for the Christian thinker. The dialectic which gave its name to the theology of the early Barth between the two wars came from Kierkegaard, Hegel's implacable opponent. And yet Hans Urs von Balthasar thought he could see in Barthian thought a kind of kinship with that of Hegel.[58] Even if his dialectic is original (which it is), it too provides a solution to the problem of evil. Our account will concentrate on that solution, taking for granted an overall acquaintance with the work of the twentieth century's greatest dogmatic theologian.

Terminology is crucial. Barth sets his thoughts on the path which will lead them to their goal by the choice of the term he uses to designate evil: *das Nichtige*, rendered in the English translation as 'nothingness',[59] in accordance with the connotations of vanity and futility brought out in the dictionaries. The word 'nothingness', used in preference to *das Böse*, indicates an *ontological* perspective; the problem of evil is being treated in terms of being, non-being, negation. This feature merits attention, for it is characteristic of Barthian thought, but often passes unnoticed beneath the biblical language that Barth brought back into theological discourse.

Barth certainly did not stop at the theme of the Absolute Other and 'the infinite qualitative difference between time and eternity', a metaphysical problem beyond the faintest shadow of doubt. In the preface to his *Römerbrief* (*The Epistle to the Romans*) of 1921, he established this as a principle, but ten years later he had changed so much that this earlier work seemed to him to have come from a different man. As Henri Bouillard pointed out, however, the conception of Barth's *Church Dogmatics* provides a striking 'parallelism' with 'that of the *Römerbrief* which it intends to leave behind'.[60] At the beginning of the doctrine of reconciliation, the centre which includes the whole, Barth defines salvation in distinctly ontological terms: it is 'the fulfilment of being', 'being in perfection in participation in the divine being'.[61] The message is summed up in these words: 'Because He *is* God he puts forth His omnipotence to *be* this other man, to *be* man quite differently, in our place and for our sake.'[62] So evil is first of all thought of as a certain negation of being.

Metaphysical notions send us back to origins. Where does evil – Barth's *das Nichtige* – come from? He is too concerned about being faithful to Scripture, either to give it the status of a second eternal principle, or to make it proceed directly from God (as a phase of the divine life, or as an element of the creation). With all due vigour he denounces the error that makes evil a natural *possibility* of created freedom: it is by that error that we begin to make evil excusable.[63] And yet evil-nothingness could not arise *afterwards*: it is not only original (sprung from created freedom after creation), it is, to use a rare word, originary, radically contemporary with created being itself. It requires a new idea for Barth to be able to hold this proposition. The divine Yes, he explains, which is manifested in the creative act, ncessarily includes a No; God 'says Yes, and therefore says No to that to which He has not said Yes', and that No brings forth what he denies. In the creation, on his right hand, as Luther put it, God affirms what he has created and chooses it; in the same moment he rejects and denies chaos or nothingness, and that rejection 'on His left hand', is 'powerful and effective', establishing and founding the reality of nothingness.[64]

Barth is not afraid to repeat himself:

> Nothingness is that which God does not will. It lives only by the fact that it is that which God does not will. But it does live by this fact. For not only what God wills, but what He does not will, is potent, and must have a real correspondence.[65]

Nothingness must not be confused with the 'shadow side' of creation, indicated in the world of Genesis by the darkness and the waters.[66] That side is part of the *goodness* of the created order. It is, however, the side that is 'contiguous to nothingness', the 'frontier' with nothingness, and which signifies the threat hovering over the creation from the fact of nothingness.[67] The devil and the demons in a way give concrete expression to the power of nothingness: 'They are', although 'their being is neither that of God nor that of the creature, neither that of the heavenly creatures nor that of the earthly'; 'they are null and void, but they are not nothing'.[68] When creatures commit evil, they give in to nothingness.

It is easy enough to discover the motive behind this Barthian construction. From about 1930, the key word of dogmatic theology for Barth was 'concentration', Christological concentration: in order to honour the freedom of grace and to drive away once for all the murky mists of natural theology (which were choking the gospel in neo-Protestant liberalism), everything must go through Jesus Christ. There is no relationship between God and mankind outside of the One who is God Incarnate. And he, indeed, is the only 'concrete' God and the only 'concrete' man. This well-known rule of Barthianism demands tremendous compression: creation, reconciliation when Christ came, and the final consummation are no longer three distinct stages. Without completely merging them, Barth tends to make creation and the end as it were shadows or reflections, prior and subsequent, of the central Event that embraces everything. For the theological understanding, reconciliation is the real *content* of all the other events. For the first of these, Barth postulates in that sense that the covenant, the covenant of grace in 'Jesus Christ, is 'the inner foundation of creation'. At once he is driven to grant an analogous structure to the work of the beginning. In Jesus Christ the Yes of God, accompanied by the No as always, wins the victory: the free grace of God, accompanied by judgment as always, triumphs over evil; it was fitting that creation too, being the prelude and type of reconciliation, should appear as a liberating victory, by the defeat of a real adversary. That is the basis for this idea of a negative, or nothingness, which is not nothing, and which emerges along with the creation, but as a hostile force.

It must also be remembered that in Barth's thinking sin is logically subsequent to the event which destroys it (just as the law is also subsequent to the gospel, being founded on it). It is always the same concentration that is operative. If reconciliation precedes creation, how much more does it precede the fall! The usual order is reversed. If these reversals are not taken into account, Karl Barth will be misunderstood. For him Jesus Christ always comes first (according to Col. 1:18, he thinks). Therefore he must be the first sinner in the eyes of God in respect of judgment: 'That this was true of Adam, and is true of us, is the case only because in God's counsel, and in the event of Golgotha, it became true first of all in Jesus Christ.'[69] The thesis is paradoxical, but Barth was never one to worry about paradoxes!

'Jesus is Victor' and the glory of his victory requires both the recognition of the power of the enemy and the assurance that nothing is left of it. But for Barth this duality has been at work since the very beginning, and is compressed into the same period of time. So he is constantly swinging back and forth between solemn or vehement denunciation of the ruinous nature of nothingness and the extreme danger of evil, and the Good News that the irruption of nothingness is 'before God absolutely powerless', 'an episode', and that sin 'is already met', 'removed from all eternity'.[70] It is only 'a receding frontier and fleeting shadow'; 'if it is inevitable, . . . it is nevertheless as such a basically contingent and transient activity'.[71] In Jesus Christ, even this 'fleeting consistency' is taken away from it, 'the permission by virtue of which nothingness could be something is abrogated' (it is unusual of Barth to use the word 'permission'); and again:

> In the light of Jesus Christ there is no sense in which it can be affirmed that nothingness . . . is still to be feared, that it still . . . implies a threat and possesses destructive power.[72]

For each and every man and woman, 'unbelief has become an objective, real and ontological impossibility', and faith a corresponding necessity.[73] So every single person is already justified and sanctified! This truth 'is the fixed star which shines unchanged above all the clouds created by him [*i.e.* by mankind]'.[74] The only thing is, that these clouds exhibit redoubtable efficacy, considering mankind in and of himself; his capacity for falsehood is lethal. And so the dialectical pendulum swings back again, even if Barth is eager to assure us that the Yes finally wins the day. That is why he never brought himself to embrace the doctrine of the *apokatastasis*, the final restoration of everyone, while at the same time coming as close to the brink as possible, and leading his followers to it.[75]

Once the origin of evil has been explained and its defeat clearly stated, we wait for Barth to reveal its rational purpose in order to round off his solution – after the why (for what cause), the wherefore (for what purpose). Barth sees the danger of a kind of Gnostic excuse; he gives a lucid criticism of the liturgical cry *felix culpa*, 'Happy fault'.[76] But the association of inevitable nothingness with the unfurling of God's grace, which as such is free, is too close for the Barthian dialectic not to end up, like others, with a theodicy. An outline appears in an important passage which is often overlooked, and which shows with what inner confidence Barth is able to unravel the logic of God's plan with respect to evil:

> [God says Yes to what He wills and No to what He does not will and] ordains that the object of His love and the witness to His glory in the universe which He has created should testify in a twofold manner – he should testify to His Yes and to what He wills, and he should also testify to His No and to what He does not will. . . . For this purpose it was *necessary* that this man should really be confronted with what God Himself repudiates. . . . And it is *inevitable* that this confrontation with what God repudiates, with evil, should mean for man, who is certainly not God and not almighty, that evil confronts him as a hostile power, a power which is, in fact, greater than his own power. In his case, then, the defeat of this evil power cannot be so self-evident as it was in God's case. In his case it *must* take on the character of an event. It must become the content of a history: the history of an obstacle and its removing. . . . *In willing man*, His man, elected man, God *wills* that this should be the case. He *wills* the confrontation of man by the power of evil. He *wills* man as the one assailed by this power. He *wills* him as the one who, as man and not God, has not evolved this power of himself but is *subjected* to it. . . . He wills Himself as the One *by whose grace* alone man *must* live.[77]

So there *had to be* evil *in order that* grace might reign: *QED*. In spite of his words of caution, Barth just as much as the Hegelians gives us a dialectical solution to the problem.

Evaluation

Our critique of the third kind of 'Christian' discussion of evil may be made more briefly than in the two preceding cases. The features to which objection can be taken are visible to the naked eye in the majority of the systems in question: their authors have chosen to extol as strengths what we consider weaknesses. They certainly make an important contribution, and not only by their critique of other thinkers. Their sense of history, of the paradoxical victory of the cross, and of the 'overturning of evil' which God causes to serve his purposes, trains the searchlight on the very heart of the question, where it should be. But the varied interpretations that they then develop trample on too many accepted biblical teachings. It is significant that not one of them subscribed to the orthodox doctrine of Scripture, even Karl Barth who set such value on Scripture.[78] The idea of a real non-being or nothingness, which is taken to be something other than the corruption or perversion of the acts of a creature, finds no support in Scripture; such a consideration does not predispose us to respect its logical obscurity as something profound.

It is to the 'pervasive ambiguity' of Tillich's language that Alan Richardson attributes the admiration that Tillich aroused among American readers despite his aridity: 'it is possible to . . . read one's own meanings into his words and thus to be hypnotized into finding great comfort in oases which are only mirages'.[79] While we admire Tillich's writings as the synthesis of a great philosophical tradition, we note the obvious absence of any concern to be biblical. With frightening equanimity he declares that he holds to 'a self-transcending or ecstatic *naturalism*';[80] this he spells out by formulating his substitute for justification by faith already quoted: 'the accepting of the acceptance *without somebody* or something *that accepts*'. His spiritual family is to be found on the side of Gnosticism, as well he knows, along with its mythologies.

Hegel's attempt represents a stronger temptation (there were Hegelians who were theologically 'on the right'). His sheer prowess inspires awe, and his determination to be Christian and to espouse specifically Christian views is attractive. Kojève, however, clearly sees the anthropotheism that emerges.[81] Jacques Maritain makes an excellent comment: 'Such an absolute immanentism is more pantheistic than common pantheism.'[82] Evangelical theology must challenge the distortion of meaning which results when the eternal trinitarian relations are identified with the creation and with the incarnation, and of the incarnation with a mutation of the divine nature turned into its opposite.

As for the great discovery of the fusion of logic and life, which is the dialectic, it has a withering effect on life, it abuses reality in order to force it into the rational mould, or else *disguises* it as a logical process; at the same time it smashes logic, leaving it at the mercy of the arbitrary and of proof by pun. Maritain calls it 'an organon . . . perfectly designed for dogmatic trickery'.[83]

The arbitrary is also seen in the identification of the negative with moral evil, which Kierkegaard denounced.[84] A fine paper by Paul Ricœur demonstrates that the passage from otherness to the tragic under the common name of 'negative' 'is an optical illusion'.[85] And if the Hegelian processes are not to deceive us, their effects are such as to horrify us: since no criterion allows us to discern good from evil in history, then everything that happens is essentially *the very work* of God.[86] And God comes to full realization as the universal State! Hegel is the supreme example of the philosopher as Pied Piper, luring his innocent followers away to be shut fast inside the monstrous granite prison of totalitarianism. The brilliant French thinker André Glucksmann is unquestionably correct when he makes this point; so also is the philosopher Jean Brun, whose perspicacity over the years has exposed this hidden aspect of Hegel's thought in his vast surveys of his writings.

There are two further specific criticisms of Hegel's theodicy that deserve to be made. First we must protest against the travesty of *forgiveness* as the justification of all crime by the progress of the Spirit, and indeed as the absolute suppression of the event as such by the dialectic. For Hegel indeed 'the Spirit can make what has happened, not to have happened'; there is no question of any 'as if', or of wiping out its consequences or the marks it has left; *the truth changes*; the old truth that such and such a transgression has been committed ceases to be true.[87] The biblical view of forgiveness, on the contrary, implies the condemnation of the sin, but the restoration of the personal relationship, which accompanies the repentance of the sinner.[88]

We must finally note that there is one form of evil which does not figure in this vast recovery process, an evil which is irreducibly bad. This 'evil' is the conscientious objection which says No to the State, which claims to judge for itself whether we should obey God rather than men. This resistance to the movement of the Spirit is the unforgivable sin.[89] The presence of an irreparable residuum, of an evil that is truly abhorred, is itself a sign of failure. (The same thing is found in other schemes: those who make evil melt away in progress abhor what is fixed, static or unchanging.) But how palpably absurd that what is truly evil for Hegel is in fact the most noble form of human courage! If Hegel, more than other philosophers, drew his inspiration from the gospel, that is simply an illustration of the saying '*Corruptio optimi pessima*' – the corruption of the best is the worst, or, as Shakespeare put it in his ninety-fourth Sonnet: 'Lilies that fester smell far worse than weeds.' If Hegel conceived the perfect theodicy, there would be grounds for suspecting every theodicy.

To the extent that Moltmann depends on Hegel, the criticism that we have just outlined is equally valid for him. To the extent that he diverges from him, the question arises: must he not answer for having borrowed part of that system? Are not Hegel's panlogism – that everything is the evolution of the abstract idea – and life-incorporating contradiction, the negative, are they not both sides of one and the same thought? Moltmann definitely leaves too many ideas up in the air, or rather in the fog. Where is his God? Who was he before he embraced non-being?[90] Any 'panentheism' – a term for which Tillich also had a certain fondness – in his thinking is quite unacceptable. This word, whose etymology is deceptively agreeable, was coined by Charles C. F. Krause (1781–1832) for a watered-down form of pantheism which took the world to be an inner modification within God.

With admirable insight Moltmann warns us against every theory that would seek to explain the problem of evil and also against every attempt to *attenuate* it. Why does he not himself conform to this insight! Is it not precisely an attenuation to suppose an unhappy admixture of non-being in the primal creation? Is it not also attenuation to associate the incorporation of the negative, of alienation, so often with personal life, including for the life of God?[91] Above all, is it not attenuation to attack the (biblical!) image of the King of heaven from one end of a book to the other, and to quote Ernst Bloch with approval: 'Where the great Lord of the universe reigns, there is no room for liberty, not even the liberty of the children of God.'?[92] Now, it is its inclusion within the framework of the sovereignty of the God who is just, that makes evil (*i.e.* disorder affecting order) such an intolerable scandal. The heart-rending pain of the problem of theodicy is the location of sin within the plan of God Almighty who is love: everything happens as if Moltmann were replacing it by the rather crude spatial metaphor of an assumption or reception into the divine being, a metaphor which gives merely the illusion of intelligibility – for *how* does God triumph over evil as he takes it into himself? Moltmann is well able to convey the horror of evil in a very moving way, but his doctrinal edifice suffers from too much ambiguity and fragility.[93]

Karl Barth's pronouncement has a very different ring of authority, avoiding any kind of complicity with Hegelian 'justifications'. His clarity concerning the common fallacy which places the 'possibility' of sin within the creation is masterly. Without challenging the whole structure of his dogmatics, we must nevertheless deplore his drift towards a pseudo-rational gnosis of evil. For him, evil is metaphysically *necessary*: how could such an utterance not call forth our deepest indignation? Concerning Barth's position on demons, George Tavard has seen clearly that his 'ontological explanation' undermines the Christian life.[94] Despite the power of the Barthian oratory, the dialectical oscillation in the end produces the reciprocal neutralization of the propositions set forth: Barth is no longer able to make us believe seriously in the ruinous nature of *das Nichtige*, even if he prevents us from looking forward with certainty to the *apokatastasis* – 'the time of universal restoration' (Acts 3:21, NRSV). As for his explanation of the first emergence of evil-nothingness, what is it but academic sleight of hand? John Hick is perfectly right to accuse him of offering 'a merely verbal and apparent solution'.[95] It is a game with words, and the idea of an 'efficacious non-will' remains irrecoverably hollow. The doctrine of evil-nothingness is a vulnerable point in Barth's whole structure, of which it is an integral part; it might provide the starting-point for a critique of the whole which we are not able to undertake here.

The dialectical solution to the problem of evil has merit in reminding us that God is able to turn the work of evil human beings to fulfil his own designs, to make it serve the good, most notably the supremely evil act of the crucifixion of his Son. But as for the problem itself, it is a pseudo-solution which is more perverse in the way it (falsely) excuses evil, than those solutions that appeal to universal order and to the autonomy of human freedom.

4

Scripture on evil, principally its origin

The failure of the explanations of evil that we have examined and exposed in our preceding chapters, taking them according to their fundamental types, shows them for what they are, when confronted with experience and when the concepts are analysed. But it is Divine Revelation which reveals truly and with complete certainty. Holy Scripture, the Word of God, the 'normative norm', is the only standard which allows us to distinguish between those insights which agree with it, and those all too human false trails in those systems of thought.

In the light of Scripture we welcome with gratitude the fruit of the discernment of those very writers whom we refuse to follow. From the Thomists we learn that evil is not a substance, that it does not exist in and of itself, but may always be defined as the absence of some good thing; hence it has a certain affinity with non-being: evil tends to destruction. From those who favour the solution by autonomous freedom, especially such apologists as C. S. Lewis and Francis Schaeffer – but also taught by those massive thinkers Kant and Kierkegaard – we understand that evil is a fact that follows from created freedom; freedom produced it and brought it into the world; it can come forth from no other source. We gladly agree with the dialectical thinkers that evil, represented supremely by the crime committed at Calvary, enters into the plan of God and serves the cause of reconciliation. For that is true, attested by the Bible.

But those writings which take hold of these truths, imagine that they are developing them, and then claim to go further and give an explanation of evil, run into the rock of Divine Revelation, and so capsize. The first type of solution blunts the biblical hatred of evil as that which is relentlessly opposed to what is good, and does not acknowledge with sufficient clarity the perfect goodness of everything that God creates; we see it as constituting the temptation of *the wise man*, respectful of hierarchies, passionately supporting order, an admirer of the balances within nature, and concerned to integrate all contingencies within the political plan. Even if he is wise according to God, the wise man always runs the risk, as seen in the sad example of Solomon, of slipping towards a wisdom which is too much of this world. He needs the prophetic reprimand, like a goad.

The second type of explanation, through autonomous freedom, can draw from freedom a *reason* for evil only by forgetting the sovereignty of God, as it is taught in the Bible; indeed, if God is Lord over human choices, one wonders why he permits tragic decisions. Perhaps this is the temptation of *the prophet*, to imagine that the autonomy of the human will explains the emergence of evil: the prophet's call is to challenge freedom in the human heart as the proximate source of evil, and summon it to be converted. But the biblical prophet distances himself from this temptation, recalling that he is to denounce and to announce according to the *tôrâ* of the covenant, by the communication of the royal *counsel* of the LORD, Yahweh.

The third type, the dialectical theologian, also launches an attack, fiercer than that of the first type, on the total and absolute goodness of God and of his work, as well as on the assertion of the wickedness of evil. Can we discern in him the temptation of *the priest*, accustomed by sacrifice to the propitiatory effects of innocent blood? The priest has to understand, from the *tôrâ* and from the prophets, that no sacrifice operates by a dialectic of reversal, that only *one* sacrifice is truly efficacious, that of the Lamb of God *freely* offered for his people, to fulfil the justice of God. Against these three temptations, Scripture raises the triple affirmation: that evil is evil, that the Lord is sovereign, and that God is good, his creation also being good with a similar kind of goodness.

We shall now study in greater detail these three branches of the biblical doctrine. Then we shall ask questions (which we shall address to Holy Scripture) on their sum, their resolution or their synthesis. And we shall conclude by considering the result that we have obtained.

The evil reality of evil

Scripture never tires of denouncing the reality and the danger of evil: it is evil totally, radically and absolutely. Respectable non-Christians grow weary or irritated at such insistence, from the third page to the very final page of the Bible. Sometimes they are shocked at the harsh reality of the picture: it is like the abscess beneath the surgeon's lamp. The biblical writers obey the apostle's exhortation: 'Hate what is evil' (Rom. 12:9).

For the cardinal evil known as 'sin', the Hebrew vocabulary, generally so restrained, is exceptionally rich.[1] As Paul was later to explain, the law is given in order to reveal the heinous monstrosity of transgressions (Gal. 3:19; Rom. 3:20; 5:20; 7:8ff., 13, *etc.*). The prophets, such as Micah (Mi. 3:8), at the risk of their lives, pour forth torrents of indignation against the misdeeds of Israel. They were treated as troublemakers (1 Ki. 18:17); but face to face with the false prophets who were stirring up the people, it is their strange 'obsession' with evil, their uncompromising strictness, their sheer intransigence on the whole matter (in fact two thirds of their utterances!) which authenticate their ministry. Nor does Jesus, *the prophet*, fail to keep up the tradition; implacable in the face of hypocrisy, he unmasks the fatal infection of the heart hidden beneath the disguises of outward religious practice. Right from the Day of Pentecost, the preaching of the apostles carries the note of accusation; it demands a complete about-turn in one's daily life and behaviour, in order to make a break with a 'corrupt generation' (Acts 2:40); and it interprets the death of Christ primarily in relation to people's sins. It carries through to the book of Revelation, with its apocalyptic visions of evil and its reverberating cries of evil and against evil. Who can read the Bible and take evil for a mere epiphenomenon, *i.e.* a secondary matter?

With the greatest obstinacy Scripture upholds the antithesis between good and evil. There is not the slightest hint of some descent into the depths to the point where the opposites meet, beyond good and evil – a dream that haunts nearly all pagan religion. Rather, there is stubborn resistance to the heady attraction of paradoxical reversals. 'Woe to those who call evil good and good evil,' says the prophet (Is. 5:20). With deliberate, didactic repetition, we return time and again to the opposition between obedience and sin, the righteous and the wicked, the faithful and the ungodly, the humble and the arrogant, the wise man and the fool. This contrast, which is systematically maintained, is an original feature of the biblical proverbs when compared with the wisdom writings of Egypt. 'In Egypt you do not come across the antithesis of "foolish" or "senseless" and wise. The antithesis of "impetuous" and "reflective" or "cool-headed, calm" is of a quite different kind.'[2] Jesus did not refuse to take up the antithesis (Mt. 7:24ff.; *cf.* 12:36, *etc.*). The very final page asserts yet again the mysterious necessity for opposites to appear as opposites with no compromise: right and wrong, holiness and uncleanness (Rev. 22:11). Paul reacted fiercely against the calumny that was being spread, falsely attributing to him the proposition of the 'fruitfulness of the negative', of evil as the source of good (Rom. 3:8). He also hastened to point out that the death-dealing effect of the divine commandment comes in reality not from itself but from sin (Rom. 7:12ff.). Paul refused to turn the antithesis into a dialectic. Over against the sheer goodness of what is good stands in all its hostility the utter malignity of evil, ultimately shown by the concentration of evil in the Evil One, the Adversary, the Prince of darkness who opposes God who is light, 'the god of this age' (2 Cor. 4:4), the Liar, at war with the true God.

Nothing shows the evil reality of evil better than the wrath of God against it and the eternal perdition of those who choose evil and remain devoted to it. Its judgment (the certainty of which is precisely what governs Paul's thought in Rom. 3:5ff.) and the requirement of expiation for that judgment to be removed, prove to what extent God takes evil seriously. Many thinkers today need to listen to Anselm's refrain in his *Cur Deus Homo*:

'You have not yet duly estimated the gravity of sin.' The fact that evil is vanity (*'āwen*) and the lack of something good (*i.e.* privation) does not remove the weight of sin, for evil makes use of the substance of created goodness, which it turns and reverses for its own purposes against that entity's Creator. Such is the weight of *untruth*, borrowed from the truth that it has travestied and perverted. It is a hideous reality which draws down upon itself the judgment of God.

At this point, however, an initial complication brings us to a halt. Is the punishment inflicted on a guilty man also an evil? The case is considered by many to be self-evident. The suffering and death which follow the fall as its due reward from Genesis 3 onwards are the very *evils* of which men and women complain, and Scripture ratifies this way of seeing them. With all due respect to St Francis of Assisi, death well deserves the name of 'the last enemy' (1 Cor. 15:26). The infiltration of pagan practices (and perhaps certain mechanisms unravelled by psychoanalysis) have brought into the mainstream of traditional Christian spirituality a tendency to prize the moral value of physical pain, and also the ascetic practice of mortification for the sake of mortification, which are quite foreign to the Bible (*cf.* Col. 2:20 – 3:11 for a corrective to these misunderstandings). But the Bible does not judge losses, frustrations, infirmities, sicknesses, or persecutions to be good. Whereas certain figures were later to court martyrdom, Jesus simply said 'Flee' (Mt. 10:23). The classical analysis seems to agree with Scripture: 'physical evil' afflicts the human race as the consequence and the penalty of sin (taken in its entirety).

Nevertheless, as the execution of the judgment of God, and as the restoration of justice, the infliction of punishments must be called *good*. It is something good as far as God is concerned, and so it is something good for the order of the world, for all its creatures, even for the one who undergoes it – the good of everyone as a created being is always to be in harmony with the Creator. Many will be shocked by such sentiments. It is because of our failure to be stirred, as were the prophets and the apostles, with zeal for the honour of God and of his holiness, that so many of our contemporaries are blind to the essential goodness of punishment.[3] They see things only from the point of view of mankind, and this anthropomorphism distorts and truncates anthropology itself. Nothing is as foreign to the Bible, and as falsely philanthropic, as Moltmann's thought: 'For love there *is* only "innocent" suffering'; punishment only adds one evil to the evil already committed.[4] The punished sinner sanctifies and glorifies the LORD, thus achieving the essential end of every person (Lv. 10:3; Ezk. 38:16). He submits to God's justice and renders it due homage. At the last day, every human being will confess the lordship of Jesus Christ, either with shame and remorse, or else with joy and love (Phil. 2:10ff., referring back to Is. 45:23). That is why punishment does not exclude a universal 'reconciliation', but is on the contrary included in it (Col. 1:20).[5] Good and evil join here *without* any dialectic: death (of a man) is evil because God did not desire it, in the sense of Ezekiel 18:32; but *once sin has appeared*, death is something good in terms of its relationship to the satisfaction of justice.

At that point other texts flood the memory. Do they not teach that sometimes evil brings the fruit of blessing, and not by way of punishment? Do they not challenge the notion of utter malignity? Are we not to consider trials as a reason for 'pure joy' (Jas. 1:2)? Does the apostle Paul not encourage us to 'give thanks in all circumstances' (1 Thes. 5:18; *cf.* Eph. 5:20)? Jesus discounts the connection imagined by the disciples between the man born blind and a particular sin, and he gives to weakness and disease, physical evils, a positive purpose: 'that the work of God might be displayed' (Jn. 9:3). Moral evil itself appears capable of a happy outcome; the most striking example of this is perhaps that of the criminal actions of Joseph's brothers against him, from which God drew forth good (Gn. 50:20; *cf.* 45:8). In a more general manner, even 'the wrath of men' will bring praise to the LORD (Ps. 76:10, RSV). One more step, it seems, and we shall be joining the procession of those who are singing *felix culpa*, the harmonious dissonance, the paradoxical fruitfulness of the negative!

Scripture, however, never takes that step, which acts as such a powerful temptation to our mind! Scripture reproves and deplores sin, even when God has found the way to overcome the situation. If the anger of man – which does not work the righteousness of God (Jas. 1:20) – ends in the praise of God, it is in a variety of ways and without any watering down of God's judgment. It does so by its resounding failure to start with, and in general when the wicked are caught in the trap they had laid for others (Ps. 9:16, *etc.*). Or again because one particular evil can counter another, as for example when the barbarous actions of the Babylonians purged the land of Judah of the crimes of King Jehoiakim (*cf.* Hab. 1). The aphorism of Proverbs 16:4 makes very good sense taken that way: the LORD has made everything for its own purpose, even the wicked for the day of disaster, that he may serve as the rod of God's wrath on the day of punishment. In so much as it is a work of wickedness, the act committed is evil; but in that it is the execution of justice, the event brings forth good. Human 'wrath' can in the end 'praise' the LORD by the results that flow from the evil action, but not from its actual malignity. (The distinction is possible here because evil always perverts something that had earlier been created as something good; underlying the malignity of the action is a creational operation.) This last thought sheds light on the case of Joseph: his presence in Egypt was the result of treachery, but it is not in that respect that it becomes a source of deliverance; it is not the evil of the action that brings forth the good. Nor does the text (Gn. 50:20) say that the evil was 'changed' into good, as some translations suggest: only that God 'thought for the good' that which the brothers of Joseph had thought as an evil. The narrative shows *the intervention of God*, mastering all the events and correcting the evil, as the sole source of the beneficial results.

It is from that angle that we read the biblical promises made to those who undergo various trials, promises which remind them of the benefit that they will be able to derive from their painful experience. The evil at the heart of the trial does not as such produce Christian patience or endurance: that is a fruit of the Spirit, a fruit of grace that allows one to endure. Never does Scripture give thanks for sins or for evils as such, but, in every circumstance, for the very present help of the LORD, and for the sovereign direction that he maintains over all that occurs. Evil only ever serves good *in spite of* its malignity, one form of it driving away another, or evil giving the *opportunity* for 'all the more grace' (Jas. 4:6, NRSV).

When an evil gives God the opportunity to reveal the supremacy of his wisdom and the power of his love, people assume that he permitted it *for that purpose*. Rightly so: this conclusion is authorized by Jesus' comment on the man born blind, and is confirmed by other biblical passages. According to Romans 9:17, God raised up Pharaoh with his obstinacy in order, by punishing him, to display his superiority over the gods of the heathen. A little further on, Romans 11:32 teaches that God has imprisoned all in disobedience so that he may be merciful to all. In the context, the meaning is clear: successively in human history the two great categories of mankind, pagans and Jews, have lived in mass disobedience towards God – the pagans when they were all idolaters, the Jews in their rejection of Jesus. God touches them, and will touch them, *in* that situation, thereby demonstrating clearly that his salvation springs from sheer mercy. Such is the plan of God.

It would, however, be exceeding the teaching of the texts to think that there we have the final explanation of evil. In all the cases considered, evil was *already* in the world. God channelled it, directed it and broke down its outworkings so that these might serve his purposes. The decision to permit evil, which is rationally justified by the end in view, concerns only particular crystallizations, transgressions and misfortunes, and the pattern that God imposes on them. But it would be an undue extrapolation to suppose a decision with a like purpose for the first permission of evil *itself*. The import is no longer the same. When evil is already present, if God makes use of that hostile reality as an opportunity to act, and even as a means to punish and to warn, the fact in no measure lessens the malignity of evil, and in no way allows for any insinuation that God might be its accomplice. Rather, it is the victory of God over evil that is proclaimed. If, on the contrary, God had permitted evil itself for the sake of the use he was going to make of it, then *evil itself*, the counterpart of something good, *would be explained and excused*, at least to some extent; instead of holding it in horror, we would have to understand that everything is for the best in the best of all possible worlds. Holy Scripture, if our reading of it is correct, never takes that path; it asserts that God, whose competence infinitely transcends the devilry of his adversaries, is well able to play off evil against evil, and overturns the stratagems of the enemy for his own glory; but that is always, once evil has come in, by way of a counterstroke.

No biblical material, studied with care, allows us to retreat from the denunciation of malignity. We may not compromise its rigour by arguing that God makes use of evil and permits it in order to bring about his purposes, for good does not proceed from evil as such, and its connection with the divine purposes is not taught in respect of the first permission, the origin of evil. Evil remains evil: totally, radically, absolutely.

The universal sovereignty of the Lord

Scripture never doubts God's command over every event, or that he determines everything that happens, in its entirety and in minutest detail: God is sovereign totally, radically, absolutely. Certain people have thought they could undermine this certainty by criticizing the translation of God's name *'ēl šadday* by the words 'God Almighty'. It is true that the old Jewish interpretation *shè-day* ('who-sufficient', the Sufficient One), who in Greek became *ho Hikanos* ('the One who is able'), derives more from a play on words than from etymology;[6] but that is not the basis for the assertion of God's sovereignty! We argued above that it flows from monotheism, and one must be the victim of an indefensible anthropomorphism in order not to see it. We appeal to the huge attestation of both Testaments to the active governing of the world by the Lord of (the cosmic) Hosts, the Lord (*despotēs*), Almighty (*pantokratōr*), from whom, through whom and to whom are all things, to whom belong for ever and ever the kingdom, the power and the glory.

The great proof-texts leave scarcely any loophole for any who would wish to doubt. But also the spontaneous, almost incidental, expressions of conviction about the sovereignty of God abound to the point of drowning by their sheer number the categorical declarations. Of course, there is no question of minimizing these: 'Our God is in heaven; he does whatever pleases him' (Ps. 115:3; *cf.* 135:6) contrasts the LORD with the idols; the gods of the Semitic world were already much stronger in the area of will than the Greek gods – they were 'masters', Baals (note the richness of vocabulary concerning the will); but the God of Israel ridicules the Baals by the power and universality of his dominion (*cf.* Ps. 103:19). The Jewish theologian Abraham Heschel discerns the contrast with the pagan gods, and even with the master of Olympus: 'To the biblical man, God is the supreme Lord Who alone rules over all things. This association of the concept of God with the idea of absolute sovereignty and supreme power may be contrasted with other ways of religious thinking. Zeus, for example . . .'[7] The dogmatic proposition of the apostle Paul leaves scarcely a loophole: God 'works out everything in conformity with the purpose of his will' (Eph. 1:11).

But the consistent language of biblical devotion bears even more eloquent witness. The Creator is not content simply to determine times and allot places (Acts 17:26); everything that happens depends on his will. It is God who makes the sun shine for everyone, and who gives forth or withholds the rain (it has been pointed out that in the Old Testament 'God is raining' has replaced 'it is raining'); it is God who clothes the grass of the field and who feeds the birds of the air, just as the lion cubs look to him for their food, as do all the animals in the vast oceans. It is God Most High who holds dominion, who makes and unmakes kings, who raises up and thrusts down, who kills and makes alive, who opens and closes the womb. The list of familiar phrases from Scripture could be extended with no difficulty.

It follows automatically that to God are attributed not only the course of nature and the overall march of history, but also the most personal events: the family misfortunes of Naomi (Ru. 1:13, 20), and the accident at work or hunting whose unwitting perpetrator may escape the avenger (Ex. 21:13).[8] In order to show that God's care extends even to the minutest occurrences (how much do our own restricted ideas limit the Lord?), Jesus teaches that not one sparrow 'will fall to the ground apart from the will of your Father' (Mt. 10:29).[9] A little story repeated in Jewish tradition and used by preachers illustrates the biblical belief. It tells of a rabbi who was able to see how birds were caught in a trap or escaped from it, according to whether a voice from heaven uttered "Mercy!" or "Destruction!"; and in this way he grasped to what degree God decides the smallest event and, *a fortiori*, for his own comfort, the fate of every individual human being.[10] Trust in God, like prayer, has no sense, except on this foundation.

The lazy and rather cowardly idea – cowardly because it lacks the courage of radical thought – that God would concern himself only with the broad outline of the course of events and not with the details, is striking by its absence. As far as Scripture is concerned, God is expressly interested in faithfulness in little things as well as in great undertakings. Is he not the God of the ant as much as the sun, of the electron as much as the Milky Way? What store does he set by our criteria of importance? Peter Geach has not overlooked this obvious point:

> God must not be conceived as ordaining a broad plan of evolution without responsibility for the unfortunate results to individual

> beings. . . . Only by gross anthropomorphism can we compare
> God to an army commander or big business executive, who is
> responsible for the main line of policy and not for the details of
> its execution.[11]

This lucidity reveals the failure of the moderate pseudo-solutions, such as
the 'limited autonomy' and the partial determinism that we found in John
Hick.[12]

It is regrettable that Geach in his turn has recourse to an anthropomorphic image, whose biblical support and whose own acuteness seems
scarcely any better. He assigns to God the role of 'the Ordainer of the
lottery', that is to say, of life, as if God could do no more than set the limits
of some ultimate chance which is independent of him.[13] And that leads us to
our next point.

The exercise of absolute sovereignty does not exclude the 'relative'
operation of secondary causes; on the contrary, it includes it, and gives it
consistency. Jacques Maritain declared: 'The world is not a clock, but a
republic of natures; and the infallible divine Causality, by virtue of its
transcendence, makes events occur according to their own conditions,
necessary events in a necessary manner, contingent events contingently, and
the events of chance fortuitously.'[14] On condition that the 'transcendence'
is not a pretext to remove all meaning from 'causality' (or better, the lord
and master's determination in the strictly monarchical 'republic' of
creation!), and on condition that chance does not take on the appearance of
an independent factor, we can subscribe to this proposition.

It is also what Calvin teaches: many things 'for us . . . are fortuitous' or 'in
a sense fortuitous. For they bear on the face of them no other appearance,
whether they are considered in their own nature or weighed according to
our knowledge and judgment.' He also preserves the distinction between
necessity and contingency in the modalities of the realization of the plan of
God: the necessity that everything happen according to God's ordinance
does not render a particular event, however certain it may be, 'of its own
peculiar nature necessary'; he notes the difference between 'relative necessity and absolute necessity', that which is linked to the nature of things as
God has created them, and necessity 'from the secret stirring of God's
hand', for example the necessity that not one of the bones of Christ be
broken, as it was foretold, even though in their nature his bones were as
fragile as ours.[15] Calvin brings out clearly the activity of secondary causes.[16]
Thus he is in full agreement with Holy Scripture, which shows the Lord
constantly sending and using *servants*, whether or not they possess a soul –
angels as swift as the winds, winds as obedient as angels. God operates *by
means of them*, he raises up an agent more often than he executes, he brings

into play laws, constants, stable properties and capacities, what Maritain calls 'natures'. This distinction removes the spectre of fatalism, and prevents anyone from drawing any objection from the activity of his creatures against the sovereignty of the Creator.

Holy Scripture also includes the decisions of free beings under divine sovereignty. In point of fact, if such realities were excepted, what would remain of human history for God to govern? The Wisdom writers recognize that to God belongs the choice that directs a man's life (Pr. 16:1, 9), and Jeremiah echoes the same thought (Je. 10:23). The New Testament confirms that God *grants* the repentance and the faith that he commands. The apostle Paul makes the point clearly: 'It is God who works in you to will and to act according to his good purpose' (Phil. 2:13). This admirable formulation immediately blocks any attempt to get round it; if Paul had said only 'to will', some would have explained that 'man's part' is to carry through to completion the impulse begun by grace; if he had said only 'to act', others would have added 'on condition that we ourselves are willing to start with'. Paul does not waver: 'to will *and* to act'! He can be almost ruthless: 'So it depends not on human will or exertion, but on God who shows mercy' (Rom. 9:16, NRSV). Such a word is hard to many people; to others it is sweet.

Objections arise from *a priori* positions that are assumed to be self-evident, rather than from actual biblical difficulties. In the whole area of the great anthropomorphic misunderstanding which overlooks the *uniqueness* of our relationship with the Creator – 'God is wholly other than another', said Jules Monchanin – the prejudgment is made that liberty is stifled and responsibility vanishes if God determines infallibly. But the subjective – and collective – conviction that this presupposition enjoys does not displace the sanction of Holy Scripture. Nowhere does the Bible endorse this alleged 'obviousness' of common sense. It is true that our decisions are free (with the freedom of a creature); it is also true that we are responsible for them; God does not treat us like puppets. Calvin exclaims: 'Who is such a fool as to assert that God moves man just as we throw a stone? And nothing like this follows from our teaching.'[17] The appeals and reproaches, the promises and threats that fill the pages of Holy Scripture are perfectly explained in this way.[18] But as for the idea that the indetermination of the will is necessarily implied, there is no trace of it anywhere. In trying to retain just a hint of it in a generally Augustinian doctrine, the Thomism of Charles Journet shows its exponent's difficulties. He seeks to uphold two contradictory propositions: that the power to sin is *essential* to free will, which is maintained under grace; and that the power to sin disappears sometimes under grace and will disappear in glory, while free will lives on now and in eternity.[19] If it can be said that an entity (in this case free will) remains even though it is deprived of its essence, then words lose their meaning! But in fact the power to sin implying indetermination does not belong to freedom in its primal integrity; it is not essential. The human will cannot escape from its dependence on God. Our minds cannot rise higher than the Dominion that sets us free, nor do they dissect the mystery of the 'how', but we unflinchingly accept Scripture's revelation of the sovereignty of God over our most private decisions and choices, over our hearts.

Under divine sovereignty Scripture *also* includes evils, calamities and transgressions. In point of fact, if such realities were excepted, we again ask, what would remain of human history for God to govern? In the case of the evil of disasters, the position is so blindingly clear, from the flood to the plagues of the book of Revelation, that there is no need to labour the point. The prophets bear witness: Amos 3:6 denounces the spiritual stupidity of those who do not recognize the LORD as the author of the disaster that strikes a city; Isaiah 45:7 proclaims that weal and woe, prosperity and disaster come forth from him; Jeremiah 31:28 (*cf.* 45:4f.) recalls God's faithfulness to his threats. The laments in the Psalms spring from the same conviction; the book of Lamentations (3:37f.) recognizes that God decides and that he indeed brings affliction on human beings (3:33).

Something that is less easily admitted, the attribution of moral evil to divine decisions is met on several occasions; God even seems to bring it forth, according to a number of texts which we shall have to consider as objections to the assertion of his goodness. Jesus does not define the necessity for 'occasions for stumbling' (Mt. 18:7, NRSV); according to the analogy of his other 'it is necessary' (*dei*) sayings, we may presume that he has in mind the necessity that the Scriptures be fulfilled, their being themselves an expression of the purposes of God. At any rate, God 'hardens whom he wants to harden' (Rom. 9:18, referring back to the narrative of the exodus); the following verse shows that blameworthy acts are not done without the will of God (Paul knows that his doctrine gives rise to the objection that he is formulating, and yet he does not put it aside as incorrect in its premises; in fact, even the sinner does not resist the will of God). Thus God successively imprisons the Gentiles and Israel in disobedience (Rom. 11:32). The historical books abound in illustrations of this: the sons of Eli reject admonishment 'for it was the LORD's will to put them to death' (1 Sa. 2:25); Shimei curses David, who understands that the LORD told him to do it (1 Sa. 16:10); it is the LORD who in his wrath incites David to number the people (2 Sa. 24:1). Calvin quite properly refers to Jeroboam's rebellion.[20] God approximates to being the *author* of Absalom's crime, saying 'I will do this thing' (2 Sa. 12:12). In Ezekiel, the LORD goes so far as to say that he himself is the deceiver or enticer of the false prophet (Ezk. 14:9), and the one who 'gave them statutes that were not good', including the abominable practice of the sacrifice of their first-born (Ezk. 20:25f., NRSV). In none of these cases is the malignity of evil allowed any leniency or excuse; on the contrary, the text condemns it utterly. What it excludes is the illusion that creatures have autonomy, even in doing evil.

Nor do creatures that are purely spiritual escape divine governance. The LORD sent the evil spirit which tormented Saul (1 Sa. 16:14, *etc.*) and the lying spirit which enticed the prophets of Ahab (1 Ki. 22:21ff.; *cf.* 2 Thes. 2:11). The devil is 'the god of this age' (2 Cor. 4:4) only in this sense: unbelievers yield to his influences as they ought to yield only to God; they make him play the part of God. He has not the powers of an anti-god and he takes nothing away from the authority of the LORD. Without God's permission he can do nothing, as is disclosed in the prologue to the book of Job. To use Luther's phrase, he remains 'God's devil'. That is why going back from human freedom to that of the Angel that became the Tempter, in order to explain evil, does not provide any solution: the problem persists and in fact increases by arising at a higher point in the scale. Why, oh why did God allow his heavenly servant to have this appalling choice which brought catastrophe on the universe? Why did he not include him, like Gabriel, among 'the elect angels' (1 Tim. 5:21)? Why did he allow him to tempt the man and the woman, and why did he not prevent them from succumbing? The fall of Satan, before that of the human race, helps us to understand certain aspects of human sin, in particular weakness and indolence; and the cosmic dimension of wickedness can be better appreciated. But with God remaining sovereign over all the participants in the drama, the enigma of its first appearance is not resolved.

The Augustinian and Reformed tradition maintains that *in one sense* God 'wills' evil, he decides that evil shall occur. Calvin, though he at times uses it, objects to the term *permission*; he considers it too weak, suggesting a God who is a mere spectator.[21] In reality, he declares, God goes so far as to *move the will* of those who do evil. Many are scandalized at this. Journet blames Calvin bitterly for speaking of 'willing'.[22] He can tolerate only the language of 'permission'. Berkouwer criticizes his own tradition on the same point: even Bavinck, he argues, ought not to have stated that God in a certain manner 'wills' evil.[23] We are obliged to refute the accusation: first of all because the audacity of writers of Scripture, such as Paul or Ezekiel, puts the boldest of Calvin's expressions in the shade; our quotations above bear that out. And then why should we argue about words? 'Having the authority to prevent, and the power, when God allows it, is that not as good as if he did it?' (Calvin).[24] There is little to gain in rejecting the verb 'to will' so long as you do not deny divine sovereignty. Berkouwer is obliged to concede that sin is never committed 'outside (*praeter*) the will of God';[25] is that not the admission of a certain will? In vain does Journet attempt to pit Calvin against Augustine on this point.[26] One may as well take one's position from the stern candour of Scripture: if evil occurs under the rule of God, then his will is involved.

The assurance of the absolute sovereignty of God contributed to 'the fear of the LORD', which is so rare amongst people, even Christians, in our day. It fostered humble faith, it poured the balm of consolation. Racked with illness, Calvin repeated, 'You are crushing me, Lord, but I am content that it comes from your hand.' It alone can bring peace, beyond that of forgiveness, for having done irreversible wrongs, for even that is in the hand of God, *etiam peccata* ('including sins'). By including that in his plan, he relieves us of the intolerable care of having the final responsibility (*cf.* Gn. 45:8). He is the First and the Last. Our God reigns.

The unadulterated goodness of God and his work

Holy Scripture rejects as a satanic calumny and as blasphemy the least hint that God be the accomplice of evil, that he should harbour its seed in his heart, or, which amounts to the same thing, that he should incorporate it in what comes forth from him. God is utterly, radically, absolutely good. Over against the 'tragic' myth of divine cruelty, and the enticement of the dialectic stands what Berkouwer calls the great biblical *a priori*.[27] The testimony to the perfect justice and goodness of God is one of the constants of Scripture (Dt. 32:4, *etc.*). Praise takes delight in it, never wearies of it; those who are victorious over the beast and his image make it their eternal theme in the song of the Lamb (Rev. 15:3ff.). Several times the assertion is reinforced in the face of doubt or false doctrine. The LORD who sent the fierce Chaldeans has eyes 'too pure to look on evil' and cannot even tolerate the sight of it without his indignation being stirred (Hab. 1:12ff.). Let no sinner imagine that he can avoid blame by imputing the causality to God: God neither tempts nor is tempted (Jas. 1:13). John utterly condemns the speculation of the proto-Gnostics, the precursors of Boehme, about the presence of darkness within God (1 Jn. 1:5). Nothing could be more clear.

If there were any need for it, the biblical definition of evil would come and corroborate this testimony. The 'cardinal' evil, as we called it earlier (p. 85) is *anomia*, the violation of the law of God (1 Jn. 3:4). What we may call 'physical' evil, which springs from it, is to be measured by its distance from God's original intention for humankind (in the sense of Ezk. 18:32). Everything therefore is evil which opposes the will of God: opposing his commandments and his 'wishes' or desires, his 'preceptive' will and his 'decretive' will. In the very depths of evil is hidden its driving force, that of hostility towards God, ever ready to emerge. David had discerned it in his repentance (Ps. 51:4). Sinners are the enemies of God (Ps. 5:10, *etc.*). Now, the God of the Bible is not divided against himself; he has no part in evil, and evil has no part with him.

The creation as such is in the image of the goodness of God, for it comes from no other origin. That is exactly what is meant by the phrase *ex nihilo* within the perspective of Scripture. In particular that signifies that no second principle, such as non-being, *mē on*, vaguely hypostatized, combines with the being given by God. The phrase *ex nihilo* itself is found only in apocryphal writings; in the canonical books, everything is *ex Deo* rather than *ex nihilo*, *i.e.* 'the world was created by the word of God' (Heb. 11:3, RSV). Therefore the work of God, in the image of its author, is 'very good' (Gn. 1:31), and that holds true for each particular element (emphasized further in 1 Tim. 4:4). In the beginning, God 'made mankind upright' (Ec. 7:29); our subtle perversities have a different origin, as has also the subjection to futility (Rom. 8:20, RSV). Similarly, Jesus contrasts the institution of God 'in the beginning' and the subsequent situation caused by the hardness of heart that had arisen amongst mankind (Mt. 19:8). At the start there is purity.

It is at this point that the debate on *possibility* holds the stage. What is more natural than to conclude that since man is fallen he was *fallible*, and that since evil arose it was *possible*? For the writers who develop this thought most readily, the potentiality of a defect in the creation provides the explanation of evil, as it implies weakness and vulnerability, one could say a crack, a fault, a hidden *germ*. The goodness of creation, therefore, is very much open to question. In order to describe this fully, it is necessary to put forward a 'real possibility' of evil, to use Kierkegaard's phrase, which would inevitably become a reality one day; the choice against God specifies *from the very beginning* a real power in real liberty.

Such a manner of imagining evil before the fall seems to us totally absent from Scripture, and scarcely compatible with its affirmation of the goodness of the creation. We are grateful in that respect for the clarity of Karl Barth: for the occurrence of sin 'there is no inner or outer necessity, and therefore there is no inner or outer possibility'; that man might perpetrate sin 'does not belong, as is often said, to his freedom as a rational creature';[28] and Barth has clearly understood what is at stake: 'Turn it how we will, if we regard this as a possibility of the creaturely nature of man, we shall always find it excusable because it is grounded in man as such.'[29] We would add that, in order to excuse, one implicitly accuses someone or something – in this case the creation and its Maker. Georges Florovsky, dealing with man in his primal integrity, also discerns that 'evil did not yet exist as an ideal possibility'.[30] He uses the term 'ideal' where we would say 'real', perhaps because he is more willing than us to use Platonic categories, but his meaning is the same; he is concerned to deny the possibility of evil in the perfection of the created order, even the slightest trace of it. Everything was *very good*.

The more common way of thinking (which we are here criticizing) tends towards ambiguity. We recognize that sin and evil were not impossible in Eden; in that sense, provided it is adhered to in the strictest measure, it was 'possible'. The slippery fallacy consists of turning what is at that point 'not impossible' into a confused 'something'.[31] 'In the beginning' the notion of evil enters the mind only as the logical negation of the *only* real good, as an abstraction; it applies to nothing in the creation, it is radically *alien* to both the strengths and the weaknesses, all of them good, of the work of God.

We are ready to admit, as we are bound to, that many times the language of Scripture appears to oppose our proposition – not, indeed, regarding 'possibility' (a significant point), but the major assertion concerning the goodness of God and the goodness of his creation. We have quoted the strongest, most scandalous texts as proof (which they are) of the total sovereignty of God over evil. We might perhaps add the meditation in Ecclesiastes on the provision of various 'times', with room for hatred and war (Ec. 3:1–8), and the praise of the bestial and tortuous monsters in the LORD's speeches to Job (Jb. 40; 41). But if we take a closer look, we see that these creatures, a giant hippopotamus and crocodile which are alien to us, represent not evil but the *incomprehensible*. Job has to learn to *worship* transcendence. Despite his uprightness and his trembling faith, even from the midst of his sufferings, Job has not been able to see on a sufficiently large scale; his complaint has kept its narrow anthropocentric perspective. God shows him what are for mankind the most disconcerting beauties of his creation, in order that he may understand that man, even in the midst of sufferings, is not the measure of all things. And Job confesses that he has spoken of wonders too amazing for him to understand (Jb. 42:3).

As for the reflections of Ecclesiastes, is anyone really confident of understanding the final significance of all he says? In our view they concern the enigmatic diversity of human experience, not the creational order. In the series of successive pairs, not all include a negative, bad pole: it can be good 'to be silent' as well as 'to speak' (Ec. 3:7). The irregular alternations show first that man does not master the flux of his unstable life: he rises high enough to be aware of the situation and to ask the question (*i.e.* he has the sense of eternity), but under the sun he cannot find the single key that will unlock everything (Ec. 3:11). Only the counsel and the work of God perfectly encompass the whole (v. 14); God alone will judge with total knowledge and perfect insight (v. 17). But what about evil, which *also* has its place in the enigmatic interplay of the contraries? We can understand '[God] has made everything beautiful in its time' (v. 11) from the ordering by which God integrates evil into his plan, uses it and turns it on its head in the service of good. We are not so far from Proverbs 16:4.

As for the rest, we notice first that evil inflicted as a *punishment*, for the re-establishment of justice, is in that situation something good; this principle, which we have already settled, resolves the difficulty of many passages. When it is a question of sins, however, even if falling into these sins is a sanction for earlier errors by God's judicial hardening, the explanation is not enough; the God whose eyes are 'too pure to look on evil' cannot 'tempt' anyone. It is here that the analogy of faith guides the interpreter. In order to respect the consistency of God's Word with itself, we have to presuppose different meanings and styles, forms of language that may depart from literal usage; when the prophets deliberately shock the reader by attributing evil to God (Is. 45:7; Ezk. 14:9; 20:25), their *sole* purpose is to bring out all the more sharply God's sovereign majesty.

Theologians distinguish between the decretive and the preceptive will of God, or the will of *eurestia* (*i.e.* what God is pleased to have his creatures do). When we read 'God wills' or 'God wishes', it is not always with the same meaning. The wicked sons of Eli did not repent 'for it was the LORD's will to put them to death' (1 Sa. 2.25), and yet we read that God takes 'no pleasure in the death of the wicked' (Ezk. 33:11). In the first case, God willed in the sense that he has written the deed in his book (Ps. 139:16), that he has included it in the programme of everything that happens, in his universal plan or decree. In the second case, we are dealing with his desire that all should be saved, and it also involves his call, commandment or precept that they should turn and be converted. We should note carefully that, even at the heart of the decree, if evil is willed in a certain manner, it is not willed *as* something good. God wills what is good directly, simply, for himself; he wills evil only in a different manner, while hating it at the same time. It is, to be sure, sovereign, but it is also a *permissive* will that is being referred to. Divine causality with respect to good is *efficient* (*i.e.* God acts efficaciously, every grace and every good gift comes down from the Father of lights, Jas. 1:17). With respect to evil, it is *deficient* (*i.e.* God is content not to act, as if he failed to assist; he *did not* bring forth the will to do good, nor the deed).[32] Whereas God himself works good by making it work, evil is always the deed of one or of several created beings, exclusively.

These distinctions, which are authorized by divine revelation taken as a whole, meet with confirmation in detailed exegesis. The condemnation that goes with the evil 'willed' by God indicates the complexity of the 'willing' in question, and suggests that only the creature *brings forth* evil. This sinning agent appears often. Thus 1 Chronicles 21:1 explains 2 Samuel 24:1 – Satan was the efficient tempter, but, since he was not acting independently of the decretive will of God, the older text had made use of the same shorthand as Ezekiel 14:9.[33] The 'deficient' rather than 'efficient' character emerges in several phrases: God 'gave them over' (*i.e.* sinners) to their depraved ways (Rom. 1: 24, 26, 28); they 'received not' the love of the truth (2 Thes. 2:10, AV, RV);[34] in the matter of the imprudence and pride of King Hezekiah, 'God

left him to himself, in order to test him and know all that was in his heart'
(2 Ch. 32:31, NRSV).[35] By insisting that it is not 'willingly' (*millibô*) that God
afflicts human beings, the inspired poet gives his support to the idea of a
permissive will, one that is paradoxical (La. 3:33); even the stark declarations
of Romans 9 tend in that direction, for the 'vessels of wrath' are those
whom God '*endured* with much patience' (Rom. 9:22, RSV), and it is not
stated that he himself prepared them for perdition. Genesis 50:20 with its
emphasis on the implied thought (*ḥāšab*) supports Calvin's analysis of the
activity of God, Satan and man in the same event: he shows the difference of
purpose and of manner between God and the agents of evil, a difference
which separates God absolutely from all evil and wickedness.[36] The great
biblical *a priori* remains firmly in place: we may praise the Lord for his
perfect, unadulterated goodness, which extends to all the works of his
hands.

The thorn in reason's flesh

The evil of evil, the lordship of the Lord, the goodness of God: these three
immovable propositions stand together as the basis of biblical doctrine. We
can picture them as a capital T: the sovereignty of God forms the stem, the
two branches being the denunciation of evil and the praise of God in his
goodness. But the great difficulty lies in holding all three together. Because
they stumbled at that point, the Christian thinkers of the three groups that
we have examined critically have obscured, rejected even, one or another of
them. Are we now about to produce the secret of their combination, like a
rabbit out of a hat?

We shall maintain that they are not strictly contradictory. If we grant the
distinctions that Scripture itself encourages on the different modes of the
divine will, no-one can prove any strict incompatibility. In order to do that,
it would be necessary to demonstrate this postulate: a God who is good and
sovereign *cannot* permissively decree that the creature shall choose against
the Creator. Many people quite uncritically take this proposition as self-
evident. It is not, and it runs straight into the biblical testimony. Such a
naïve extrapolation of rules that are doubtless valid for human conduct is in
point of fact the very thing that *needs to be demonstrated*. But with what
means, with what criteria? How can a mere man – and a sinner at that – lay
down the law, without appearing ridiculous, about what God is able to do?
Listen to the great Pascal's reasoned mockery of the pretensions of human
reason.[37] And mankind, *homo* who modestly confers on himself the title of
sapiens sapiens, has in recent times made his reason swallow too much arrant
nonsense, not to sit still and keep quiet.

For all that, we are not congratulating ourselves on a comprehensive
victory. We admit that we have only narrowly escaped contradiction. The

nagging problem persists. Distinctions that are both necessary and legitimate do not resolve it, but in the end present it in different terms. How do
these different wills combine in God?[38] How does God simultaneously wish
and not wish the hardening of the sinner and his death? How can we
reconcile God's perfect goodness, his love for us his creatures and his hatred
of evil with the fact that he does not work in everyone the desire for good
and the doing of good? What is the meaning of sovereignly permitting? The
thorn of these questions is deeply and sharply embedded in the human
mind, even the renewed mind of the believer; as the individual thinker
clings to the 'I' of Christian teaching, he feels his mind under fearful strain,
almost to breaking-point.

Scripture teaches us that we shall not find, at least in this life, the rational
solution that so many have sought after. It does not give us the answer. In
fact it goes much further than that: it turns its floodlights on to the
difficulty, and invites us to take a different step. That is at least one of the
purposes of the book of Job. The wisdom of Job's friends shatters into tiny
pieces under the reproof of God. The authentic function of the suffering of
Job, the condition of a testimony that glorifies God, does not answer the last
question on the first permission given by God: it is once evil has entered the
world that God makes use of it as he did in this case; but it would be
repugnant of him to have permitted the origin of evil to that end. That is
why Job will know nothing about the scenes set in heaven, and why the
divine discourse accompanying the vision of God which crowns the book
says nothing about it. In that theophanic disclosure there is no rational
solution, but a Presence that is sovereign, humbling and that, as such, brings
peace and healing. Habakkuk raises the problem of theodicy: in his 'complaint' are found the three scriptural convictions. First, he shudders at the
horror of evil; he learns and confesses that God determines the acts of the
Chaldeans or Babylonians; he is well aware, however, that God's eyes are
too pure to look on (tolerate) evil. What does he get from the long-awaited
reply? He too receives no knowledge of the 'why' or of the 'how' of God's
permission of evil: God calls him, in the dark times that he is passing
through, to live *by faith* (Hab. 2:4). And the apostle Paul, who of course is
very well aware of the protests of the 'natural' mind – 'It is unjust!' and
'How can we still be held responsible if God is directing everything?' (*cf.*
Rom. 9:14, 19) – likewise fails to satisfy our questions. He puts the creature
of clay back in its place, as if to say: 'You cannot understand'; he simply
glorifies the mastery of the sovereign Potter.

For pilgrims such as we are,[39] there is no rational solution to the problem
of evil: the theoretical problem of the origin of evil.[40]

Inscrutability, the cross, hope

The agony of the Christian mind wrestling with the problem of evil seems at first sight a sign of weakness. Is it not an admission of its inability to resolve the principal objection, its powerlessness even to begin chipping away at the 'rock of atheism'? On reflection, however, we would suggest that things appear differently.

If we bowed to the incomprehensible as a way out every time that we found ourselves in difficulties, there would be grounds for suspicion about such a procedure – it would be sheer irresponsibility, the abdication of reason. People are too ready to fall back on the action of 'mystery', and also to confuse mystery with the absurd – which Scripture never does. But we would argue that the mystery of evil is the one unique inscrutable mystery, as unique as evil itself, *sui generis*. Far from being absurd, it corresponds precisely with the experience of evil, with its two facets: unjustifiable– reality. Engraved in the decree of God, evil has a certain reality; but being contrary to his precept and his will, it is unjustifiable. As we have said, it does not imply contradiction. All the other mysteries that transcend our understanding, those of the Trinity, the union of the two natures of Christ, created freedom, are all luminous mysteries: if the mind tackles them biblically, it simply revels in them. Only the 'opaque' enigma of evil causes it pain.

If the solutions put forward in place of the scriptural response were capable of satisfying the human mind and spirit, they would be unquestionably superior. But surely it is the opposite that we have shown from a broad enough selection. Analysis reveals that what are called solutions turn out to be so many attempts to gloss over one or other of the aspects of the problem, to deny evil, or to 'forget' the initial, more reliable apprehension of the reality of evil that everyone experiences with indignation and shame. Scripture *alone* is free of that. Surely such purity is nothing short of miraculous. No discourse strips the guilty of excuses like this Book. Water down one of the three affirmations, and evil to some extent becomes excusable, as we have demonstrated. Would Scripture be so true to reality if its origin were solely human?

We may take these thoughts further. The sense of evil *requires* the God of the Bible. In a novel by Joseph Heller, 'while rejecting belief in God, the characters in the story find themselves compelled to postulate his existence in order to have an adequate object for their moral indignation'.[41] Molt-mann too has perceived that you suppress all protest against suffering, if you suppress God: 'Since that time no atheism can fall below Job's level.'[42] When you raise this standard objection against God, to whom do you say it, other than *this* God? Without this God who is sovereign and good, what is the rationale of our complaints? Can we even tell what is evil? Perhaps the late John Lennon understood: 'God is a concept by which we measure our pain,' he sang.[43] Might we be coming to the point where the sense of evil is a proof of the existence of God?

We do not understand the why of evil. But we can understand that we cannot understand. Human reason is made to trace the connections in God's created order, and to weave harmonious patterns from them; to understand means to integrate. A rational solution to the problem of evil would necessarily imply that evil was an integral part of the harmony that came forth from God! Similarly, to go back from sin to its 'real possibility', before it came into the world, means applying to it the logic of continuity which obtains in the processes of the creation.[44] But evil is disruption, discontinuity, disorder, alienness, that which defies description in creational terms (except negatively!). Seeking its causal explanation, its ontological reason, its why, is tantamount to seeking, by the very nature of that seeking, to reconcile it with the rest, in other words to justify it. (The 'rest' is in fact what is 'just'.) To understand evil would be to understand that evil is not ultimately evil. The French have a saying, that to understand all is to forgive all; here, understanding all would mean to *excuse* everything.

Evil is not there to be understood, but to be *fought*. The absence of any solution to the theoretical problem of the emergence of evil is one side of the coin; the other side, something still more precious than righteous indignation, is the solution to the *practical* problem of the *suppression* of evil. What you appear to lose on the speculative level you gain on the existential level. And we have in mind particularly the far *horizon* of the practical task, the *end* of evil, something of far greater interest than its origin. Then will end the cries of 'How long?' which express a far heavier burden than the cries of 'Why?' Only the complete combination of the three propositions, the capital 'T' of biblical teaching, gives assurance of that victory. If beneath the outward appearance of evil there were hidden something good, why would anyone want to see it disappear? If God were not sovereign, how would he bring under his control what is not dependent on him? If God concealed darkness within himself, how would it not be eternal, like him? But 'God's solid foundation stands firm' (2 Tim. 2:19). When wild hopes disappear into thin air, the foundation of hope comes into view, the sovereignty of the God who fights against evil, and who invites us to join him in the battle.

God battles with evil, and will conquer it. Or rather, God *has battled* with it and he *has conquered* it. We have kept the supreme consideration to the end: that other 'T' formed by two small beams of wood on the hill called Golgotha, Skull Hill. There the darkness of the mystery deepened, from the sixth hour until the ninth, the place from which shines forth the light.

In the light of the cross, how could there be any doubt about the three propositions at the heart of the Christian position? The *sheer and utter evilness of evil* is demonstrated there: as hatred in the mockery of the criminals who also hung there; as hateful in the weight of guilt which could be removed only by the sacrifice of the Lamb of God. Even if I think of the benefits for myself, when I see my Lord suffering there, I cannot say: *Felix culpa*. Rather, I feel shame and indignation, against evil and against myself. The *complete sovereignty of God* is demonstrated there: all this happened 'by God's set purpose and foreknowledge' (Acts 2:23), for it was necessary that the Scriptures be fulfilled, those which bore witness to the destiny that the Lord had assigned to his Servant. If there is a revolting 'scandal', it is unquestionably that of Judas's betrayal, and like the squalid reconciliation of Herod and Pilate it accomplished 'what your power and will had decided beforehand should happen' (Acts 4:28). Of no other event is it attested so fully that God 'willed' it. The *unadulterated goodness of God* is demonstrated there. At the cross, who would dare entertain the blasphemy of imagining that God would, even to the slightest degree, comply with evil? It brought him death, in the person of his Son. Holiness stands revealed. Love stands revealed, a pure love; there is no love greater. Because of the cross we shall praise his goodness, the goodness of his justice, the goodness of his grace, through all eternity. At the cross, God turned evil against evil and brought about the practical solution to the problem. He has made atonement for sins, he has conquered death, he has triumphed over the devil. He has laid the foundation for hope.

What further demonstration do we need?

5

Evil and the kingdom

Does our dark question grow even darker? Has a new twist increased the mystery? The absence of any theoretical solution to the problem of evil is, in Scripture, like the reverse side of the practical solution: it allows us to hope for the elimination of evil. The biblical form of this hope is called the *expectation of the reign*, or kingdom, of God – 'Thy kingdom come.' But surely the good news carried by the heralds of Christianity is that *the kingdom has come*. The church preaches the establishment of the kingdom through the ministry, death and resurrection of Jesus. And yet, *evil has not disappeared* since then; some would say it is flourishing as never before. We cannot avoid facing this difficulty which grows like a shoot out of the base of the problem of evil: no longer is the problem that evil exists by sovereign permission of a God who is good, but that after the victory of Christ and the appearance of his kingdom, evil persists.

We shall first of all put forward the apparent support for the assertions just made, which would seem to involve considerable tension among themselves. If it were possible right away to rebut merely one of the three, the difficulty would disappear. But if all three have to be taken seriously, if room must be found for all of them at the outset (at least *pro tempore*, after this preliminary glance), then the theologian cannot avoid a detailed examination of them.

Evil abolished in the kingdom

The suppression of evil is a vital part of the coming of God's reign or kingdom;[1] this first point is scarcely contested. George Eldon Ladd, who devoted his career to studying this subject, concludes his review of the gospel texts with this quite straightforward comment: 'The coming of the kingdom of God will witness the complete expurgation of evil from God's creation.'[2] There we have the distinguishing mark between the reign or kingdom heralded by the gospel and which is at the heart of all Christian preaching (Acts 20:25), and the abiding imperial rule of the *Pantocrator*, the Ruler of the universe, ruling without change, decline or failure for all time and eternity. That is the difference between the kingdom which *is* and the kingdom which *is coming*. The first mysteriously *embraces* evil, while the other *drives it out*. The former ensures that God's *decretive* will is carried out, while the latter perfectly embodies the fulfilment of his *preceptive* will, 'on earth as it is in heaven'. Of course, evil is defined in the Bible by its failure to conform to the wishes and commandments of God: the realization of that will, flouted by the rebellious choice of the creature who has been so damaged by the consequences of his rebellion, is by definition the end of evil.

The prophets whose words gave rise to this hope certainly understood it in that way. Whether they are proclaiming the eschatological rule of Yahweh, the LORD, or that of the expected Son of David – it comes to the same thing, since the prince, in this filial relationship with God, acts as his viceroy (2 Sa. 7:14; Ps. 2:7) – they associate it with the triumph of justice and peace. Hosea looks forward to the harmony of universal reconciliation (Ho. 2:18–23) in that time 'afterwards' when the Israelites will return to Yahweh, their God, and to the (new) David, their king (Ho. 3:5). For Amos, heavenly prosperity and security will accompany the restoration of 'David's fallen tent', at the coming of Messiah whom the Rabbis, on the basis of that oracle, could call 'the Son of decadence' (Am. 9:11–15; *Sanhedrin* 96b). Micah links together healing and peace with the rule of Yahweh, King and Shepherd (Mi. 4:6ff.; *cf.* 4:3ff.; 2:12ff.), which it would be quite wrong to separate from the rule of the child from Bethlehem, who will shepherd the people 'in the majesty of the name of the LORD' and will in his own person be *šālôm*, peace (Mi. 5:2, 4f.).

Micah's young contemporary, the mighty Isaiah, bears the same testimony. His eyes have seen the King (Is. 6:5), and he gazes at the future rule of the king 'in his beauty' (33:17ff.): Yahweh's accession as King (and saviour) coincides with the healing of all sickness and the absolution of all sins (33:22, 24). To the shame of the arrogant 'powers in the heavens', the moon and the sun (24:21ff.), it will be the time of the feast of God: 'he will swallow up death for ever, . . . will wipe away the tears from all faces', and will kill with his great and powerful sword the adversary, 'Leviathan the fleeing serpent, Leviathan the twisting serpent' (25:6–8; 27:1, RSV). The promised child, the Davidic prince of peace, so at one with Yahweh that he will bear the divine name of 'Wonderful Counsellor, Mighty God, Everlasting Father', will be invested with the sovereign power of this rule (9:6): under his government 'he will neither harm nor destroy' on all the holy mountain, hereditary enemies will be perfectly reconciled, and 'the earth will be full of the knowledge of the LORD as the waters cover the sea' (11:6–9). Two elements in this last passage are taken up in such a way that it may be connected with the vision of the new heavens and the new earth, of Jerusalem re-created: there shall past troubles be forgotten, weeping and crying will be heard in it no more, the hazards and frustrations of life will be over, and the sentence pronounced on the serpent (Gn. 3:14) will be fully executed (Is. 65:16–25). It is true that some read verse 20 as predicting the continuation of death, sin and God's curse, in spite of the rest of the passage, but that surely shows a poor exegetical feel. In the lofty rhetoric of this piece, the function of verse 20 is quite different: it is not there to take anything away from the thrust of the other assertions (as if to say, there will after all be some tears and wrongs), but to bring out the vast scale of the cataclysm, the radical change of the new creation; our own scale of values will no longer operate. Whereas today the centenarian is the longevity champion, and passes for a good man who has been exceptionally blessed, in the new Jerusalem it will all be different: dying at the age of a hundred would be like dying while still a youngster, like a sinner cursed and cut off by God. It is just not possible to take these words as a piece of information, a report presented literally on the permanence of death in the new order![3]

Several interpreters consider that the theme of Isaiah 40 – 66 is the kingdom of Yahweh, from Mount Zion to the ends of the earth, whose triumphal appearance is imminent. 'Your God reigns!' in Isaiah 52:7 gives us the key to the whole message: 'It is not a *potentia absoluta* which is in focus, but it is the covenant-relationship and the kingdom of grace, love, righteousness, and divine power in the service of the realization of this ultimate goal';[4] sorrow and sighing will have vanished away (51:11).

And the other prophetic books confirm this. Zephaniah echoes the promises in Micah by celebrating the presence amongst his people of Yahweh, the King of Israel, 'mighty to save' (Zp. 3:15ff.). Ezekiel describes the covenant of peace, when the LORD himself will become the one Shepherd-King of Israel, and his servant (the new) David will be that one shepherd (Ezk. 34:11–16, 23–31; 37:21–27; the apparent contradiction between God *himself*/David is resolved only in Jesus). Zechariah is perhaps the most eloquent: he associates the wonderful day when Yahweh is King over the whole earth (Zc. 14:7, 9) with the removal of every curse (v. 11, RSV), then with the holiness of even the most common of objects, like cooking-pots and the bells of the horses (v. 20). It will identically be the rule of Messiah: the LORD will open a freely flowing fountain for the cleansing of sin and will achieve his purposes (13:1, 9), by virtue of the sufferings of another 'Shepherd' who 'stands next to' God, one with him (11:4–13; 12:10; 13:7), who must, according to Zechariah's strict framework,[5] be identified with the new Solomon, now 'humbled' (*'āni*, not simply *'ānāw*, 'humble'), 'the bringer of salvation' (*nôšā'*; 9:9f.). Without the slightest doubt, the kingdom, according to the prophets who are the reference point of the New Testament, entails *victory over evil*, over folly and war, sin and suffering, sickness and death.

The kingdom that has come in Jesus Christ

According to Scripture, has the rule or kingdom already come? This second proposition is broadly admitted, whether in full or in a modified form. It is at the heart of the 'realized eschatology' school in the field of New Testament studies, which first came to prominence in the English-speaking world through C. H. Dodd's *The Parables of the Kingdom* (1935). He argued that for Jesus the kingdom is not only near but actually present; the crisis which is coming like a thief in the night coincides with his own ministry at the very time that he is speaking, and it is then the final time of harvest (the sowing having occurred in the Old Testament). Scholars of note, particularly in Britain, such as John A. T. Robinson, have followed in Dodd's footsteps, and his influence can be seen in many less radical writers. According to this approach, we must not allow ourselves to be misled by the apocalyptic dress in which the message appears; it is easy enough to imagine Jesus and the writer of the fourth gospel making full use of imagery and not limiting themselves to the literal sense of their words.

Among dogmaticians, Karl Barth has in certain respects joined the advocates of realized eschatology as a result of his christological concentration: he constantly asserted with great vigour that reconciliation had already been brought about, that all people were already justified and sanctified, that evil had already been abolished and that the kingdom is already established. The fact of the sanctification of all mankind in Jesus Christ 'is the ground on which we stand, the horizon that surrounds us and the air which we breathe'.[6] The man of sin, who has 'been displaced, overcome and put to death in Jesus Christ', is no longer anything but 'an arbitrarily conjured shade'; this truth 'is the fixed star which shines unchanged above all the clouds created by him [man], pursuing its own course without deviation'.[7] 'All the tears are already wiped away from our eyes (Rev. 21:4), and in very truth there can no longer be amongst us any mourning or crying or pain;' there has been manifested 'the Kingdom of God (that link inserted into the chain of history) come with power – not in a restrained, reserved way, but *totally*, with power'.[8]

These triumphant tones do not lack encouragement in Scripture. Certainly, the translation of the perfect tense *ēngiken*, usually rendered 'has come near' ('The kingdom of God *ēngiken*', Mk: 1.15, *etc.*) by 'has arrived' is somewhat tendentious. It is likely that the verb keeps its reference to closeness, a notion that has its rightful place in a discourse on the end of time ('near, right at the door', Mk. 13:29). But the imminence dramatically proclaimed at the *start* of Jesus' ministry, and even before that in the preparatory work of John the Baptist, suggests the coming of the kingdom in the subsequent months that were filled with the works of Christ, or at least in the years which saw the unthinkable crucifixion of the Son of God, and the first man that conquered death! This is confirmed by Jesus: some of his hearers 'will not taste death before they see the kingdom of God *come* [the perfect participle] with power' (Mk. 9:1). To the Sanhedrin he declares '*From now on* you will see the Son of Man seated at the right hand of Power and coming on the clouds of heaven' (Mt. 26:64, NRSV).

Christ is even more categorical when he discloses the meaning of his exorcisms: 'the kingdom of God has come to you' (Mt. 12:28; Lk. 11:20, NRSV), which implies the defeat of 'the strong man', the devil, who is henceforth bound, tied up. Satan falls from heaven 'like lightning' (Lk. 10:18)! And Christ also added, 'The kingdom of God *is* among you' (Lk. 17:21, NIV margin, NRSV), a word which may not justifiably be reduced to the meaning of imminence. The Greek text uses the preposition *entos* instead of the usual preposition *en*, which would have been sufficient to express 'in the midst'. What is the significance of the choice of term? *Entos* speaks of inwardness. It is unlikely that Jesus is asserting that the kingdom is an inner reality in the hearts of his hearers, for he is addressing Pharisees. He is undoubtedly referring to the unperceived presence of the kingdom *at the heart* of the situation in which he is found with them: the presence of the kingdom in his own person and in his works. With the NIV, we understand the enigmatic saying of Matthew 11:12 in a similar way, by taking *biazetai* as a verb in the middle voice: since the days of John the Baptist, 'the kingdom of heaven has been forcefully advancing, and forceful men lay hold of it'.[9]

The passion narratives lay emphasis on the kingship of the man crucified, and the promise made to the dying thief who repents suggests that Jesus' entry into his kingdom is the very 'today' of his answer (Lk. 23:42f.; is the paradox already to be found underlying the dialogue of Mk. 10:37f.?). These passages taken together bear considerable weight, and prepare the way for the Johannine emphasis on the judgment that has already been decided, the passage from death to life already achieved, the casting out of the prince of this world (Jn. 3:17f.; 5:24f.; 12:31). They also agree with Paul's use of the phrase 'the kingdom of God' for the reality experienced by Christians (Rom. 14:17; 1 Cor. 4:20; Col. 1:13), and the teaching of the letter to the Hebrews on the 'kingdom that cannot be shaken' that is received by those who hear and believe the word of the new covenant (Heb. 12:28). Sin has been condemned in an effective manner at last, something which was impossible for the law (Rom. 8:3). Christ has triumphed over the hostile powers (Col. 2:15). He has destroyed the works of the devil (1 Jn. 3:5, 8). He has triumphed over evil. The kingdom is already here.

The persistence and growth of evil

Who would not wish to be able to refute the third point, the affirmation that evil persists? No-one can turn a blind eye to all the atrocities committed and the horrors endured *since* Christ's earthly ministry. There is scarcely any suggestion these days that the influence of Christianity is constantly changing the world for the better. The optimism of progressive thinkers and movements seems to have died in the wake of the First World War and the economic crisis of the 1930s. In Europe its funeral oration was given by dialectical theology, and in America by the social realism of Reinhold Niebuhr. Pictures of such suffering as Auschwitz and the Gulag, the Vietnamese boat people and the destruction of Beirut, discourage any return to it. Nowadays the tendency is rather to point an accusing finger at Christianity and its impact on history; the myth of the noble savage (or, perhaps, the happy savage) has captured a new generation. There is a longing for traditional cultures, and for the pristine balance, before the time of Christ, between mankind and nature, when the human being was not yet an individual and had not been divorced from the world of nature. Others are more radical, rejecting the affirmation of the world and of time that has characterized Western civilization, and looking for peace in the void of Eastern religion. The most sarcastic will demand to know whether we think the churches have contributed more to the suppression of evil than to the suppression of mankind. The Christian resists the temptation to blame the message of the Scriptures for the evils that afflict civilization; but he also sees these evils spread out in full view. And to this must be added the lethargy of the churches, their quarrels and their blunders. Above all, the Christian is aware of the evil that he still commits, even while living in the kingdom. Having uttered the triumphal cry that we quoted above, Karl Barth quickly asks, 'Is this all imagination?' He admits that these positive assertions 'do not answer the question why, seeing there is no doubt that we must confidently ascribe this total, universal and definitive power to the Easter event, its efficacy should not be manifest very differently in the form of the world and our own existence'.[10] In the face of the evil that is still at work, faith wants nothing to do with pious schizophrenia.

When believers recognize the present reality of evil after the inauguration of the kingdom, they also find further support from Holy Scripture. More reliable than human experience, the Scriptures call this present age 'evil', and do not depict the 'last days' in a very favourable light (*cf.* 2 Tim. 3:1ff., *etc.*). Jesus foresees that in the days following his ministry wickedness will increase and the love of many will grow cold (Mt. 24:12). When he returns, will he even find faith on the earth (Lk. 18:8)? And how can we forget the beasts and the great prostitute of the book of Revelation? These considerations do not resolve the difficulty, on the contrary they sharpen it. They show it there, within Holy Scripture, and summon us to closer examination of the biblical text.

An unforeseen postponement?

Two doctrines call for our attention. Both attack the central thesis which we have provisionally admitted, that the kingdom of God has already come. For both, the traditional teaching on this subject rests on a major *error*: no account has been taken of the unforeseen postponement of the expected coming of the kingdom. The similarities between the two analyses cause something of a surprise: the first, 'dispensationalism', emerges from one of the reputedly 'hard' wings of fundamentalism; the second, known as 'consistent eschatology', is a product of the most corrosive liberalism. In the view of the first, only the *readers* of the Bible were mistaken, and the postponement was 'unforeseen' only by the prophets of the Old Testament, owing to the structure of history. In the view of the second, Jesus was the first to be mistaken, misled his disciples, and was himself disappointed in his expectation. But whether one or the other is right, the whole formulation of the problem is completely altered.

The 'dispensationalist' division of history

Dispensationalism sprang from the amazing genius of John Nelson Darby (1800–82). The popularizing skills of the lawyer C. I. Scofield, so evident in his explanatory notes to what became known as the Scofield Bible, first edition 1909, gave wide circulation to Darby's views. Its principal academic stronghold is Dallas Theological Seminary, founded by systematic theologian L. S. Chafer, and renowned for the lectures and writings of Charles C. Ryrie and John F. Walvoord.

According to their teaching, preaching 'the kingdom of heaven is at hand' to their compatriots meant, for John the Baptist and for Jesus, *offering* it to the nation. Had his people welcomed him, then the rule of the Davidic Messiah, his political and religious reign of righteousness and peace, and Israel's consequent hegemony over the pagan world, would have been inaugurated.[11] But the Jews refused the offer and rejected the kingdom: 'We don't want this man to be our king' (Lk. 19:14). Thereupon, the Lord, withdrawing the offer but unable to break his unconditional promises in the Old Testament, put off their realization until later. The kingdom has been adjourned, or, as it is usually put, *postponed*.[12] A recent spokesman for the movement prefers the terms 'delay' or 'suspension'.[13] The kingdom will be established on earth, after the return of Christ, for a thousand years, *i.e.* the millennium.

The system is supported by the two great doctrines of dispensationalism. First, the insistence on literal interpretation,[14] which is the principle according to which Israel has only earthly promises,[15] so that, for example, 'a real King will sit on a material throne (Is. 33:17)'.[16] Second, the strict separation between Israel and the church, the latter enjoying heavenly promises and being a stranger to the Old Covenant, 'intercalated' like a 'parenthesis' unforeseen by the prophets.[17] This separation is the 'touchstone', 'the essence of dispensationalism'.[18] It is clear that the kingdom of heaven, as conceived by dispensationalists, has not been set up; they therefore suppose that it has been postponed. The church, which would not have been born if the Jews had accepted the offer,[19] fills the gap; it does not inherit Israel's prerogatives. Dispensationalists could adopt the famous saying of Alfred Loisy, 'Jesus foretold the Kingdom and it was the church that came.' Loisy meant that the change signified the denial which events inflicted on Jesus' illusions, whereas for dispensationalists it represents the divine response to the unbelief of the first people of God.

Our critical examination must concentrate on the theory of the postponement of the kingdom, leaving aside related doctrines.[20] This limitation does not turn to the advantage of dispensationalism. Its formal declaration can be accommodated only by a somewhat startling distinction between 'the kingdom of heaven' and 'the kingdom of God', despite the equivalence supported by parallel passages in the synoptic gospels and a passage like Matthew 19:23–24.[21] Only a passionate *a priori* approach can prevent anyone from recognizing in the substitution of 'heaven' for 'God' a respectful euphemism, typically used by the Jews at that time.[22] Even on distinguishing the two kingdoms, dispensationalists have difficulty taking into account the attribution of all power to Christ from the moment of his ascension (Mt. 28:18).[23] They are obliged by the parables in Matthew 13 to speak of the 'kingdom (of heaven) in mystery', or 'the mystery form of the kingdom', for *the present time*, that pure 'parenthesis' (according to them), having no connection with the Davidic kingdom![24] They are scarcely agreed on the reiteration of the offer to Israel in the book of Acts.[25]

What is the support for the major assertions in particular? Where do we see that Jesus *offered* the kingdom to the people of Israel? John the Baptist and Jesus announced its imminent coming as an event that depended on God alone. In Donald Guthrie's words: 'Man is not even invited to comment on it. It is simply announced as a *fait accompli*. God has acted in history.'[26] A decision of *metanoia*, of conversion, is demanded, for the coming of the kingdom brings about the great separation foretold by the prophets. But it is not on that decision that the coming of the kingdom depends! It advances in its own power, and the individual human being will be either chaff blown away by the wind of judgment (the carnal part of the people, represented in Romans 11 by the branches broken off from the olive tree), or, if he or she repents, grain gathered into God's storehouses (the believing remnant, which inherits the promises).

The dispensationalist suggests: 'At the time of the first announcement of the kingdom, Christ understood there was contingency. The offer of the kingdom was genuine, but so also was the human contingency (Mt. 10:5–7; 15:24). "If you are willing to accept it, [John] is the Elijah who was to come" (Mt. 11:13–15; 17:10–13).'[27] Is that really so? You have only to re-read the texts referred to in order to see whether they contain the slightest trace of the idea of contingency with respect to the coming of the kingdom or of that Elijah, of whom Jesus asserts: 'But I tell you, Elijah has already come'! Was he depending on the good will of his hearers for the thing to be true? As little as the axe consults the root of the tree which it attacks (Mt. 3:10)!

Where, likewise, do we see that the rule or kingdom has been 'postponed' because of the unbelief of the Jews (in the mass, and of their authorities)? It is true that many Israelites rejected the kingdom, which was so different from the picture of it that they had imagined. Christ himself drew attention to that difference, as he recalled the possibility for stumbling that his ministry meant to his compatriots, in spite of the fulfilment of prophecy (Mt. 11:2ff.). In the same way he emphasized that the kingdom comes in an unseen manner (Lk. 17:20f.).

Would the Jews of that time have rejected the kingdom if it had been offered to them in the form described by dispensationalists? After the miracle of the loaves and fish, did they not believe that they could reach out and touch this kingdom, in that very form, and did they not want to make Jesus king? Jesus was the one who made the refusal (Jn. 6:14f.)! The Jews, then, rejected God's purpose, but only 'for themselves' (Lk. 7:30). Their hostility had no more effect on the inauguration of the kingdom than the Jewish deputation to Rome against the rule of Archelaus had on the continuance of the Herodian dynasty (*cf.* Lk. 19:14). Having ascended to the Father, the Ancient of Days, the Son of Man was invested with kingship, and forty years later his enemies underwent their punishment. Jesus made no secret of the immediate consequences of rejection, and of the measures that God would take concerning the kingdom. Israelites merely 'according to the flesh', those who are the natural heirs of the kingdom by the fact of their birth, are thrown outside and lost (Mt. 8:12). The kingdom is *taken* from Judaism; it is not deferred as to its date, but *transferred* to the nation that is Israel according to the Spirit, which bears the fruit of faith (Mt. 21:43).[28] There is emphatically no adjournment. Luke 10:11 appears even to teach the exact opposite: whatever reception it gets, the kingdom is established with the same majestic certainty – 'You may be sure of this: the kingdom of God is near.' The zeal and dexterity of dispensationalist interpreters cannot achieve very much in the face of such textual material.

The liberal school of Albert Schweitzer

For Loisy and for 'consistent eschatology', if the church came instead of the kingdom, it was because Jesus himself had been badly mistaken. The name 'consistent eschatology' (in German '*consequente Eschatologie*') was adopted because its advocates considered that they alone were 'consistent', or 'thoroughgoing', with their double discovery of the importance of the imminent end for Jesus, and of the realization of his error. Johannes Weiss was the first scholar to explore this particular path in his short, highly influential *Jesus' Proclamation of the Kingdom of God* (1892), but it was Albert Schweitzer (1875–1965) who made the decisive leap. Before setting off for the hospital at Lambaréné in tropical Africa to begin the work which was one day to earn him the Nobel Prize for Peace, Schweitzer had published a book on the history of (liberal) research into the life of Jesus (1906). This won him recognition as a leading figure in the field of New Testament criticism. Martin Werner and Fritz Buri can be named amongst his successors; but we should especially note that it was with this book that the idea of the mistake made by Jesus, and of the formative part played in primitive Christianity by the ill-acknowledged failure of the second coming of the Messiah, postponed indefinitely, filtered through into more than two thirds of New Testament criticism.

'Consistent' eschatologists see clearly that Jesus borrowed from Jewish apocalyptic of his own day, and that he took more than a mere outer shell of imagery. Unless we are to be engulfed in self-destructive scepticism towards the historical testimony of the gospels, we must admit that Jesus expected within a very short time the great cosmic revolution which would include the enthronement in glory of the Son of Man. According to Schweitzer, Jesus first of all thought he would bring it about by sending disciples into the towns and villages of Israel (Mt. 10:23). He had to revise his ideas. Coming to the understanding in his own mind that his suffering and death would constitute the 'Messianic sufferings' necessary to bring the kingdom to birth, he gave himself up, certain that the end of the world would ensue at once (Mk. 9:1; 14:62 and parallel passages). The disciples, carried away by the spiritual experiences they had enjoyed, still clung to the illusion. Eagerly they expected Messiah's coming in glory for their own generation (Mk. 13:30 and parallels; 1 Thes. 4:15, 17). Paul derived a whole new mysticism from this interim situation. It was necessary, without admitting it, to strike a more sober note, face up to the hard facts, return to life in the real world and make do with the sacramental presence as a substitute for the one that had been promised – this was 'proto-Catholicism'. This outline thus deals with the material for a 'realized' eschatology in the following way: either it is interpreted only in the sense of imminence (which is illusory), as in Luke 17:21, or else it is exposed as the additions and embellishments made by the church when the delay started to become an embarrassment. There is no hope of bringing the literal sense of the original simple message back to life, especially as we wish to be 'consistent'; the only way to save anything from it is through some kind of hermeneutic – mystical, moral, existential, political or what have you.

We shall have to make do with a brief glance at the specialists' debate on 'consistent' eschatology and the crucial arguments that it elicits.[29] Frankly, even this ought to be unnecessary for *Christian* readers. One would hope that believers would react instantly against the hypothesis that their Master had got it wrong! When those who are 'learned' according to this present age believe that they can ascribe illusions to Jesus, even if they think they are doing him some kind of favour, as far as a *disciple* of Christ is concerned, they have ruled themselves out of court. Our desire is, at all times and in all places, to be nothing more or less than disciples. The Lord is not our Lord only in certain areas, his authority does not stop at the outer limits of the academic world. Academic refutation, however, carried out in the shadow of trust and obedience, has its proper place. Jesus did it, and he taught his disciples to practise it in their turn, demonstrating the weakness of opposing arguments. It removes any excuse for error, and it strengthens faith. A brief reminder of the weaknesses of the so-called 'consistent' view can be of help.

Despite the wealth of scholarship lavished on it, what has actually been gained from all the work done on 'consistent' eschatology? It has certainly brought out the future expectation of the New Testament; it is now impossible to reduce everything to past realization. It is also impossible to explain the imminence of the king's coming simply by the metaphysical pressure of eternity: 'there is no trace of a vertically suspended eternity-concept that absorbs the eschaton in permanent, timeless relation and leaves no room or meaning for the continuity of history as such'.[30] But imminence, without breaking loose from chronology, does not imply a definite delay; a storm can linger 'menacingly' on the horizon ('imminent' and 'menace' have the same etymological root). We must not overstate the eschatological excitement of the first community of believers: 'The very primitive speeches at the beginning of the Acts of the Apostles give absolutely no impression of a feverish, anxious expectation of the end; they put more weight on what the disciples have already received than on what they do not yet possess.'[31] When he writes of 'we who are still alive' (1 Thes. 4:17), Paul expresses himself in the way that every Christian does naturally, in every generation. It is quite inadmissible to exclude *a priori* the textual evidence that contradicts the argument; it is too easy to cut out as unauthentic the words and deeds of Jesus which assume that time still has some way to run before the end, of which nobody knows either the day or the hour (Mt. 24:36). Luke differs less from the other gospel writers in this respect than has been suggested;[32] prejudice apart, there is no compelling reason to rob Jesus of his authorship of those parables in which the growth of the crop requires an interval of time, or those in which the master or the bridegroom delays his coming.[33]

The texts which state that the End is already here, and that the kingdom has already come, which are referred to by the 'realized' eschatology school, deserve closer consideration. Of supreme importance here is the Easter event, swept away by the self-styled 'consistent' eschatology with the illusions of the time. Karl Barth is quite right to take it as the basis of his position, by asserting one single return (*Wiederkunft*) of Jesus who had descended to the dead, but in three interdependent forms: at Easter, at his appearing at the Last Day, and between the two as the Paraclete.[34] Heinrich Ott points out that this is not an apologetic produced for the occasion, but simply 'the product of his fundamental theological discovery',[35] a discovery which we by no means despise. As for the signs of the kingdom and of the end, they suggest that a delay can occur, nevertheless without contradicting its imminence and suddenness. They are indeed *signs*, not merely 'signals'; wars, famines, earthquakes, lawlessness, immorality, apostasy – the function of these is not primarily to signal the exact moment of the final phase, but to indicate the decrepitude of the old world, surviving on a precarious reprieve.[36] 'Consistent' eschatology forces the New Testament in all its rich complexity to undergo a disastrous mutilation; the surgery carried out by Dr Schweitzer and his team has left the patient in a pitiful condition.

The handful of verses that are still quoted can surely be explained without having to claim that Jesus was mistaken. Matthew 10:23 – 'I tell you the truth, you will not finish going through the cities of Israel before the Son of Man comes' – undoubtedly does not only mean that Jesus himself is going to visit the towns of Israel within a short time, having sent his disciples on ahead as trail-blazers.[37] Might Jesus have had in mind the special judgment of Israel that occurred in AD 70?[38] A different position is presented by A. L. Moore, who sees a warning against undue optimism or a hankering for martyrdom; in other words, the mission to the Jews will fail, you will not have managed to convince them before Messiah's return.[39] We prefer to understand it either like Barth, taking Jesus to refer to his resurrection, following which the mission of the twelve will expand from the towns of Israel to reach to the ends of the earth;[40] or else, like Guthrie, taking it to be reassurance from Jesus to his disciples when threatened with persecution.[41]

In the case of another passage, there is no doubting the intention of the evangelists: the declaration of Mark 9:1 – 'I tell you the truth, some who are standing here will not taste death before they see the kingdom of God come with power' refers to the transfiguration, which they proceed to relate straight away, and which is a preliminary revelation of the resurrection and of the glory of Christ that we shall see at his second coming.[42] The answer given to the high priest (Mk. 14:62 and parallels): 'You will see the Son of Man sitting at the right hand of the Mighty One and coming on the clouds of heaven' combines two quotations that Jesus particularly liked, because they refuted the idea of the kingdom and of the Messiah allowed by official Judaism. These are Daniel 7:13 and Psalm 110:1. In neither passage is it a case of a return to earth. The scene in Daniel 7 in which the Son of Man on the theophanic clouds is advancing *towards God* describes his enthronement.[43] Before his accusers Jesus proclaims his impending rehabilitation and justification by God, in which we may distinguish three main stages: the resurrection on the first Easter Day, the judgment brought upon Jerusalem in AD 70, and the final return.[44]

That leaves us with the difficult statement in the discourse on the Mount of Olives that 'this generation will certainly not pass away until all these things have happened' (Mk. 13:30 and parallels). Our own interpretation is along the following lines. In spite of the appeal of R. T. France's brilliant interpretation, showing that the first thirty-one verses could be quite simply concerned with the destruction of Jerusalem in AD 70,[45] we are inclined to see the chapter as a fusion of the two ends, described in plain language, superimposed one upon the other, answering the double question which leads into the discourse (Mt. 24:3): the end of the Jewish world and the end of the world. This association of the two is rich with meaning; it reflects the function of Israel as the representative of humanity (in grace and in judgment), and the theological importance of the destruction of the temple and of the city, which it would be hard to overestimate. Jesus' intention is not to dictate the timetable. The repetitions of the warning 'Take heed' (Mk. 13:5, 23, 33, RSV), translated in a number of ways in the latest versions, but the same word each time in the Greek (*Blepete*), which punctuate the passage as it develops, draw this penetrating comment from Dom Jacques Dupont:

> A discourse which began by presenting itself as an apocalyptic revelation ends up becoming what has been called an 'anti-apocalyptic discourse'. In place of the curiosity with which apocalypses seek to know what the future will be, it establishes a Christian attitude which comprises suspicion of people who are too well informed on the subject and constant vigilance in view of the fact that the Lord's coming can occur at any moment.[46]

Read from such an angle, Mark 13:30 makes perfectly good sense, provided that the verb *genētai* is taken as what the grammarians call the 'ingressive' aorist, to be rendered 'begin to happen'. Jesus is referring 'to the complex of events that may be called "signs of the end" and which will be experienced by his own generation, without necessarily exhausting them'.[47] Take heed! All this will begin to happen during your own lifetime, but it will be only the beginning of the birth-pains (vv. 7–8). When these different passages are taken in this way, one is tempted to endorse Karl Barth's ruthless comment on 'consistent' eschatology: 'in its way the greatest triviality of any age'.[48]

Can we still believe in the imminence of the event after nineteen centuries? If we have properly understood the passages quoted above, imminence is no longer primarily a question of a fixed date; imminence expresses the essential connection between our present and that future, which is the next act of salvation and which arises as the first corollary from the work of Christ accomplished in the past.

> The Parousia is near, not because it must necessarily come within a set number of years but because, however long it might delay on account of God's patience and purpose of grace, it remains that which necessarily belongs to what has already happened in Christ, as it is the unveiling of the mystery of the incarnation and the revelation of the glory of the Christ.[49]

Furthermore, just as the Old Testament knows of the 'days of YHWH' to bring a *partial* conclusion, to judge or save a particular people at such and such a moment in history, and just as it can speak of a 'coming' of Yahweh *on a cloud* (Is. 19:1), the New Testament can set its sights not only on the final coming of the Lord, but also on other intervening 'comings', like minor tremors preceding a great earthquake. It is now widely accepted that the judgment of AD 70 prefigures the end of the world; the letters to the seven churches speak of a localized coming, for judgment, of Christ in his glory (Rev. 2:5, 16).[50] We must always take this into account in connection with both the imminence of the Last Day and the need to be always watching; the end is already encroaching on the present in the form of those personal or collective crises and denouements of which only the Father knows the day and the hour. In contrast with the dogmatism of 'consistent' eschatology, we may always be alert, knowing in what way 'the Lord is near'. John Henry Newman pictured it as follows:

> Up to Christ's coming in the flesh, the course of things ran straight towards that end, nearing it by every step; but now, under the Gospel, that course has (if I may so speak) altered its direction, as regards His second coming, and runs, not towards the end, but along it, and on the brink of it; and is at all times near that great event, which, did it run towards it, it would at

once run into. Christ, then, is ever at our doors; as near eighteen hundred years ago as now, and not nearer now than then, and not nearer when He comes than now.[51]

The unfolding of the ages

Our examination of the theories of postponement allows us to maintain that the reign or kingdom *has come*; but it brings out the other side of the teaching of Scripture, which is by no means illusory but is true to reality: the kingdom has still *to come*. As the church continues to pray, 'Your kingdom come!' This twofold structure can shed light on the phenomenon of the persistence of evil.

The duality of the present and future aspects of the kingdom, the 'already' and the 'not yet', is a truth that is widely recognized, a middle path between realized eschatology and consistent eschatology. Theologians like Joachim Jeremias and W. G. Kümmel incline to the 'already'; O. Cullmann maintains the balance, along with such evangelical scholars as Herman Ridderbos, G. E. Ladd and I. H. Marshall. R. N. Longenecker has highlighted the way that both stages are regularly presented together: Acts 2:16ff. is complemented, after 3:18, by 3:20f.; Hebrews 1:1 by 2:5; Hebrews 9:26 by 9:28b; 1 Peter 1:20 by 1:5.[52] We would gladly add the parallel and the distinction of the two resurrections, the first spiritual, occurring in the present age; the second corporeal, being the general resurrection at the end, John 5:25 and 28, *cf.* the clear wording of 1 John 3:2: 'Dear friends, now we are children of God, and what we will be has not yet been made known. But we know that when he appears, we shall be like him, for we shall see him as he is.'

C. H. Dodd himself modified his position,[53] and accepted Jeremias's formula *'sich realisierende Eschatologie'*, meaning eschatology in the process of being realized.[54] We prefer the phrase of Georges Florovsky, *inaugurated* eschatology.[55] This expression seems to us the one that corresponds best to the biblical image of the *firstfruits*, used for the risen Christ (1 Cor. 15:23) and for the gift of the Spirit (Rom: 8:23), and to the metaphor of a down payment or deposit (found in 2 Cor. 1:22, 5:5; Eph. 1.14). There is more in the notion of firstfruits than just anticipation or prolepsis, a concept favoured by Wolfhart Pannenberg[56] and Jürgen Moltmann.[57] The idea of anticipation lends itself to the conceptual dexterity in which these two theologians excel; in Pannenberg's work its foundations are unsteady,[58] and in Moltmann's case it encourages a strangely *spatial* treatment of the future or of time; he constantly writes as if the future were a space ahead in which things are already occurring. But the future *does not exist!*[59] This idea favours the *future* aspect, which is detectable in Moltmann's reticence towards the idea of fulfilment already realized;[60] by contrast, the biblical 'firstfruits' enjoy qualitative pre-eminence over the future harvest! As for the last point, our censure is precisely the opposite of the one that can be made of Karl Barth, for whom the 'time fulfilled' of the resurrection (*plērōma tōn kairōn*) shines with such intensity that it eclipses the consummation yet to come.[61] We suggest that the term 'anticipated' eschatology be given to the institution of the kingdom from the time of John the Baptist onwards, when it made its way forward vigorously (*biazetai*, Mt. 11:12), and the term 'inaugurated' eschatology for the system in force since Easter and Pentecost. In that way we may distinguish 'times and periods'.

One characteristic makes the distinction of the 'times' of the rule or kingdom precise and clear in the New Testament, but too many writers leave it out of the picture. The presence of the kingdom, which is as inconspicuous as a seed, *is experienced only in the Spirit*, and the apostle Paul, who chiefly among the New Testament writers structures his theology in terms of his anthropology, sets out the correlation with the 'levels' of human life. The Spirit gives life to the 'inner' man (*anthrōpos*), while the kingdom is simply future for the external order of the world, of which our body makes us an integral part. Jean Héring had already pointed out, with reference to the kingdom, 'that it is realized at the present time [for the gospels], in so far as it is spiritual, in the heart of those who accept the Preaching with Faith and who repent', adding that this 'partial' realization 'will remain in the moral sphere'.[62]

Without this clarification, the 'already' and the 'not yet' become entangled one with the other, striving against one another in confusion. You swing from one to the other, honouring this instability with the title 'dialectical', without reaching any clear conclusion or even finding a landmark to give you your bearings. When you have to derive from this guidelines for the Christian's conduct and mission, you cannot avoid reaching arbitrary conclusions. Who is to say what is the correct proportion of the 'already' and the 'not yet'? It is certainly acknowledged that the kingdom was established in veiled fashion, so that it may be perceived by faith, not by sight, but further than that no-one dare go. Anthropological monism, *i.e.* the refusal to distinguish body and soul as constituents of the individual's make-up, so congenial to the modern mind and, between 1930 and 1960, enjoying the prestige of reflecting the alleged Hebrew mind, stands in the way of further progress. Nobody wants to be accused of 'Platonism for the people', or at least of idealism; and that produces inverted idealism! We must find the way back from these excesses.[63] Unity does not exclude duality; the individual person *is* his body, but he also *has* it – such is the 'mystery' of our incarnation. He *has* this lump of clay, in common with the whole visible creation, as a part of his being which is distinct from the inner self; by it he expresses himself and suffers, receives and gives, and he must keep it in check (Jas. 3:2). In spite of their constant interaction, the two levels always remain distinct. Never does the New Testament say that the regeneration of the *world* is already achieved, nor the liberation of the body. (Miraculous healings are only the signs of a kingdom which we cannot yet see.) Never does the New Testament tell the believer that he must still wait for the resurrection of the *inner* man, or for his partaking of eternal life, the life of the kingdom. The kingdom of God is righteousness, peace and joy *in the Holy Spirit*, the Spirit who is in close union with the spirit of the inner person (Rom. 8:10, 16; 2 Cor. 4:16). Conversely, since the form of this world is passing away, the body is still waiting for its redemption, being part and parcel of the creation which is groaning, and the outer nature is disintegrating with the passage of time (1 Cor. 7:31; Rom. 8:20–23; 2 Cor. 4:16). Here too, we perceive God's times!

If the kingdom, with its victory over evil, comes at several times, and if it is present now only in the Holy Spirit, the persistence of evil after the institution of the kingdom no longer gives the same cause for stumbling; for not everybody has the Spirit, and the old world, corrupted by sin, is still running its course. Although death has been conquered in the one who is the pioneer of life, and in the spiritual resurrection of his people, it is not yet 'put under his feet' (1 Cor. 15:20–28). The enemy has been cast out and has been bound in such a way that he cannot prevent the evangelization of the world, yet he is spreading his fury across the face of this earth in the short time that he has left (Rev. 12:12).

Indeed, several Old Testament prophecies of the kingdom implied that the elimination of evil would not happen in an instant, just as in the typology of the Hebrew kings: the warrior David precedes Solomon's reign of peace. In his reign, Messiah will make use of valour as well as retributive justice (Mi. 5:4f.; Is. 11:24; *cf.* the use made of this latter verse for one of the terminal acts of the economy of grace, 2 Thes. 2:8). The LORD sets him on his throne, commanding him to subdue his enemies (Ps. 110:1f.). This is the first phase of the kingdom, one of battle or conquest, concerning which the apostle Paul emphasizes, against those who deny the resurrection, that it entails victory over the final enemy, death: 'he must reign [according to the prophetic psalm] until he has put all his enemies under his feet', therefore until the resurrection of his own people (1 Cor. 15:25f.). May one suggest that it takes a good while for the small 'stone' of the kingdom of God to grow and fill the earth, whilst the statue that it struck crumbles (Dn. 2:34f., 44, NRSV; *cf.* the enigmatic prolongation of life permitted to the first three beasts in the parallel vision, 7:12)? It is not certain. But the prophet Ezekiel announces unequivocally that *after* the coming of the prince/king David, the one shepherd of the one flock, after the covenant of peace, after the fulfilment of the promises of return and of security (Ezk. 37:24, 26; 38:8,

11f., 14), then against the people of God will arise the great horde of Gog. In its initial phase, in the Holy Spirit, the kingdom of God is not established in the form that the majority of people were expecting; it does not put an end to evil at a single blow, but its liberating march of conquest extends over a period of time. For that period of time, evil continues to thrive.

The virulent counter-attack

The temporal structure of the establishment of the kingdom eases the tension felt between the two assertions, 'The kingdom has come' and 'Evil has not disappeared'. But how are we to explain the increased virulence of evil? If only we could see Christ's enemies finally struck down, one after another, and left as powerless as a footstool! But we see instead the intensification of their efforts and their undertakings, which furthermore we find in some of the prophecies of Scripture.

In point of fact, the question is not so easy to resolve. Since the time of Christ, has evil made progress in the world? We commonly uphold that view in our preaching, but we must acknowledge that there is strong psychological pressure in favour of pessimism. Optimism is automatically suspected of being soft towards those evils which it refuses to magnify; it is easier to rouse Christians to action by sounding an alarm; and in Christian circles there is the fear of appearing less spiritual, more worldly if you do not blacken the picture – after all, the true prophet's message must be one of condemnation.

In these conditions, it takes courage for a theologian in the Reformed tradition, Loraine Boettner, to uphold the view that 'marvelous progress' has been realized in nineteen centuries of history, in both the material and the spiritual realms.[64] It is easy to forget the appalling moral degeneracy of the pagan world, and to underestimate the advantages in all areas of life that our present generation enjoys. If detractors of our own society were put aboard a time machine and whisked back to an earlier age, few of them would turn down the chance of an early flight back. But moving on from that to asserting an overall improvement of life for everyone on this planet is a different matter altogether. It does not take long to recall so many horrors in this twentieth century. And on the scale of world history, who is able to measure the quantity and the atrocity of the sum of those evils? That would require infinite powers.

The only Judge who has such powers has given us in his revealed Word a carefully balanced verdict. After the sowing of the seed by the Son of Man, the weeds grow, as does also the corn (Mt. 13:24–30; 36–43). Good and evil grow together. The kingdom of God moves forward, and the building of the church brings benefit also to the world (*cf.* 1 Tim. 4:10). Simultaneously mankind's revolt against God moves towards its frenzied climax, increasing in its virulence and malignity. This is the enemy backlash (Mt. 13:28). Despite being defeated and confined to strict limits, the enemy hits out wildly, precisely in order to react against this defeat and restriction. This consideration can help us to interpret the increase in wickedness and suffering in this 'present age', since the death and resurrection of Christ.

It is the book of Revelation that unmasks this counter-attack. Its secret lies in a satanic caricature. A false trinity promotes its own worship on earth: the dragon, the beast and the false prophet. It is allied with Babylon, the prostitute, an obscene travesty of the Bride, Jerusalem. The beast, an amalgam of the beasts in the book of Daniel, apes the figure of Christ: it establishes its kingdom by what resembles a sacrificial self-offering and by an ersatz resurrection (Rev. 13:3); it receives an imitation divine name (it once was, now is not, and yet will come, Rev. 17:8), which implies a 'parousia': 'It will come' (*parestai*) is the verbal form which corresponds to the noun *parousia*, meaning the coming or advent, the word regularly used for the coming of Christ.

This beast, Satan's Messiah, is in our view to be identified with the antichrist spoken of in the first letter of John, and with the 'son of perdition' (RSV) or 'man doomed to destruction' (NIV) foretold by Paul in his second letter to the Thessalonian church. You can observe the same pattern in all three passages: an influence here and now, and a climactic eruption in the future.[65] For the paradox of the beast is that it 'is' the eighth of its own heads (to come), and also one of the seven (Rev. 17:11).[66] The attribution of the ordinal number 'eighth' seems likewise to be a mimicking of Christ, for eight is the symbolic number that belongs to him. He rose on the eighth day, which opens up the new creation after the seven days of the old one. In Greek the numerical value of the name 'Jesus' is 888. The writings of Peter allude to this symbolism (1 Pet. 3:20; 2 Pet. 2:5).

The antichrist of 1 John 2:18, who is both the one who opposes Christ, and the one who seeks to be the substitute for Christ (according to the two meanings of the Greek preposition *anti*), represented by the apostate teachers of early Gnosticism, seems nevertheless to be a figure that is to come.[67] Similarly, the operation of the mystery (or, secret activity) of lawlessness at work already, then its release from all restraint, will be followed by the coming (*parousia*) of the lawless one, the man of ultimate godlessness (2 Thes. 2:7–9). This man who brings to its peak the Adamic claim to be equal to God does so by imitating Christ. The man who makes himself god mimics the God who became man; not only is he a sinner, he is also apostate, not only is he pagan, he is also antichrist. These teachings extend Jesus' warning about false Christs and false prophets (Mk. 13:22). This duality is preserved in the book of Revelation and is also detectable in the mention of the spirit of antichrist in 1 John 4:3 (the false prophets are mentioned in v. 1), and in the reference to the power of Satan which will aid and abet the coming of the man of lawlessness (2 Thes. 2:9). Such is the operation of evil after the death and resurrection of Christ.

It is in the subtle mimicry of Satan's counter-attack that its deadly power is hidden. We must not be surprised if evil becomes evil beyond measure in the 'post-Christian' world. According to the saying that we have already quoted, '*corruptio optimi pessima*', the corruption of the best is the worst. The devil, incapable of creating anything, considers what is most beautiful and perfect, and produces its most attractive – and therefore most pernicious – imitation.

This understanding helps us to discern the evil of our time. We are undoubtedly seeing the 'return of Dionysus', as the French philosopher Jean Brun has so brilliantly shown in his book of that title.[68] For the eighth king is already the sixth, the beast of paganism which comes back to life at the end; the antichrist brings to realization the design of original sin. But the distinguishing characteristic of contemporary evil is that it is post-Christian. Humanism secularizes the biblical pre-eminence of the human race (Ps. 8:4–8), historicism secularizes the biblical emphasis on history, and politic-ization secularizes the message of the kingdom of God. Secularization itself is an imitation of the desacralization of the world achieved by Christianity. The arrogance of the man who makes himself god and destroys the earth (Rev. 11:18) would not have been possible without the awakening brought about by the gospel message, which lifted the world out of the morass of paganism, and out of slavery to the 'basic principles of the world' referred to by the apostle Paul (Gal. 4:3, 9; Col. 2:8).

Paul Schütz provides an impassioned demonstration of this, focusing on the importance of two kinds of person: the scientist and the politician. From several different angles he develops the paradox formulated by C. F. von Weizsäcker, '*Christus ermöglicht den Anti-Christ*': Christ renders possible the antichrist.[69] He explains how the schema subject–object which is character-istic of humanistic thought is deeply rooted in the consciousness of sin that was brought in by Christianity. It is typical of modern man to set his self over against the world, and even to set it (the self as the object of psychological study, for example) over against his 'I'. There you have a transposition of that duality which is brought out clearly by the Christian confession of sin permeating human nature: the individual divides into two not only as in the act of reflection, but goes so far as to dissociate himself from himself by accusing his 'hateful' self. He makes it an object that he pushes away from himself into the distance, and which he nevertheless is himself. The theme of the new creation is secularized in revolutionary thinking; the revolutionary is the one who will make 'all things new' (*cf.* Rev. 21:5). Even the theology of the Absolute Other is a form of anti-Christian thought in disguise.[70]

The last observation can be given widespread application. The most pernicious form of post-Christian evil is apostasy. The evil of evils, since the death and resurrection of Christ, is false Christianity, what Karl Barth calls 'a sham church',[71] and which begins with the adulteration of Christian truth in the church. That is exactly what the letters of John give us to understand by calling false teachers 'antichrists'. When people are shocked at so many evils laid at the door of 'Christianity' down the centuries, has any examination been made of its claim to this title? Has anyone identified the 'little flock', to whom the Father has been pleased to give the kingdom (Lk. 12:32)? In the field of this world, while waiting for the Son of Man to weed out of his conquering, mediatorial kingdom everything that causes sin (Mt. 13:41), the wheat and the tares are difficult to tell apart. The only conclusion that is easy to draw is the practical command of our Lord: 'So be on your guard; I have told you everything ahead of time'; 'What I say to you, I say to everyone: "Watch!"' (Mk. 13:23, 37).

The necessity of faith

There remains one final, mysterious question: Why has God chosen to delay the full realization of his kingdom, leaving the way open for an execrable counterfeit version of it? Why has he established it only in a hidden form, in the Spirit? 'How was it possible that the world's future already made present there in that event should not at once engulf the whole world like a tidal wave?'[72] Why did God not remove evil from the world at a single stroke? Why did he not prevent it from perfecting its methods, to the misery of so many human beings? Why did he allow the devil time for his counter-offensive, with all the allurements of a false Christianity? We do not have access to the counsel of God to explain all his ways. If the answer is part of 'the secret things' that 'belong to the LORD our God' (Dt. 29:29), we shall submit without demur; but if 'the things revealed' throw any light on the question, then it is our duty to gather from there what we can.

Karl Barth, the preacher of the message of the once-for-all fulfilment, grapples with the difficulty. After taking into account answers that are true without being adequate – the invisible nature of the transformation being wrought, the 'not yet', the scale of the church's advance – Barth reaches the essential question: God wanted to give the being he had created time 'not merely to see, but actively to share in the harvest which follows from the sowing of reconciliation'; we 'should not merely be the objects of His action but that we should be with Him as independently active and free subjects'.[73] He did not want to complete his work by going 'over the head of man'.[74] Without our response of faith, reconciliation would have been 'dictatorial', 'a sovereign overpowering of humanity'; without the delay willed by God before finally executing the sentence passed on evil, his grace would have been 'brutal grace';[75] the decision would have shown 'to the world and men only the kind of lop-sided favour which European nations used to exercise without consulting them to the peoples of their colonies'.[76] That implies that 'the defeated enemy still has power and opportunity to lash out in its death-throes'; hence the persistence of evil, and of Jesus Christ we understand that 'It is He who is surprised and startled that it is not removed'.[77] In spite of this strange assertion, which is by no means commonplace in his writings, Barth is greatly concerned to show that everything comes from Christ, who is not himself a combatant in this battle, but who makes it proceed from his fulness, from the perfection of the reconciliation.[78] He explains that, otherwise,

> God should have withheld from Himself and from us His presence and action in the form of His provisional promise in time, and the demonstration of His power in our present, under the conditions and in the limitations and problems of our present, and in the vulnerability of our existence, refraining from being our God or having us as His people in this way.[79]

So there we have the answer: evil has been left at large in order that man may respond freely; the glory of the God of grace required that it be so.

How are we to appraise the construction? Berkouwer, for whom the rationality of world and life was not all that transparent, concluded that the explanation was a failure.[80] At any rate, Barth's final reason looks in some respects like theological indiscretion; it appears presumptuous to define what God 'should' have done, and offensive to suppose that evil should be granted a temporary reprieve ('Hate what is evil', Rom. 12:9) for the sole purpose of serving as a foil or backcloth for grace. With reference to man's free response we seem to be on more solid ground; for it is clear that God requires it from us in this present age, and that the full implementation of the kingdom would have excluded its possibility. So we can be glad that Barth does not fall into the errors of Arminius or Pelagius on human freedom, and that he does not make it a factor that is independent of God.

But objections spring up as we read other passages of Barth. For is it not this same theologian that resolutely includes the subjective, *i.e.* the response of man, *in* the objective, *i.e.* the work of Christ once for all? Is he not the one who reduces the role of faith to the awareness of the fact of the salvation which already includes ontologically (in their real being) all human beings? Has he not described it as an *epiphenomenon*?[81] If everyone, as Barth asserts, *is in Christ* without faith, justified and sanctified, is grace nevertheless not 'dictatorial', 'a sovereign overpowering', even – worst of all – 'brutal'? In the same discussion, Barth excludes the possibility that the dam of unbelief can stand firm before the 'living stream' of grace, which is 'too strong' for it; he can envisage only 'the onrush of the waters'.[82] The image suggests a physical constraint, and it is no coincidence that Barth has a kind of predilection for such language: he speaks of 'the physical force of its fulfilment' (*i.e.* of the atoning death of Christ on the cross).[83] What in another writer would be stylistic licence corresponds in Barth's case to propositions concerning ontology. What weight, then, does freedom have, swept along like a wisp of straw by the rising tide?

If we correct his doctrine of faith, Barth's effort perhaps will bear fruit. Scripture moves in that direction. To the martyrs who would like to shorten the delay of the final judgment, the reply is given that the number of their fellow-servants is to be completed first (Rev. 6:11). God in his patience consents to appear negligent with respect to his promises and to endure human jeers and insults on the postponement of the coming of Christ, in order that all may come to salvation (2 Pet. 3:9). Before the end, the good news must first be preached to all nations (Mk. 13:10).[84] This gospel age is the proper (*idios*) time for giving the testimony (1 Tim. 2:6) established by the God who desires all people to be saved. We are able to understand that God wishes no other entry into his kingdom than that of faith; not by automatic incorporation, but by faith which responds to the Word and receives the Spirit, the faith which is brought to birth by the Word and engendered by the Spirit. Faith needs time, hence the old world has been given a stay of execution, during which the Word will spread, the power of God that is ludicrously weak in the eyes of the world: '"Not by might nor by power, but by my Spirit,"' says Yahweh *ṣᵉbā'ôt* (Zc. 4:6, lit.).

The way of the kingdom

Further than that we do not think we can go. We simply confess that the *times* of the kingdom, the *method* of its institution, and its *nature* cannot be separated. The way of faith, the way of love and not of constraint (Jn. 14:23) is the same one that God followed to establish his rule. If the kingdom comes in a way that is hidden from human eye, that is because it is hidden beneath the cross. It is *essential* for it to come by the cross: it had come by the cross, not only in order to fulfil the Scriptures, but in order that evil might be truly conquered.

Those who belong to the kingdom hate evil as the enemy of that kingdom. They know the reality of evil and can no longer align themselves with idealism or any kind of utopian position. They see through its strategy and they attack the sophisticated evil of the end time, which is the adulteration of Christianity. They can already relish its defeat in the Holy Spirit. The imminence of the kingdom speeds them on their way and the energy of grace is constantly being renewed in them. The way of the kingdom, however, remains one of unremitting conflict: 'We must fight throughout life under the cross.'[85]

Conclusion

Just as evil still torments people, casting a dark cloud over their happiness, polluting and plaguing their mind and conscience, so too the problem of evil remains without any rational solution. It is stuck fast in their mind like a thorn, even when that mind has been renewed by grace and belongs to the most faithful disciple. Now that the time has come to sum up what we have gained from our investigations, that is, the conclusion that we find ourselves obliged to draw. If we look to remove the thorn completely, we simply drive it in deeper, and a poisonous abscess forms, that of some kind of deceitful Gnosticism. The explanations put forward by theologians with the very best of intentions simply amount to concealing the real evil of evil and titivating its ugly horror, even when they do not go so far as to insult the pain of the victims by providing the criminals with excuses. Holy Scripture alone completely resists this temptation. The Bible says nothing which might in the least measure diminish the offence of evil; it refuses any attenuation, whether optimistic or pessimistic. Such faultlessness, as we have earlier pointed out, is nothing short of miraculous and deserves our notice; it indicates a source of inspiration which is of a different kind from human reflection. What have we discovered?

Inscrutability

At the heart lies the inscrutable mystery of the first appearance of evil. Why? How? Where does it come from? It cannot be explained by being made an initial ingredient of existence, or the price that has to be paid, on our microscopic scale, for universal harmony. These so-called solutions, which cut the nerve of human indignation and give cheap relief to the sense of guilt, run straight into the testimony of Scripture. The Lord God is preparing to judge a world that is overflowing with all kinds of abomination – he does not underestimate the gravity of what is intolerable – but on the sixth day of the creation he had rejoiced to behold a created world which 'was very good'. It contained not the slightest embryonic presence of evil, since it was in its entirety 'from him and through him and to him'. From the source of goodness there could not flow anything that was bitter (cf. Jas. 3:12). Even less could it be conceived that God would become the accomplice of evil by raising it up for the *purpose* of acting as his instrument or as a convenient foil.

Then, if it is true that evil arises from the misuse of created freedom, that of the devil and then that of human beings, that does not give us any final explanation either. How was evil born of a freedom that was good? To argue that evil is there and therefore was possible, and that doing evil was a real possibility arising from that freedom, is to cover up the discontinuity of that singular fact – singularly singular. It is completely to pass over its monstrous unwarrantedness; evil is already interpreted as a natural ingredient of existence, if it is taken as something that is consistent with goodness. Scripture bears the opposite testimony, and denies that the human will may ever become independent of God. It is God who rules his creation as sovereign, in accordance with his own design, according to the revelation he has given us in his Word written, even the choices that are aimed against him. The sovereignty of God, which is affirmed times without number in his own revelation, makes his permission of evil an impenetrable mystery.

Divine sovereignty, however, is indispensable to the denunciation of evil, for it alone can guarantee the order with respect to which evil is denounced as disorder. It is short-sightedness together with an absent-minded dash of anthropomorphism which plays with the empty notion of a form of divine sovereignty to which God himself has set limits. It is better to observe that the three branches of the capital T of the biblical doctrine, *i.e.* the abhorrent nature of evil, the goodness of God, and his absolute sovereignty, assign to evil its position of utter loathsomeness, of being an unjustifiable reality, and ratifies our initial, wholesome reaction against it of shame and indignation.

When we join the book of Job and the ninth chapter of Paul's letter to the Romans by forgoing the rational explanation of the origin of evil, we find ourselves moving on to the answer to the question, 'What is evil?' It is, of course, formally defined as something that is contrary to the will of God and yet permitted by him; but if we ask what is its 'essence', its 'nature', the elucidation runs up against the impenetrability of the mystery. The phenomenon does not belong to the order of the creation; neither is it an independent principle, for it draws its force from the created realm that it corrupts. It is neither really 'something' (for it is not from God, from whom all things come forth), nor really 'nothing'. It is neither a metaphysical datum nor a surface effect that can be easily dispersed. Georges Florovsky commented on this radically disturbing alienness in these terms:

> Evil is divided within itself; it is a discord and a disharmony, *inordinatio*. Evil is ambiguous, unstable, variable. It has no charac-ter of its own. . . . Nature itself is affected, nature itself is no longer pure. It is a dynamic disorder, a dynamic or functional perversion which is not yet consolidated in a metaphysical transformation. . . . The existence of evil is a parasitic existence,

evil lives by means of good, *ex ratione boni*. The elements are the same in the original world and the fallen world. But the organizing principle has changed. And although it is dynamic, the perversion is irreversible. Whoever has gone down into the abyss of evil, of his own will, is unable to climb back out.[1]

Here again, theological analysis agrees with the simple experience of ordinary people.

The absence of any theoretical solution, as we have perceived, opens the way for the practical answer to the question: 'Lord, how long?' The three inseparable biblical truths form the springboard of hope. They alone authorize us to expect the suppression of evil. But the inscrutable enigma puts forth a horrifying new shoot, which lengthens into the persistence of evil, even its revival, after the death and resurrection of Christ. If the Messiah has come, the Saviour, if he has won the victory over evil, if he has set up his kingdom, how are we to account for the succeeding nineteen centuries? Could the kingdom not have reached us, in spite of Matthew 12:28?

Light in the darkness

A ray of light pierces the gloom. It comes from the cross. The impenetrable mystery of evil meets the paradoxical mystery of the cross. The mystery of Golgotha is that of the darkness which turns to light, as the Psalmist said, for God and for us – for us *by* God (Ps. 139:11f.). We understand that we cannot understand, and even a little more. At the cross we find the verification of God's mastery over evil, of his incorporating it within his plan, of his using evil men, and of his freedom from all suspicion of complicity in it. The mere mention of this last hypothesis, even though it is made in order to brush it aside, is profoundly disturbing, as if we were on the verge of blaspheming. At the cross we find confirmation that evil does not belong *metaphysically* to the condition of the human race; to a catastrophe in history, God reacts in human history. At the cross is revealed how his kingdom comes about: not by might (of weaponry), or by power (of worldly means), but by the Spirit of sacrifice (Zc. 4:6); not by the subjection of multitudes to slavery, in the manner of the great rulers of this world, but by the service of the Son of Man (Mt. 20:25–28); for the kingdom is not of this world (Jn. 18:36). The way of the kingdom requires that it spread most unobtrusively, by spiritual influence. It conquers people's hearts, by their unconstrained acceptance of, and adherence to, the Word, its preaching and its call. Hence the stay of execution for the old world, the permission of continuing evil, and the margin of freedom left to the devil who is giving vent to his great fury, for he is aware how little time he has left (Rev. 12:12).

Hence the association of the kingdom with the suffering and the *patient endurance* in Jesus (Rev. 1:9).

Evil conquered as evil

But why is the kingdom set up in such a way, if another way could have spared so much weeping, so much bloodshed? We have come to the threshold of the secret and hidden wisdom, revealed by the Spirit, in words taught by the Spirit, and that none of the rulers of this age understood, what has not been conceived by any human mind (1 Cor. 2:7ff.). We have a special wisdom to seek out in the mystery of the cross. Not that this mystery gives us leave to overturn the concepts of orthodox Christian doctrine, such as downplaying the omnipotence of God as stated in Holy Scripture (after the death of Christ, as well as before it), and promoting a 'powerless God'; that is the kind of 'wisdom' that the rulers of this age endorse. The Pied Piper philosophers of our world will gladly take that path, reflecting as it does the vagaries of their humanism, their ideological manoeuvres and their all too human resentment.[2] The wisdom of God in the event of the cross maintains its unique, concrete character, spelt out with total clarity by what the cross achieved: perfect redemption and propitiation. In short, at the cross evil is conquered *as evil*.

The wisdom of the way of the cross is that it attacks evil according to the ambiguity of its unique nature, and its illegitimate status. If evil simply boiled down to the 'local' imperfection of every finite being, exaggerated by an optical illusion, Christ would have had to do no more than teach, or else initiate his disciples into the liberating vision, like a Zen master; but evil is something other, and it is at the cross that it is conquered, in quite another manner. If evil were a substance, an entity, comparable to some great power in the created order, it would have been sufficient to deploy a superior force against it, assuming that the opposing parties had enough in common for such a meeting to be conceivable; but evil is something other, and it is at the cross that it is conquered, in quite another manner.

At this point a misunderstanding arises for some people. They imagine Christ overcoming the devil at the end of a spiritual duel by his superior strength; or they speak of the elimination of evil, swallowed up by love, as if it were some kind of chemical operation of absorption and dissolution. Scripture is careful to avoid these misleading images. It speaks of the evil one being disarmed by the expiatory blood which alone washes away sins. The power of the devil over human beings is that of accusation, as his name, Satan, the accuser, indicates (Rev. 12:10ff.; Col. 2:14f.).

Lastly, if evil corresponded to a necessary moment in the forward movement of a dialectical sequence of events, it would be left behind by its own progression to a higher synthesis. But evil is something other, and it is at the cross that it is conquered. Good Friday is anything but speculative. The free sacrifice, unique and once for all, is the reverse of the illustration of the fruitfulness of the Negation in a universal chain of logic. At the cross evil is conquered as evil: corruption, perversion, disorder, a parasite, and yet also weighed down with the load of the people it has led astray and deep in debt from the responsibility incurred.

Evil is conquered as evil because God turns it back upon itself. He makes the supreme crime, the murder of the only righteous person, the very operation that abolishes sin. The manoeuvre is utterly unprecedented. No more complete victory could be imagined. God responds in the indirect way that is perfectly suited to the ambiguity of evil. He entraps the deceiver in his own wiles. Evil, like a judoist, takes advantage of the power of the good, which it perverts; the Lord, like a supreme champion, replies by using the very grip of the opponent. So is fulfilled the surprising verse: 'With the pure you show yourself pure; and with the crooked you show yourself perverse' (Ps. 18:26, NRSV).

It is exactly this, the sin of sins, the murder of the Son, which accomplishes this work in a double manner. It provides the opportunity for love to be carried to its very peak, for there is no greater love than to give one's life for one's friends (Jn. 15:13). And as this gift contains no element of a romantic suicide (like Tristan or Romeo), the death unjustly inflicted becomes the 'wages' earned by the sin of the world, borne by the Lamb of God. It constitutes the ransom paid to liberate sinners, for they are prisoners of the law of God, the One who is Son of God and Son of Man, the head of the new humanity taking upon himself the debt of his own people (Mt. 20:28; Gal. 3:13, 21; Col: 2.14, *etc.*). It is in this way that he triumphs over sin, guilt and death. It involves a double coincidence. Evil culminates in murder; by *taking away* the life of the other person, sin brings about the successful conclusion of its essential intention, the rejection of the Lord and of whoever bears his image. By contrast love, which is 'being for the other person', culminates in the *gift* of one's own life in favour of someone else. Furthermore, the requirement of right order, which is the order of love according to God, is that evil be punished by death, but it permits the brother and head to intervene in love and take over the debt in place of the guilty party. Here lies the mystery of the victory:

> I see the depths of my pride, curiosity, concupiscence. There is no link between me and God or Jesus Christ the righteous. But he was made sin for me. All your scourges fell upon him. He is more abominable than I, and, far from loathing me, feels honoured that I go to him and help him. But he healed himself and will heal me all the more surely.[3]

The secret and hidden wisdom of the Lord has caused to coincide the ignoble murder and the act of supreme love of the righteous for the unrighteous, the expiation, by his death in their place, of their sins. At the cross, evil is conquered by the ultimate degree of love in the fulfilment of justice.

A more elaborate treatment of evil would expose, in addition to its reversal (the suppression of the other person), the twisted leer of counterfeit love, false love, perverted love in which the warped outlines are still recognizable. It would also show how death, the secret goal of sin from the very beginning (Jn. 8:44; Rom. 8:6), is of necessity the retribution that befalls it, rather than any other punishment; and also how the primacy of love, which is the foundation of humanness, permits the transfer of responsibility. It would thus further elucidate the connection between Calvary and the problem of evil. But we have seen enough to recognize in the mystery of the cross *the* divine answer to the unanswerable question of evil: *de profundis*, 'out of the depths' (Ps. 130:1), springs light, despite the impenetrability of the enigma.

Such is the glory of the cross that one would be tempted to explain the permission of evil *by this end*, that love, put to the test, reveals itself in its ultimate intensity. One last time, we must resist the attraction of this thought, for it would cause us to fall back into a pseudo-rational Gnosticism; it would attribute to a holy God a calculating mind which would utterly appal him. We have no other position than at the foot of the cross. After we have been there we are given the answer of the wisdom of God, which incenses the advocates of optimistic theodicies or of tragic philosophies. God's answer is evil turned back upon itself, conquered by the ultimate degree of love in the fulfilment of justice.

This answer consoles us and summons us. It allows us to wait for the coming of the crucified conqueror. He will wipe away the tears from every face, *soon*.

Notes

Introduction

1 *Le Mythe de Sisyphe* (1942), ET *The Myth of Sisyphus* (London: Hamish Hamilton, 1955); *La Peste* (1947), ET *The Plague* (London: Hamish Hamilton, 1948; Penguin, 1960); *La Chute* (1956), ET *The Fall* (London: Hamish Hamilton, 1958; Penguin, 1963).

2 'Les nouveaux philosophes' are a group of writers who became disenchanted with Marxism in their student days, in particular following the events of May 1968. The best known are André Glucksmann and Bernard-Henri Lévy.

3 *Religion, Revolution and the Future* (New York: Charles Scribner's Sons, 1969), p. 55, cf. pp. 62, 204.

4 According to John Hick, *Evil and the God of Love* (London: Collins, Fontana Library, 1968), p. 5, n. 1, Epicurus formulated it by tying it to the dilemma: either God is good and unable, or he is able and not good.

5 Plotinus, *First Ennead* 8, quoted by Charles Journet, *The Meaning of Evil* (1961–2; ET London: Geoffrey Chapman, 1963), p. 29, n. 9. Augustine, *De Natura Boni* ch. 4, in Philip Schaff (ed.), *The Nicene and Post-Nicene Fathers*, vol. 4 (Grand Rapids: Eerdmans, 1974).

6 Quoted in French translation in P. Béguerie *et al.*, *Etudes sur les prophètes d'Israël* (Paris: Cerf, 1954), p. 35.

7 Etienne Borne, *Le Problème du mal* (Paris: PUF, 1958), p. 67.

8 *Ethics*, Preface to Part IV, *Everyman's Library* (London: Dent, 1910), p. 143.

9 *First Ennead* 8, 15 and *Third Ennead* 2, 17, quoted by Charles Journet, *op. cit.*, p. 22, nn. 9, 10.

10 *Op. cit.*, p. 52.

11 Aristotle, *Metaphysics*, E2 1027 a 8f.

12 Charles Werner, *Le Problème du mal dans la pensée humaine* (Paris: Payot, 1944).

13 G. C. Berkouwer, *Sin* (ET Grand Rapids: Eerdmans, 1971), p. 20.

14 Ananda K. Coomaraswamy, *Buddha and the Gospel of Buddhism* (London: Harrap, 1916), pp. 39f.

15 J.-P Sartre, *L'Etre et le néant* (Paris: Gallimard, 1943); ET *Being and Nothingness* (London: Methuen, 1957).

16 Philippe Nemo, in *Job et l'excès du mal* (Paris: Grasset, 1979), holds that the exceeding quality of evil – the failure of every technical solution being, as it were, a breach in this world through which a beyond is revealed – awakens the soul. Such is the intention of the Intention, and then we discover the good, the Father who dwells outside this world. He is a soul related to our own, and is pure weakness: 'He is, for us, *nothing other than the excess of good and evil*, inexplicably merged' (p. 194).

17 Ananda K. Coomaraswamy, *Hinduism and Buddhism* (Westwood, Connecticut: Greenwood Press, 1971 reprint), p. 45.

18   Albert Camus, *The Myth of Sisyphus*, the concluding sentence.

1. The solution by universal order

1   Gottfried Leibniz, *Essais de théodicée* (1710), I, 92 and 30; II, 241f.

2   Henri Gouhier, 'Situation contemporaine du problème du mal' in *Le Mal est parmi nous* (Paris: Plon, 1948), p. 12.

3   Werner Post, 'Théories philosophiques sur le problème du mal', *Concilium* 56 (June 1970), p. 96, n. 2.

4   Georges Friedmann, *Leibniz et Spinoza* (Paris: Gallimard, 2nd edn. 1962), p. 32.

5   Claude Tresmontant, *Introduction à la théologie chrétienne* (Paris: Seuil, 1974), pp. 685, 688, 694.

6   *The Christic* is published in English translation in the volume *The Heart of Matter* (London: Collins, 1978), pp. 80–102; this passage appears on p. 92. The same symmetry and affirmation are to be found in his *Introduction à la vie chrétienne* (Paris: Seuil, 1969), p. 184.

7   *The Phenomenon of Man* (ET London: Collins, 1959), pp. 292f.

8   *Introduction à la vie chrétienne*, p. 183, *cf.* also p. 156.

9   *Le Milieu divin* (ET, retaining the French title, London: Collins, 1957).

10   *Cf.* the second and third of the 'Three stories in the style of Benson' (1916) in *Hymn of the Universe* (ET London: Collins, 1965), pp. 46–55; and *The Christic*, p. 94. *Cf.* also *Le Milieu divin* (ET), pp. 113ff.

11   *Esquisse d'un Univers Personnel* in vol. 6 of his collected works, *Oeuvres* (Paris: Seuil, 1962), p. 73.

12   *Note sur quelques représentations historiques possibles du péché originel* (1922), *Ouevres* vol. 10, p. 69.

13   *Chute, Rédemption et Géocentricité* (1920), *Ouevres* vol. 10, p. 53; *Le Christ évoluteur* (1942), *Oeuvres* vol. 10, p. 175.

14   *The Phenomenon of Man*, p. 313; *Notes sur les modes de l'action divine dans l'Univers* (1920), *Oeuvres* vol. 10, p. 43.

15   *Ibid.*, p. 44; *Christologie et Evolution* (1933), *Oeuvres* vol. 10, p. 103 n.

16   *Letters to Léontine Zanta* (ET London: Collins, 1969), p. 115. The English version in fact reads 'Physics' for 'the physical', an understandable slip in the overall context.

17   *E.g. Réflexions sur le péché originel* (1947), *Oeuvres* vol. 10, p. 227: '*Statistically* . . . it is absolutely inevitable [the French word is '*fatal*', *i.e.* 'fated']; *The Heart of Matter*, p. 51.

18   *Notes sur les modes de l'action divine*, p. 42 n. 4; *ibid.*, p. 43.

19   The explanation is given clearly in a number of places, appearing as early as the appendix on evil in *The Phenomenon of Man*. On the other hand, Teilhard gives scarcely any explanation on the first emergence of non-being/the pure multiple; the fullest treatment is in the carefully worked out essay of 1948, *Comment je vois*, *Oeuvres* vol. 11 (1948).

20   *Le Milieu divin* (ET), p. 65 (*cf.* the whole section).

21   *Ibid.*, pp. 67ff., also *The Heart of Matter*, p. 51.

22   *Esquisse d'un Univers Personnel*, pp. 107ff.

23   Quoted in Georges Crespy, *La Pensée théologique de Teilhard de Chardin* (Paris: Editions Universitaires, 1961), p. 231.

24   *Esquisse d'un Univers Personnel*, p. 111; *The Phenomenon of Man*, p. 308.

25   *The Phenomenon of Man*, p. 257.

26   *Esquisse d'un Univers Personnel*, p. 99.

27   Teilhard's laborious debate with himself can be followed in the last part of *La Place de l'Homme dans la nature. Le Groupe zoologique humain* (Paris: coll. 10/18, Union Générale d'Editions, 1962), pp. 160–169.

28   *Ibid.*, pp. 142ff.

29   Texts quoted by Jean-Marie Domenach in *Esprit* 326 (March 1964), p. 327.

30   *Comment je vois* in Crespy, p. 121.

31   Gustave Martelet, *Libre Réponse à un scandale. La faute originelle, la souffrance, la mort* (Paris: Cerf, 1986), pp. 44 (49ff.), 79f.; references to Teilhard, pp. 124f., 128.

32   *Ibid.*, p. 136 (our italics); pp. 41f., 79, 82f.

33   *Ibid.*, pp. 33, 49f.; p. 63: Genesis and Paul had only 'historically precarious' information on Adam.

34   *Ibid.*, p. 87; *cf.* pp. 133f.

35   Charles Journet, *The Meaning of Evil*, 1961 (ET London: Geoffrey Chapman, 1963), pp. 31ff., details the patristic writers who present this view.

36   Etienne Gilson, *The Spirit of Mediaeval Philosophy* (ET London: Sheed and Ward, 1950), p. 115.

37   *Summa Theologiae*: The Creation, Iª qu. 48, arts. 2, 3 and 5, translated and annotated by A. D. Sertillanges (Paris: Desclée, 1972).

38   Journet, p. 42, criticizes the confusion of the German philosopher.

39   *Ibid.*, p. 47.

40   Jacques Maritain, *De Bergson à Thomas d'Aquin* (Paris: Hartmann, 1947), p. 295.

41   *Op. cit.*, p. 151.

42   Maritain, *op. cit.*, p. 280; the same image is used by Gilson, *op. cit.*, pp. 116f.

43   Doctrinal note in the section of the *Summa* referred to above (n. 37).

44   *Summa* Iª qu. 48, art. 2 *cf.* qu. 49, art. 2 (ET London: Burns Oates and Washbourne Ltd, 1921), vol. 2, p. 267. Having quoted the same proposition, John Hick comments: 'One might well inquire into the grounds of the view that what can fail sometimes will fail. Is this an empirical generalization reflecting our observation that things that are capable of failing sooner or later do so? Or does it, more narrowly, simply restate the circumstance that man, created free, has in fact fallen? Or again, does it postulate some necessity that a fallible creature must fail? Or that out of a collection of free beings a certain proportion must fail? On neither type of interpretation can Aquinas' statement do more than gloss over a major difficulty. For if a free creature *necessarily* fails, the Being who created him must at least share the responsibility for his failure. If, on the other hand, it is just an observable fact that free beings have fallen, to report this does not serve to *explain* anything, and we are left with the undiminished paradox of a being who is created good but who spontaneously becomes evil.' *Evil and the God of Love* (London: Collins, Fontana Library, 1968), pp. 102ff.; *cf.* also pp. 196ff.

45   Maritain, *op. cit.*, p. 274; Journet, *op. cit.*, p. 255.

46   *Op. cit.*, p. 218, Sertillanges' italics.

47   Iª qu. 48, art. 2, ET p. 268.

48   Gilson, *op. cit.*, p. 120.

49   Maritain, *op. cit.*, p. 274, also p. 275.

50   *Ibid.*, p. 277.

51   Journet, *op. cit.*, p. 147; *cf.* p. 82.

52   *Ibid.*, p. 147.

53 *Ibid.*, pp. 13f.; 176–182; 219ff.; *cf. Summa* Iª qu. 48, arts. 5 and 6.

54 *Op. cit.*, pp. 278, 282.

55 *Op. cit.*, pp. 82ff., especially p. 85.

56 *Ibid.*, p. 147.

57 *Ibid.*, p. 279.

58 *Op. cit.*, pp. 282–298; Maritain comments on *De Malo* I, 3, to which *Summa* Iª qu. 49, art. 1 corresponds; ET pp. 277–280. Gilson refers to the same passage in the original edition, *L'Esprit de la philosophie médiévale* (Paris: J. Vrin, 1932), vol. 1, pp. 264ff., n. 25; unfortunately it is one of a number of lengthy notes omitted from the English translation. Journet refers to the passage briefly, *op. cit.*, p. 72.

59 *Ibid.*, pp. 284ff.

60 *Ibid.*, p. 285.

61 *Ibid.*, p. 287.

62 *Ibid.*, p. 288.

63 *Ibid.*, p. 293.

64 *Ibid.*, p. 298.

65 *Ibid.*, p. 300; Journet, *op. cit.*, pp. 83, 162f.

66 *Cf.* our study 'La foi et la tentation du néant' ('Faith and the temptation of non-being') in *Pour une Reformé permanente* (Rencontres Protestantes 1973; Geneva: Société Evangélique de Genève), p. 28.

67   Haec tua sunt; bona sunt quia tu bonus ista creasti.
             Nil nostrum est in eis, nisi quod peccamus amantes,
             Ordine neglecto, pro te, quod conditur abs te.
    Quoted in Henri Marrou, *Saint Augustin et l'augustinisme* (Paris: Seuil), p. 141.

68 *E.g.* the orthodox Protestant dogmatician Herman Bavinck, according to G. C. Berkouwer, *Sin* (ET Grand Rapids: Eerdmans, 1971), pp. 63f. John Hick notes the concept of evil as privation in Calvin's writings, *op. cit.*, p. 121, n. 2.

69 Journet, *op. cit.*, p. 77.

70 Georges Florovsky, '"Tenebrae noctium". Position d'un chrétien de l'église orthodoxe russe' in *Le Mal est parmi nous* (Paris: Plon, 1948).

71 Paul Claudel, 'Du mal et de la liberté', *ibid.*, p. 277.

72 Søren Kierkegaard, *Christian Discourses* (ET Oxford University Press, 1939), p. 108.

73 *Summa*, section referred to above.

74 John Hick has seen that the concept of 'non-being' is a source of conceptual confusion: *op. cit.*, p. 48, *cf.* pp. 188, 190ff.

75 Quoted by Florovsky, p. 251.

76 *Job et l'excès du mal* (Paris: Grasset, 1979), p. 28.

2. The solution by autonomous freedom

1 Nikolai Berdyaev, *Freedom and the Spirit* (ET London: Geoffrey Bles, 1935), p. xix.

2 *Ibid.*, p. 160.

3 *Ibid.*, *cf.* p. 307: 'a deep and ineffable source', *etc.*

4 *Ibid.*, p. 165. The dark void is Jakob Boehme's *Ungrund* (see further ch. 3, p. 67); but Berdyaev points out that he locates it outside God, whereas Boehme locates it in God: quoted by Charles Journet in *the Meaning of Evil* (London: Geoffrey Chapman, 1963), p. 101, n. 108.

5 Journet, p. 101, makes a curious mistake on the meaning of 'meonic' by linking it to the

Latin *meo*, 'I pass', to mean 'a Freedom which is always on the move', but in the next paragraph he reproduces a clear explanation from Berdyaev, who writes that 'Man is . . . the child of freedom – of nothing, of non-being, *to mē on*', *The Destiny of Man* (ET London: Geoffrey Bles, 1937), p. 25. *Cf. Freedom and the Spirit*, p. 128: 'Liberty is bound up not with the form but with the matter of life . . .' (classical Greek dualism).

6 *The Meaning of the Creative Act* (ET London: Gollancz, 1955), pp. 15f.

7 *Freedom and the Spirit*, p. 160.

8 Journet's expression, *op. cit.*, p. 100.

9 *Freedom and the Spirit*, p. 129.

10 *Ibid.*, p. 165.

11 *Ibid.*, p. 166.

12 *The Meaning of the Creative Act*, p. 148. He adds: 'Theodicy, the justification of God, is also a justification of the meaning of evil.'

13 *Ibid.*, pp. 148–150.

14 Charles Werner, *Le Problème du mal* (Paris: Payot, 1944), p. 64; pp. 62–65 give an excellent summary of Monod's theodicy.

15 Wilfred Monod, *Le Problème du bien. Essai de théodicée et Journal d'un pasteur* (Paris: Félix Alcan, 1934) I, pp. 139, 169, 226.

16 *Ibid.*, I, p. 691; *cf.* p. 186.

17 *Ibid.*, I, pp. 733f.

18 *Ibid.*, I, p. 122; for the preceding assertion, p. 127; *cf.* the summary, p. 246.

19 *Ibid.*, I, pp. 120, 230 (*cf.* p. 134).

20 *Ibid.*, II, p. 729; *cf.* I, p. 245.

21 *Ibid.*, I, pp. 108, 120 ('The dogma of the incarnation, by humanizing God, divinizes humanity; there are profound insights, expressed in ridiculous forms, in the "Cult of humanity", that is to say "of life"').

22 *Ibid.*, III, p. 155 ('The prayer which hears and answers God' is the title of the chapter); *cf.* I, p. 132.

23 *Ibid.*, I, p. 158.

24 'Dieu selon la "Process Theology"', *Etudes Théologiques et Religieuses* 55 (1980), pp. 197ff.

25 A. N. Whitehead, *Religion in the Making* (Cambridge University Press, 1926), pp. 89, 98f., 153.

26 *Ibid.*, p. 154.

27 See *The Spirit and Forms of Love* (New York: Harper and Row, 1968), discussed by Carl F. H. Henry in 'The Reality and Identity of God: A Critique of Process Theology', *Christianity Today* 13 (1969), pp. 523–526 and 580–584. Henry's article is well worth consulting.

28 *God, Power and Evil: A Process Theodicy* (Philadelphia: Westminster Press, 1976), pp. 201ff.

29 See Carl F. H. Henry, *art. cit.*, quoting Peter Hamilton, *The Living God and the Modern World* (London: Hodder and Stoughton, 1967), p. 226.

30 Stephen T. Davis, 'God the Mad Scientist: Process Theology on God and Evil', *Themelios* 5 (1979), p. 22.

31 Whitehead, *op. cit.*, p. 155.

32 *Process Theology: An Introductory Exposition* (Philadelphia: Westminster Press, 1976), p. 71, as quoted by Stephen T. Davis, *art. cit.*, p. 22 (see pp. 20f. for the presentation of the ideas).

33 *Letters and Papers from Prison* (ET London: SCM Press, 1953; Fontana Books, 1959), p. 166.

34 Dorothee Sölle, *Christ the Representative. An Essay in Theology after the 'Death of God'* (ET London: SCM Press, 1967), pp. 151f.

35 *Le Conflit des interprétations. Essais d'herméneutique* (Paris: Seuil, 1969), p. 297.

36 *La Symbolique du mal, finitude et culpabilité*, vol. II (Paris: Aubier-Montaigne, 1960), p. 126.

37 *Le Conflit des interprétations*, pp. 297ff., 422ff.

38 *Ibid.*, p. 424.

39 Quoted by Werner Post, 'Théories philosophiques sur le problème du mal', *Concilium* 56 (June 1970), p. 97. A. J. Rasker, in his thesis on the problem in Kant's writings, *De Ethiek en het probleem van het booze. Een studie naar aanleiding van de ethische en godsdienstphilosophische geschriften van Immanuel Kant* (Assen: Van Gorcum, 1935), pp. 111ff., considers, over against Emil Brunner, that radical evil is not inconsistent with human autonomy, because of the difference between the transcendental self and the empirical self; however, as he shows, Kant himself is in some difficulty with the tension between his strong pronouncements on radical evil and the corruption of moral maxims on the one hand, and upholding the freedom of the will and its power to bring about moral amendment on the other hand (pp. 113–118); what is at question here is the influence of Christian dogmatics (pp. 118f.).

40 François Laplantine, *Le Philosophe et la violence* (Paris: PUF, 1976), gives him due attention, Part II, chs. 3 and 4.

41 *Le Problème du mal* (Paris: PUF, 1967), *e.g.* pp. 80ff., 105f., 113.

42 S. A. Kierkegaard, *Fear and Trembling* (ET London: Oxford University Press, 1939), p. 100. *Cf. The Sickness unto Death* (ET London: Oxford University Press, 1941), p. 188: 'Thou shalt [is] the only regulative principle . . . in man's relationship to God.'

43 *The Concept of Dread* (ET London: Oxford University Press, 1944), p. 21; '. . . freedom gazes down into its own possibility, grasping at finiteness to sustain itself. In this dizziness freedom succumbs . . . . That very instant everything is changed, and when freedom rises again it sees that it is guilty'; p. 55; 'The relation of freedom to guilt is dread'; p. 97. No English word renders *Angst* adequately. Walter Lowrie uses 'dread' in the translation we quote from. Denzil G. M. Patrick prefers 'anguish', *Pascal and Kierkegaard*, vol. 2 (London: Lutterworth Press, 1947). John Macquarrie argues for 'anxiety', 'dread' being misleading in its suggestion of fear, and 'anguish' in its suggestion of acute pain; *Existentialism* (Harmondsworth: Penguin, 1973), pp. 164f.

44 *The Sickness unto Death*, p. 22.

45 *The Concept of Dread*, p. 100.

46 *Ibid.*; *cf.* p. 99 n.: 'The distinction between good and evil certainly exists for freedom, but not *in abstracto*'; *cf.* p. 45: 'abstract *liberum arbitrium* . . . is a non-sense to thought'.

47 *Ibid.*, p. 55.

48 *The Sickness unto Death*, p. 19.

49 Emil Brunner, *The Christian Doctrine of Creation and Redemption* (ET London: Lutterworth Press, 1952), p. 20.

50 *Le Philosophe et la violence*, p. 197.

51 C. S. Lewis, *The Problem of Pain* (London: Collins, Fontana Books, 1957), pp. 68f.

52 Francis Schaeffer, *The God Who is There* (London: Hodder and Stoughton, 1968), p. 103.

53 Stephen T. Davis, *art. cit.*, p. 22 and (for the crucial distinction) p. 19.

54 On this debate, see, for example, John S. Feinberg, 'And the Atheist Shall Lie Down with the Calvinist: Atheism, Calvinism and the Free-Will Defense', *Trinity Journal* new series 1 (1980), pp. 142–152; Keith Burgess-Jackson, 'Free-Will, Omnipotence and the Problem of Evil', *American Journal of Theology and Philosophy* 9 (1988), pp. 177–185.

55 *Dieu sans idée du mal. La liberté de l'homme au coeur de Dieu* (Limoges: Critérion, 1982).

56   *Evil and the God of Love* (Collins, Fontana Library, 1968, 1st edn. 1966), pp. 302ff.

57   *Ibid.*, p. 311.

58   *Ibid.*, p. 302.

59   *Ibid.*, pp. 310f.

60   *Death and Eternal Life* (Macmillan, 1990, 1st edn. 1976) p. 164.

61   *Ibid.*, p. 246. He defines Johannine predestination with a hardness that smacks of caricature: 'a predestination involving a fixed and impassable gulf between those marked from birth for eternal life and those marked from birth for eternal death' (pp. 246f.).

62   *Evil and the God of Love*, p. 313: it 'contains within itself tensions and pressures which it cannot withstand'.

63   *Ibid.*, p. 376.

64   *Ibid.*, p. 379.

65   *Ibid.*, pp. 379, 380.

66   *Ibid.*, p. 172; *cf.* p. 35 with regard to J. S. Mill.

67   *Ibid.*, p. 234.

68   *Ibid.*, p. 262.

69   *Ibid.*, pp. 150, 262 and 265: 'The Augustinian thinks it impious to state explicitly what his doctrine covertly implies [God's responsibility since he is confessedly sovereign]; the Irenaean, in a more rationalist vein, is willing to follow the argument to its conclusion.'

70   *Ibid.*, p. 311.

71   *Ibid.*, p. 312.

72   *Death and Eternal Life*, pp. 254ff. The phrase is used, for example on p. 256.

73   *Evil and the God of Love*, p. 313.

74   *Ibid.*, p. 312.

75   *Ibid.*, p. 295, n. 1.

76   *Ibid.*, pp. 174f.

77   *Ibid.*, p. 175.

78   *Ibid.*, pp. 297, 372, 399 respectively.

79   *Ibid.*, p. 268.

80   *Ibid.*, p. 290; *cf.* pp. 217ff. for Irenaeus.

81   *Ibid.*, p. 291.

82   *Ibid.*, pp. 314ff.

83   *Ibid.*, p. 317.

84   *Ibid.*, p. 318.

85   *Ibid.*, p. 319.

86   *Ibid.*, p. 323.

87   *Ibid.*, *loc. cit.*

88   *Ibid.*, pp. 275f.

89   *Ibid.*, p. 211.

90   *Ibid.*, p. 284.

91   *Ibid.*, pp. 318ff. (the phrase appears on p. 320), *cf.* p. 209.

92   See Henri Blocher, *In the Beginning. The Opening Chapters of Genesis* (Leicester: Inter-Varsity Press, 1984), especially chapter 7.

93   *Evil and the God of Love*, pp. 128f., 180f., 228, 238, as well as pages referred to earlier.

94   *Ibid.*, p. 221.

95   *Ibid.*, p. 223.

96   *Ibid.*, pp. 225f.

97   *Ibid.*, p. 387.

98   *Ibid.*, p. 388.

99   *Ibid.*, p. 365.

100 *Ibid.*, p. 366.

101 *Ibid.*, p. 397; *cf.* pp. 324f.

102 *Ibid.*, pp. 369f.

103 *Ibid.*, p. 371

104 *Ibid.*, p. 389.

105 *Ibid.*, p. 399.

106 Thus the criticism of too naïve a vision of a dreamlike harmony which in the end turns out to be bland and dull to the point of aimlessness.

107 An apprenticeship through suffering, according to the play on words in Hebrews 5:8 (*emathen/epathen*), does not imply cognitive distance. Hick, *ibid.*, p. 299, seems to acknowledge the sinlessness of Jesus, and remains vague about his divinity.

108 We have noted its recurrence, *ibid.*, pp. 103, 116, 145, 165, 182, 218, 265, 280, 323, 400.

109 Peter Geach, *Providence and Evil* (Cambridge University Press, 1977), p. 80.

110 *Ibid.*, pp. 69f., over against C. S. Lewis, in whose book Geach rightly detects 'a slight Manichean strain' (p. 133).

111 On this question, ch. XV of John Hick's *Evil and the God of Love* is one of the least satisfactory in the book; see also the interesting appendix in John W. Wenham, *The Enigma of Evil. Can We believe in the Goodness of God?* (Leicester: Inter-Varsity Press, 1985), pp. 196–205.

112 Alvin C. Plantinga, *God, Freedom, and Evil* (New York: Harper and Row, 1974), p. 147, as quoted by John S. Feinberg, *op. cit.*, p. 30.

113 Colin E. Gunton, *Becoming and Being. The Doctrine of God in Charles Hartshorne and Karl Barth* (Oxford University Press, 1978), pp. 31, 34, 81 (the quotation in inverted commas), 103f. He provides a study of Hartshorne who, following Whitehead, was a founding father of process theology.

114 For other criticisms of Plantinga, see Kenneth Surin, *Theology and the Problem of Evil* (Oxford: Basil Blackwell, 1986), pp. 71ff.

115 John Hick, *op. cit.*, p. 391, sees clearly that in Scripture 'evil is related in a dual way to the divine will' (*cf.* the emphasis on God's responsibility, the word remaining ambiguous); we shall return to this duality, but for the moment we point out what appears to us to be lacking in Hick's understanding: he does not make sufficient distinction between the *decretive* and the *preceptive* will of God; according to John Hick, God wills evil not only in a permissive and radically mysterious manner, but positively, as an indispensable means of soul-making, from which he derives good.

116 On this distinction, see Jacques Maritain, *De la grâce et de l'humanité de Jésus* (Paris: Desclée de Brouwer, 1967), and, on the whole subject, Henri Blocher, *Christologie* (Vaux-sur-Seine: Edifac, 1986), ch. III, particularly section C, pp. 194–228.

117 François Laplantine, *op. cit.*, pp. 126f.

118 John Hick also, *op. cit.*, p. 359, can write: 'Man's fallenness is thus the price paid for his freedom . . . .'

3. The solution by dialectical reasoning

1   Ernst Bloch, *La Philosophie de la Renaissance* (Paris: Petite Bibliothèque Payot, 1974), p. 79:

tin was consecrated to Jupiter, hence 'Jovian'; *cf.* p. 77 for the Gnostic influence. Our account of Boehme follows this great neo-Marxist thinker.

2   Quoted by Bloch, p. 85.

3   Quoted in *ibid.*, p. 95 (the text is taken from the *Six Theosophical Points*).

4   *Ibid.*, p. 86.

5   Quoted by Bloch, *ibid.*, p. 87.

6   *Ibid.*, p. 93.

7   *Ibid.*, p. 94.

8   *Cf. Systematic Theology* I (University of Chicago Press, 1951), p. 235.

9   *Ibid.*, p. 202, then p. 187.

10   *Cf. ibid.*, p. 253; vol. II (1957), pp. 20ff.; *cf. The Courage to Be* (London: Nisbet, 1952), p. 31f., the reference to the 'me-ontic' freedom of Berdyaev.

11   *The Courage to Be*, p. 32; *Systematic Theology* 3, p. 209; *Love, Power and Justice*, (London: Oxford University Press, 1954), pp. 37–40.

12   *Systematic Theology* I, p. 242.

13   *The Courage to Be*, p. 31.

14   This is the perceptive thesis put forward by Frederick D. Wilhelmsen in *The Metaphysics of Love* (New York: Sheed and Ward, 1962); we are not, however, ready to follow Wilhelmsen and to treat Tillich as an exemplary representative of the direction in which Protestantism is moving.

15   *The Courage to Be*, p. 170.

16   *Ibid.*, pp. 32f., 37–51.

17   *Systematic Theology* I, pp. 198–201.

18   *Ibid.*, pp. 259, 255, 202, respectively.

19   *The Courage to Be*, p. 32.

20   *Ibid.*, p. 171. The Trinity is explained by the dialectic of this life, in relation to the world, *Systematic Theology* I, pp. 53–59.

21   *Systematic Theology* I, pp. 134, 133 respectively; *The Courage to Be*, p. 176, also p. 178 (where Tillich speaks of 'the Church under the Cross').

22   Certain people think that in the end Tillich gave up the idea of the superiority of Christianity to Eastern religions, *cf. Christianity and the Encounter of the World Religions* (Columbia University Press, 1964); the question is much disputed. Tillich makes a certain distinction between Christianity and Jesus as the Christ (although the phrase 'as the Christ' refers to the understanding of the figure of Christ in the historical Christian community). Christianity stands at the personal pole of religious bipolarity, at the opposite pole to impersonal mysticism and the characteristic themes of Eastern thought, but Christ remains supreme in his kenosis and thus can be Lord of this very duality.

23   *Hegel* (Paris: Seuil, 1968), p. 13 (*cf.* p. 164).

24   *The Phenomenology of Spirit*, quoted in the preface to *Principes de la philosophie du droit* (Paris: Gallimard, 1973), p. 11.

25   Alexandre Kojève, *Introduction à la lecture de Hegel* (Paris: Gallimard, 1947) p. 574, also p. 541.

26   *Ibid.*, p. 539.

27   *Ibid.*, pp. 566ff. (long quotations from the *Lectures* of 1803–4); then p. 560, from a piece on *Natural Law* of 1802 (Kojève's brackets). See *Principes de la philosophie du droit*, pp. 353ff., also *Morceaux choisis* II (Paris: Gallimard, 1969), pp. 235ff.

28 *The History of Philosophy*, to be found in the French translation, *La Raison dans l'histoire* (Paris: UGE, 1965), pp. 100ff.

29 *Principes de la philosophie du droit*, pp. 171f.

30 K. Papaioannou, in the introduction to *La Raison dans l'histoire*, p. 17.

31 Dominique Dubarle, 'Absolu et histoire dans la philosophie de Hegel' in J. L. Leuba and C.-J. Pinto de Oliveira (eds.), *Hegel et la théologie contemporaine* (Neuchâtel/Paris: Delachaux et Niestlé, 1977), p. 110.

32 *La Raison dans l'histoire*, p. 17.

33 *Ibid.*, p. 100. If clarification is needed: 'Reason cannot dwell for ever on wounds inflicted on individuals, for particular ends are lost in the universal end.'

34 Jürgen Moltmann, 'The Right to Meaningful Work', ch. 3 of his *On Human Dignity* (ET London: SCM Press, 1984), p. 51.

35 Jean-Michel Palmier, *Hegel, Essai sur la formation du système* (Paris: Editions Universitaires, 1968), pp. 15ff., 72f., shows how deeply rooted this influence was. F. Châtelet, *op. cit.* (n. 23), pp. 121ff., quotes the most telling texts of his mature work. Dominique Dubarle, *op. cit.*, pp. 111f., examines the problem closely, showing the ambiguity of the relationship of Hegel's Christ to the historical fact of Jesus.

36 'Théologie politique de la libération' in *L'Espérance en action* (French tr. Paris: Seuil, 1973), p. 174; *cf.* 'Resurrection as Hope' in *Religion, Revolution and the Future* (New York: Charles Scribner's Sons, 1969), p. 61: in the new creation 'being and nonbeing are no longer intertwined' (as in the present); 'Towards a Political Hermeneutic of the Gospel', *ibid.*, p. 106: 'The ontological ambivalence determined through the creation *ex nihilo* is overcome in the *participatio in Deo*'.

37 Quotation from 'Gottesoffenbarung und Wahrheitsfrage' made by Gerhard Sauter in *Théologie de l'espérance II: Débats* (French tr. Paris: Cerf-Mame, 1973), p. 320, n. 11, referring to p. 224 where Sauter emphasizes the proximity to Hegel.

38 *Theology of Hope* (ET London: SCM Press, 1967), pp. 84, 170. In *The Crucified God* (ET London: SCM Press, 1974), p. 4, Moltmann speaks again of the 'cross of reality', and in the same breath mentions 'the sufferings of Christ, in the world's sufferings' (p. 5).

39 *The Crucified God*, pp. 17f.

40 *Ibid.*, pp. 151f.; here Moltmann follows C. Schmitt; pp. 193, 227.

41 *Ibid.*, pp. 202, 273, 338.

42 *Ibid.*, p. 218.

43 *Ibid.*, p. 254.

44 *Ibid.*, p. 239.

45 *Ibid.*, p. 245.

46 *Ibid.*, p. 247; but 'One cannot pray to an event' . . . Indeed, '[one] prays *in* God.'

47 *Ibid.*, p. 278.

48 *Ibid.*, p. 255.

49 'L'Absolu et l'historique de la doctrine de la Trinité', in *Hegel et la théologie contemporaine* (*op. cit.*), p. 193; Moltmann tries to balance (in a symmetry that is open to question) what he said with respect to the End and to the cross as an anticipation of the End, with a new emphasis on origins; *The Trinity and the Kingdom of God* (ET London: SCM Press, 1981) pp. 107, 111f., 152f., 159.

50 *The Trinity and the Kingdom of God*, pp. 105f., 151f., 159ff.; as for creation, Moltmann goes so far as to revive the idea of emanation (p. 113).

51 Being nineteen years old, in Germany, in 1945 . . . Moltmann recalls the memory of the

war, and also the disappointments that dampened his hopes in 1968, in *The Crucified God*, pp. 1f.

52   'Towards a Political Hermeneutic of the Gospel' *op. cit.* (n. 36), p. 100.

53   *Cf.* on this point his reply to Ernst Bloch, added to *Théologie de l'espérance* (French tr. Paris: Cerf-Mame, 1970), pp. 382ff. Contrast with Hegel, see Alexandre Kojève, *op. cit.*, pp. 523f., 538, 552f.).

54   A contribution to *Théologie de l'espérance II: Débats*, p. 268.

55   Reply to Bloch, *op. cit.* (n. 53 above), p. 387, n. 48.

56   *The Trinity and the Kingdom of God*, p. 49.

57   On universalism, as the result of the dialectical reversal, without faith being presented as the necessary means, *cf.* for example *The Crucified God*, pp. 102, 176, 178, 194f., 242f. On the unification of God and the world, see 'L'Absolu et l'historique de la doctrine de la Trinité, *op. cit.*, p. 200; *The Trinity and the Kingdom of God*, pp. 96, 159.

58   Quoted by Henri Bouillard, *Karl Barth, Parole de Dieu et existence humaine*, 2nd part (Paris: Aubier-Montaigne, 1957), p. 297.

59   'We have finally had to make do with "nothingness". It must be clearly grasped, however, that it is not used in its more common or abstract way, but in the secondary sense, to be filled out from Barth's own definitions and delimitations, of "that which is not".', *Church Dogmatics* (*CD*) III 3, p. 289, Editor's Note 1.

60   *Karl Barth, genèse et évolution de la théologie dialectique* (Paris: Aubier-Montaigne, 1957), p. 238.

61   *CD* IV 1, p. 7.

62   *Ibid.*, p. 12 (our italics). This position on the problem explains the Barthian rejection of the traditional distinction between the *person* and the *work* of Christ, p. 127.

63   *CD* IV 1, pp. 409f.

64   *CD* III 3, pp. 351f.

65   *Ibid.*, p. 352.

66   *Ibid.*, pp. 297, 352.

67   John Hick, *op. cit.*, pp. 134ff. (on death, p. 138), gives a good account of Barth's statements on the 'shadowside' of creation; he could have shown more clearly, however, that this shadowside signifies the threat of *das Nichtige*, originally, over creation.

68   *Ibid.*, p. 523 (Barth rejects the idea of the fall of angels, taught in Jude 6; *cf.* p. 530).

69   *CD* II 2, p. 739.

70   *CD* IV 1, pp. 46, 48. IV 3, p. 328, speaks of epiphenomenon.

71   *CD* III 3, p. 361.

72   *Ibid.*, p. 363.

73   *CD* IV 1, p. 747.

74   *CD* IV 3, p. 475.

75   We do not think it necessary to repeat the proof of this point which is commonly agreed on (*cf.* H. Bouillard, *Karl Barth, Parole de Dieu et existence humaine*, 1st part, pp. 243f.). We shall simply point out two references in the penultimate tome of his *Dogmatics*: *CD* IV 3.1, pp. 364f., 477f.

76   *CD* IV 1, p. 69.

77   *CD* II 2, p. 141 (our italics, of course).

78   See the studies by Pierre Courthial, reissued in *Fondements pour l'avenir* (Aix-en-Provence: Kérygma, 1981), pp. 17–41, 89ff.

79   *Religion in Contemporary Debate* (London: SCM Press, 1966), p. 50.

80   His response in Charles W. Kegley and Robert W. Bretall (eds.), *The Theology of Paul Tillich* (New York: Macmillan, 1952), p. 341 (our italics).

81   Alexandre Kojève, *op. cit.* (n. 25), pp. 572f.; *etc.*

82   J. Maritain, *Moral Philosophy* (ET London: Geoffrey Bles, 1964), p. 186. We warmly recommend the whole section on Hegel (except for his misconstruction of Luther), pp. 119–208, the most interesting part of the book and one of the finest things that he wrote.

83   We are summarizing the mocking criticism of Kierkegaard in *The Concept of Dread*, pp. 12f. (earlier on p. 10); and of Maritain, *op. cit.*, pp. 122ff., 132ff. (the quotation is from p. 134).

84   *The Concept of Dread*, pp. 12f.

85   'Negativité et affirmation originaire' in *Histoire et Vérité* (Paris: Seuil, 2nd edn. 1964), p. 320.

86   Picked up by Maritain, *op. cit.*, p. 192, n. 1.

87   'Der Geist kann das Geschehene ungeschehen machen', 'The Spirit can make what has happened not have happened', German quotation and ET in Maritain, *op. cit.*, p. 181, n. 5.

88   Carlos-Joseph Pinto de Oliveira, 'Conclusion' in *Hegel et la théologie contemporaine* (n. 49), p. 241 brings this out strongly, over against Hegel; on forgiveness, see Jacques Buchhold, *Le Pardon et l'oubli* (Méry-sur-Oise: Sator, 1989).

89   Shown clearly by Jacques Maritain, *op. cit.*, pp. 162ff., 201f.

90   These questions emerged in the Swiss symposium, *Hegel et la théologie contemporaine*, pp. 224, 225 ('The question is inescapable: what happens within God before the event of the Cross? Moltmann does not seem to us to be able to say.').

91   *L'Espérance en action* pp. 19f., 128 ('A life lived is a life which contains contradiction within itself'); *The Crucified God*, p. 218; *The Trinity and the Kingdom of God*, p. 174 (Hegel approved); p. 106 (a God who was not a creator would be imperfect, but creative love 'communicates itself by overcoming its opposite', *cf.* pp. 57f.), and p. 111 (creation implies alienation).

92   *The Trinity and the Kingdom of God*, p. 203; however, Moltmann discerns that ambivalence is not essential to freedom: 'true freedom . . . is simple, undivided joy in the good', 'the self-communication of the good' (p. 55).

93   *E.g. The Crucified God* is built on a rarely defended interpretation of the cry, 'My God, my God, why have you forsaken me?'; however, Moltmann recognizes that Luke understands it differently (p. 147), and does not dare even to consider the cry as historically authentic ('certainly an interpretation of the church after Easter', p. 146).

94   *Les Anges (Histoire des dogmes II-2b)*, translated from the German into French (Paris: Cerf, 1971), p. 236.

95   *Evil and the God of Love*, p. 148. *Cf.* p. 142: 'the particular speculation in which Barth indulges is mythological rather than rational'.

4. Scripture on evil, principally its origin

1   Among studies well worth reading we would mention that of Louis Ligier, *Péché d'Adam, péché du monde. Bible, Kippur, Eucharistie* vol. 1 (Paris: Aubier, 1960), part 1.

2   André Barucq, *Le livre des Proverbes* (Paris: Lecoffre-Gabalda, 1964), p. 34.

3   John Hick, *Evil and the God of Love*, p. 112 (*cf.* p. 94), criticizes Journet's argument about punishment restoring order; it 'arises out of an impersonal and legalistic way of

thinking'; what is not simple rhetoric in his objection depends on the exaggerated antinomy between personal and impersonal, which governed Hick's thought at the time (the book first appeared in 1966). On sin as chastisement, he follows Schleiermacher and his subjective reduction (pp. 233f.).

4 *The Trinity and the Kingdom of God* (ET London: SCM Press, 1981), p. 51.

5 *Cf.* Henri Blocher, 'Everlasting Punishment and the Problem of evil', in Nigel M. de S. Cameron (ed.), *Universalism and the Doctrine of Hell* (Carlisle: Paternoster, 1993), pp. 283–312. We try to deal there with Hick's objections.

6 The etymology remains a subject under discussion. It will be recalled that the prophets commonly made a play on words by announcing the *šōd* (from the root *šādad*) *šadday*, 'the devastation of *šadday*' (Is. 13:6, *etc.*).

7 *The Prophets* II (New York: Harper and Row, 1975), p. 18.

8 Curiously, Calvin quotes the parallel passage, Dt. 19:5, which does *not* refer the accident to the will of God (*Institutes* I 18.3); however, Calvin had earlier quoted the right text, Ex. 21:13 (*Institutes* I 16.6).

9 There has been discussion of the proper meaning here of the Greek *aneu tou patros*. Some translations restrict the meaning to 'without your Father knowing' (Jerusalem Bible, *cf.* J. B. Phillips); NEB gives 'without your Father's leave'; older translations give 'without your Father' (AV, RV, *cf.* NRSV); here we follow NIV (*cf.* RSV, and the robust wording of Moffatt, 'unless your Father wills it'). The context – reassuring the disciples and promising them protection – shows that it is a question of God's control of situations, not merely his knowledge of them. W. F. Arndt and F. W. Gingrich, *A Greek–English Lexicon of the New Testament* (Cambridge University Press, 4th edn. 1957), give for *aneu* 'without the knowledge and consent of'. Heinrich A. W. Meyer, *Kritisch exegetisches Handbuch über das Evangelium des Matthäus* (Göttingen: Vandenhoeck und Ruprecht, 1858), p. 239, gave an excellent comment on this: 'The reading *aneu tēs boulēs tou patros hymōn* is an ancient and accurate gloss. See the classical *aneu theou* and *sine Diis*.' The Lukan parallel, *i.e.* Lk. 12:6, does not carry a different meaning; for 'to forget' and 'to remember', when God is the subject, refer to his efficacious action.

10 According to Marvin R. Vincent, *Word Studies in the New Testament* (Grand Rapids: Eerdmans, 1949) I, p. 61.

11 Peter Geach, *Providence and Evil* (Cambridge University Press, 1977), pp. xii and 71.

12 *Op. cit.*, p. 312.

13 *Op. cit.*, p. 120.

14 'Réflexions sur la nécessité et la contingence', quoted by Charles Journet, *The Meaning of Evil* (London: Geoffrey Chapman, 1963), p. 114.

15 *Institutes* I 16.9; Calvin seems to follow Thomas Aquinas in *Summa* 1ᵃ qu. 19 art. 3, on the difference between absolute necessity and necessity *'ex suppositione'*. Calvin distinguishes further 'necessity . . . of consequent and consequence', that is to say of the event which follows by virtue of God's plan, and necessity of the consequential link itself (*i.e.* absolute or essential necessity).

16 *Institutes* I 17.6.

17 *Institutes* II 5.14.

18 See his most carefully balanced synthesis, *Institutes* II 5.9–11.

19 Journet, quoting Thomas Aquinas and Jacques Maritain, postulates, p. 149, that the capacity to sin belongs by nature to the essence of free will; p. 152, that elevation 'by initial grace' does not remove this 'basic faculty', for 'providence is not a corrupter but a

saver of Natures'; that is why, pp. 156ff., 'the normal, *ordinary* way' in which grace acts is 'to stir our souls', at which moment we may 'reject his loving-kindness', but it will bear fruit by its 'sovereignly efficacious influence' only if we receive it properly; in this way grace takes account of 'the treatment required by the nature of free creatures'. And yet in the state of glory the capacity to sin will cease, without our being deprived of free will (p. 153)! Above all, Journet has to admit an *'exceptional and extraordinary'* exercise of divine power, according to which God sends first of all an 'irresistible influence of grace' (pp. 158f.); then God converts rebellious wills by a miracle, as 'when he gives sight to a blind man or brings a dead man to life' (p. 160). No doubt God does this often but could not do it *always* in the world that he chose to make (p. 168). Quite apart from the contrast with Scripture where 'resurrection' is the very work of saving grace ('God made us alive', Eph. 2:5, 6, *etc.*), Journet's confusion seems insuperable: if the irresistible influence ['*motion imbrisable*', literally 'unbreakable motion'] 'corrupts' free will, how can God make use of it, even once? What is a statistical relationship doing here – 'often' but not always (40%, 70%, 95%?) – with the aim of resolving such a question of principle? (We shall not go into the question of his interpretation of Thomas Aquinas, except to say that the texts he appeals to do not appear to support his position conclusively; they may be read in such a way that they support the Augustinian position, pp. 160f., n. 31, 171.)

20 *Institutes* I 18.4.

21 *Institutes* II 4.3; *cf.* I 16.8 ('permit' can for Calvin have the sense of 'abandon' or 'give up'; in I 17.11 Calvin says that we can 'permit ourselves to God', *i.e.* '*com*mit' ourselves, or hand ourselves over, to him.) The term 'permission' is also used in his *Commentary on Genesis* (ET Edinburgh: Banner of Truth, 1975), I, p. 144, with an explanation to forestall any misunderstanding.

22 *Op. cit.*, pp. 162ff.

23 *Sin* (ET Grand Rapids: Eerdmans, 1971), pp. 52ff. Berkouwer is unfair to treat the use of the verb 'to will' as an attempt to explain evil.

24 Eighth sermon on Job, as quoted by Richard Stauffer, *Dieu, la création et la providence dans la prédication de Calvin* (Bern, Frankfurt and Las Vegas: Peter Lang, 1978), p. 148, n. 206.

25 *Op. cit.*, p. 148.

26 *Op. cit.*, pp. 162f., n. 37. Journet, however, takes no notice of a text in Augustine such as the following from ch. 43 of *On Grace and Free Will*: 'God works in the hearts of men to incline them after the pleasure of His own will, whether to good deeds . . . or to evil', in *The Anti-Pelagian Works of St Augustine*, vol. 3 (Edinburgh: T and T. Clark, 1876), p. 62. The preceding pages supply numerous examples from Scripture, which are also to be found in Calvin. Journet, furthermore, has not spotted that, for Calvin, God acts only in a privative manner (support for which is found in Jb. 12:16–25) and/or a punitive manner, without malignity ever proceeding from him: the stench that arises from a putrefying corpse is not to be blamed on the rays of the sun (*Institutes* I 17.5). On the non-necessity of the fall of man, see from a different angle the end of *Institutes* I 15.8, which answers Journet's misconstruction of III 23.8 (Journet, *op. cit.*, p. 83).

27 *Op. cit.*, ch. 2.

28 *CD* IV 1, pp. 409f.

29 *Ibid.* What liberated Barth to make this biblical discernment was, of course, his (unacceptable) idea of *das Nichtige* as the correlative of the creation but not belonging to it, opposing it. (Here is another instance of one evil used against another: one erroneous

idea puts another one to flight and thereby releases an insight that is indeed correct.)

30 'Solution à un problème éternel?' in *Le Mal est parmi nous* (Paris: Plon, 1948), p. 256. In the company of two such eminent theologians as Barth and Florovsky, we do not feel so isolated in our stand on this point. Pierre Gisel, *La Création. Essai sur la liberté et la nécessité, l'histoire et la foi, l'homme, le mal et Dieu* (Geneva: Labor et Fides, 1980), p. 43, n. 59, answers us only by the argument from tradition.

31 This logic is to be found operating particularly in the work of John Hick. Without seeing the problem we are raising, he insists on the proof which the fall is supposed to supply of the *prior* presence of the *posse peccare*, *e.g. Evil and the God of Love*, p. 316.

32 On this distinction, see the work of Reformed dogmaticians, *e.g.* Auguste Lecerf, *Introduction à la dogmatique réformée* I: *De la nature de la connaissance religieuse* (Paris: Je Sers, 1931), p. 253, and H. Bavinck, quoted by Berkouwer, *Sin*, pp. 52ff. Its origin is medieval, but the Scholastics applied the distinction to the will of man.

33 This is not a trick devised to force an agreement; when Calvin says that 'all this agrees well together' (R. Stauffer, *op cit.*, p. 197), it is the heart of his doctrine that he recognizes in the complementarity of the two verses.

34 This reading in the older English translations is retained in NASB, while NEB renders differently: 'they did not open their minds to love of the truth'.

35 The anthropomorphism in the phrase is obvious (or else one would have to deny the knowledge that God has of the heart); 'know' must mean 'bring out', 'bring to light'. Here we are concerned with the negative aspect, 'God left him to himself'.

36 *Institutes* II 4.2.

37 'The mind of this supreme judge of the world is not so independent as to be impervious to whatever din may be going on near by. It does not take a cannon's roar to arrest his thoughts; the noise of a weathercock or a pulley will do. Do not be surprised if his reasoning is not too sound at the moment, there is a fly buzzing round his ears; that is enough to render him incapable of giving good advice. If you want him to be able to find truth, drive away the creature that is paralysing his reason and disturbing the mighty intelligence that rules over cities and kingdoms. What an absurd god he is! Most ridiculous hero!' Blaise Pascal, *Pensées* (ET A. J. Krailsheimer, London: Penguin, 1966), no. 48, p. 43.

38 Calvin maintains that God's will is not 'two contrary wills', but is 'one and simple in him', *Institutes* I 18.3.

39 Berkouwer, *Sin*, p. 39, excludes it even in the state of glory.

40 This is essentially Calvin's position, as shown in R. Stauffer, *op. cit.*, pp. 123, 280.

41 Quoted by E. L. Mascall in *Theology and the Future* (London: Darton Longman and Todd, 1968), p. 62. Mascall's thought goes in the same direction as ours.

42 *The Trinity and the Kingdom of God*, p. 48.

43 Quoted in *Time* magazine, 22 December 1980, p. 25.

44 John Hick, *op. cit.*, does not stop repeating the unfortunate phrase 'the self-creation of evil *ex nihilo*' (pp. 68f., 72, 75, 180, 183, 238, 315, 368); what in fact he is doing is rejecting the singular discontinuity of evil (the qualitative leap, according to Kierkegaard). Hick quite simply asserts his wish to treat evil within the continuity of good.

5. Evil and the kingdom

1 Exegetes today give preference to the sense of 'reign', but several point out that to it

should be added the idea of the sphere in which it operates, *cf.* Donald Guthrie, *New Testament Theology* (Leicester: Inter-Varsity Press, 1981), p. 409, with support from Herman Ridderbos, *The Coming of the Kingdom* (Philadelphia: Presbyterian and Reformed Publishing Co., 1962), pp. 26f. The emphasis certainly falls on the lordship of God recognized and honoured; the *malᵉkût* or *basileia*, however, is not the abstract principle of authority, but a reality which God 'gives' to his little flock, which one can receive by becoming like a child, which one may 'enter' or be 'not far from'. The remarks of Rudolf Otto, *The Kingdom of God and the Son of Man* (ET London: Lutterworth Press, 1938), p. 53, are pertinent to this: 'Since the expression kingdom of God does not cover a strictly unified conception, but rather a complex of connotations, one must not ask how the kingdom is to be defined, but to what objective the whole of this term is directed.' N. Perrin, quoted by Guthrie, *op. cit.*, p. 431, suggests that it is to be taken as a symbol rather than a concept.

2 'The Kingdom of God' in Carl E. Amerding and W. Ward Gasque (eds.), *Dreams, Visions and Oracles* (Grand Rapids: Baker Book House, 1977), p. 135.

3 *Cf.* Alec Motyer, *The Prophecy of Isaiah* (Leicester: Inter-Varsity Press, 1993), p. 530.

4 Dirk H. Odendaal, *The Eschatological Expectation of Isaiah 40 – 66 with Special Reference to Israel and the Nations* (Philadelphia: Presbyterian and Reformed Publishing Co., 1970), pp. 61, 92 and *passim*. The whole of ch. 2, pp. 59–170, is entitled 'The Coming of the Kingdom'.

5 The rigorous double chiasmus which structures Zechariah 9 – 14 is magnificently illuminated by Paul Lamarche, *Zacharie IX – XIV, Structure et messianisme* (Paris: Gabalda, 1961).

6 *CD* II 2, p. 777.

7 *CD* IV 3, pp. 475 and 466.

8 *CD* IV 3, p. 302.

9 The NIV translation is preferable to that of RSV and NEB, following the fine argument of R. Otto, *op. cit.*, pp. 108–112, and G. E. Ladd in *Dreams, Visions and Oracles* (see n. 2 above), pp. 137f. One of the reasons for rejecting the other translation is that men of violence, being evil, quite simply cannot take the kingdom by force.

10 *CD* IV 3, pp. 302, 307.

11 Lewis S. Chafer, *Systematic Theology* (Dallas: Dallas Seminary Press, 1947–48), V, pp. 340ff.

12 *Ibid.*, pp. 347ff.

13 Herman A. Hoyt, 'Dispensational Premillennialism' in Robert G. Clouse (ed.), *The Meaning of the Millennium: Four Views* (Downers Grove: InterVarsity Press, 1977), pp. 87 and 90 (the kingdom 'in a position of abeyance or suspension', p. 90); *cf.* G. E. Ladd, *Jesus and the Kingdom* (London: SPCK, 1966), pp. 137ff.: 'the usual dispensational word is "postponed"', p. 94.

14 C. C. Ryrie, *Dispensationalism Today* (Chicago: Moody Press, 1965), ch. 5 (pp. 86–109).

15 Chafer, I, p. xix and *passim*.

16 Hoyt, *op. cit.*, p. 78 (also, 'It will be a *literal* kingdom', *ibid.*).

17 Chafer, I, pp. xixff., 39, 44; IV, pp. 10, 23f., 41ff., 47f., 127 (the woman of Yahweh is not the betrothed of the Lamb); V, pp. 349f.; VI, p. 81, *etc.* (Chafer, taking Phil. 3:1 to heart, never wearies of repeating the same things.)

18 Ryrie, *op. cit.*, pp. 45, 47, 132 (*cf.* pp. 137ff.).

19 *Ibid.*, p. 163.

20 For an evaluation of the whole, except for particular points of eschatology, see our course material *La Doctrine du péché et de la rédemption* (Vaux-sur-Seine: Faculté Libre de Théologie Evangélique, 1982, 1989), pp. 118–134. The hermeneutical literalism, which is sometimes more ingenious than it is coherent, finds itself up against the New Testament's treatment of Old Testament texts, and the separation between Israel and the church runs head first into the obvious meaning of numerous passages; that is the opinion of the theologians of all other schools including, for example, 'classical' premillennialists such as G. E. Ladd.

21 Chafer, IV, p. 26 (*cf.* p. 215); Scofield's note on Matthew 6:33; Ryrie, *op. cit.*, pp. 169f., who minimizes its importance, however, and quotes E. Sauer and A. J. McClain as writers who refuse to make the distinction; Hoyt, *op. cit.*, p. 84, like these last two, recognizes that the two terms are interchangeable.

22 This is the general opinion, which does not prevent our making an additional distinction. Oswald T. Allis, *Prophecy and the Church* (Philadelphia: Presbyterian and Reformed Publishing Co., 1945), pp. 300f., n. 11, observes: 'It is significant that Matthew uses the expression "heavenly Father" or "Father in heaven" repeatedly (about a score of times). This may indicate that his special reason for using the phrase "kingdom of heaven" was to stress the heavenly origin and nature of God's kingdom. The kingdom proclaimed by John and Jesus was not to be an earthly but a heavenly kingdom.' This is the opposite of the usage of the terms by dispensationalists, who, curiously, make the kingdom of *heaven* into a kingdom that is exclusively *earthly*.

23 *Cf.* its reduction in Ryrie, *op. cit.*, p. 172.

24 These confused phrases, which are not biblical, are to be found in Chafer (I, p. 45), Scofield, and even today in Hoyt, *op. cit.*, p. 86; *cf.* the criticisms made by O. T. Allis, *op. cit.*, pp. 84ff. Because Hoyt discerns that 'kingdom of heaven' and 'kingdom of God' are synonymous, his difficulty is to be seen again later on; admitting the participation in the kingdom by Christians today, in accordance with Col. 1:13, he explains: 'they are becoming a part of that phase of the kingdom which will serve as the aristocracy and ruling nobility when it is fully established on the earth at the Second Coming of Christ', p. 90.

25 *Cf.* the debate with the 'ultra-dispensationalists' on this point, Ryrie, *op. cit.*, pp. 194ff.; independently from him, the difficulties brought to light by Allis, *op. cit.*, pp. 139ff.

26 *New Testament Theology*, Donald Guthrie, (Leicester: Inter-Varsity Press, 1981), p. 419.

27 Hoyt, *op. cit.*, pp. 85f. *Cf.* pp. 147f. on Mt. 11:14.

28 It is in light of that passage that we understand the question of Acts 1:6: 'Are you at this time going to restore the kingdom to Israel?' It must have to do with the 'kingdom of God', in view of v. 3; and also the phrase is always used in Acts for the central content of the apostolic preaching. Rather than imagining the disciples, at the end of the forty days, still imbued with the Jewish ideas that Jesus had fought against, we think they were referring to *the opposite operation of the withdrawal* spoken of in Mt. 21:43, to the return to God by Israel, by recognition of the Christ (as Jesus gives reason to hope, Lk. 13:35, and as Paul proclaims in Rom. 11 under the image of the branches that have been cut off being grafted back into the olive tree).

29 For an overview, see André Feuillet, 'Parousie' in *Supplément au Dictionnaire de la Bible* VI (1960), cols. 1331–1419; Colin Brown, 'Parousia and Eschatology in the New Testament', in *The New International Dictionary of New Testament Theology* 2 (Exeter:

Paternoster, 1977), pp. 901–931 (*cf.* also B. Klappert on *basileia*, *ibid.*, pp. 381ff.; Donald Guthrie, *New Testament Theology*, pp. 409–431, 790–818, 868–874).

30 G. C. Berkouwer, *The Return of Christ* (ET Grand Rapids: Eerdmans, 1972), p. 83. Fritz Buri rightly takes 'crisis theology' to task for this flight into verticality, *Die Bedeutung der neutestamentlichen Eschatologie für die neuere protestantische Theologie* (Zurich and Leipzig: Max Niehaus, 1935). In Berkouwer's book, note the excellent response to Käsemann on 2 Pet. 3 (pp. 79ff.).

31 A. Feuillet, *art. cit.*, col. 1411 (*cf.* col. 1356).

32 *Cf.* Colin Brown, *art. cit.*, pp. 917ff., particularly pp. 920f., based on the work of E. Earle Ellis. *Cf.* also A. L. Moore, 'The delay of the Parousia in the New Testament', *TSF Bulletin* 52 (Autumn 1968), p. 14, which presents the substance of his major work, *The Parousia in the New Testament*, Supplement to *Novum Testamentum* (Leiden: E. J. Brill, 1966).

33 See the fine demonstration of this by I. H. Marshall, *Eschatology and the Parables* (London: Tyndale Press, 1963; 2nd edn. Theological Students Fellowship (IVF/UCCF), 1973). Throughout the work Marshall responds in particular to E. Grässer.

34 *CD* IV 3, pp. 292ff. This telescopic compression is, in our opinion, already present in Jn. 14. We are, however, reticent with respect to the trinitarian analogy proposed by Barth (pp. 294, 296 refer to the perichoresis); this enthusiasm for symmetry is not without its dangers.

35 *Eschatologie: Versuch eines dogmatischen Grundrisses*, *Theol. St.* 53 (Zollikon: Evangelischer V., 1958), p. 24.

36 *Cf.* Pierre Maury, *L'Eschatologie*, *Théol.* new series 8 (Geneva: Labor et Fides, 1959), pp. 62ff.

37 J. Stafford Wright, 'Times and Seasons' in *Dreams, Visions and Oracles* (*op. cit.*, n. 2), p. 168.

38 A. Feuillet, *op. cit.*, col. 1341.

39 *Art. cit.*, p. 13. Guthrie, *op. cit.*, p. 797, n. 26, quotes E. Schweizer with a similar meaning.

40 *CD* III 2, pp. 499f.

41 *Op. cit.*, p. 797. With one difference: Guthrie explains that there will be plenty of opportunity to flee, plenty of places of refuge available (*cf.* n. 4). We think rather that it is the coming of the Son of Man in the sense of a liberating intervention which could reassure the disciples, in accordance with the thought that 'for the sake of the elect those days will be shortened', 'he will see that they get justice, and quickly', *etc.*

42 *CD* III 2, pp. 499 and 478f. also A. L. Moore, *art. cit.*, p. 13.

43 Emphasized by R. T. France, *Jesus and the Old Testament* (London: Tyndale Press, 1971), pp. 139ff., 145ff., 169, 235.

44 *Ibid.*, pp. 145, 235.

45 *Ibid.*, particularly pp. 227–239 on vv. 24–27.

46 'La ruine du temple et la fin des temps dans le discours de Marc 13' in *Apocalypses et théologie de l'espérance*, *Lectio divina* 95 (Paris: Cerf, 1977), p. 257.

47 A. L. Moore, quoted and defended by Colin Brown, *art. cit.*, p. 912.

48 *CD* IV 3, p. 295.

49 A. L. Moore, *art. cit.*, p. 15.

50 Feuillet, col. 1397, comments: 'Thus no more than in the synoptics is the eschatological coming of the Son of Man restricted here to a univocal meaning.' Geerhardus Vos, *The Teaching of Jesus concerning the Kingdom of God and the Church* (Nutley, New Jersey: Presbyterian and Reformed Publishing Co., 1972), p. 85, also quotes Mt. 18:20 in this sense.

51 Quoted with approval by F. F. Bruce in his Foreword to *Dreams, Visions and Oracles*, p. 9. Every image has its limits, of course; it remains true that within time we are day by day approaching the Day (Rom. 13:11).

52 'The Return of Christ' in *Dreams, Visions and Oracles*, p. 145.

53 See F. F. Bruce, 'C. H. Dodd' in Philip E. Hughes (ed.), *Creative Minds* in *Contemporary Theology* (Grand Rapids: Eerdmans, 1st edn. 1966, 2nd edn. 1969), pp. 248f.

54 C. H. Dodd, *The Interpretation of the Fourth Gospel* (Cambridge University Press, 1953), p. 447, n. 1; J. Jeremias, *The Parables of Jesus* (ET London, SCM Press, 1954), p. 159.

55 Quoted by Dodd, *ibid.*

56 In *Revelation as History* (ET London: Sheed and Ward, 1979), pp. 134, 141 ('*Vorweg-nahme*'), and subsequently; in his Christology, it is the prolepsis of the end of history (the self-revelation of God) in the historical resurrection of Jesus which is the foundation of everything, the extension of the anticipatory character to the pre-Easter ministry and the eternal divinity (ontologically retroactive). That does not prevent Pannenberg from following 'consistent' eschatologists in part: 'There is no doubt that Jesus erred when he announced that God's Lordship would begin in his own generation' *Jesus – God and Man* (ET London: SCM Press, 1968), p. 266.

57 See, for example, *Théologie de l'espérance II: Débats* (French tr. Paris: Cerf-Mame, 1973), pp. 269, 273f. This language, however, is more characteristic of Pannenberg than of Moltmann; the latter prefers to speak of the resurrection as promise, of the promised future of Christ already manifested in the present, even of Jesus 'raised into God's future', 'into the final judgment of God', *cf. The Crucified God* (ET London: SCM Press, 1974), p. 168. The difference with Pannenberg comes in part from the blurred focus which affects the outline of the 'historical' event.

58 If the meaning and the self-revelation of God are the totality or the totalization of history, how will a totality be anticipated? It is difficult to see how that may be. (*Cf.* Moltmann's criticism of Pannenberg, *Theology of Hope* [ET], pp. 76ff.). Pannenberg feels the danger, and in order to allow for anticipation he distinguishes the final event and the totalization, *cf.* Ignace Berten, *Histoire, révélation et foi: Dialogue avec Wolfhart Pannenberg* (Brussels: Cep, 1969), pp. 30ff. (and n. 25). But the relation is not clear; Pannenberg's declarations appear to diverge from one another, to say nothing of the other difficulties arising from a Hegelianism deprived of its rational Necessity.

59 Peter Geach, *Providence and Evil* (Cambridge University Press, 1977), p. 54, underlines this with incisive clarity.

60 Moltmann rejects the idea of the fulfilment of the promise, speaking only of its confirmation and validation (*Theology of Hope*, p. 228); he expresses reservations concerning the present reign in heaven of the glorified Christ (*ibid.*, p. 158), considers that neither eternal life nor 'the eternal Spirit of heaven' is yet given to believers (*ibid.*, p. 162). We sympathize with his reaction against a vertical and a sacramental realized eschatology, but he patently takes it too far. In reality, Moltmann protects the dialectical identity which he posits between the crucifixion and the resurrection, and which makes him say later that the resurrection is not 'an event which followed his death' but that the death on the cross is the 'proof' of the resurrection, its immanent dimension (*The Crucified God*, pp. 73, 186, 182f.).

61 The use of the trinitarian analogy contributes to this, whether applied to the three forms of the return (see n. 34 above), or in terms of Creation, Reconciliation and Redemption (that is to come): *stemming from the christological concentration*, from the

method which infers the other 'moments' from the central moment. Creation is like a shadow cast before it, the final parousia like a subsequent reverberation.

62 *Le Royaume de Dieu et sa venue* (Neuchâtel and Paris: Delachaux et Niestlé, 1959), p. 48.

63 James Barr, *Old and New in Interpretation* (London: SCM Press, 1966), pp. 52ff., has denounced the cliché with his customary vigour (the dichotomist point of view attributed to the Greeks is well attested in first-century Judaism). Moltmann, *Theology of Hope*, p. 213, n. 1, expresses himself suitably on the subject, under the influence of Käsemann. Robert H. Gundry, *Sōma in Biblical Theology with Emphasis on Pauline Anthropology* (SNTS Monograph 29; Cambridge University Press, 1976), has launched the most devastating attack on the anthropological monism of Pedersen, Bultmann, J. A. T. Robinson and the like. *Cf.* Donald Guthrie, *New Testament Theology*, p. 176 (*cf.* p. 177, the 'dual idea' in Paul).

64 'Postmillennialism' in *The Meaning of the Millennium*, pp. 125ff.

65 The same outline is to be found again in Rev. 20:1–3, 7–10: Satan restricted, then briefly let loose. We interpret the passage in a similar way.

66 That the beast is Rome, whether more or less literally, there is no doubt. But we base our reading on the primacy of biblical symbolism in the book of Revelation and on the influence of Dn. 7, and so consider that the heads are not, or not only, successive emperors. Is it possible to imagine that they represent the seven great empires that we meet in Scripture? The five which have fallen: Egypt, Assyria, and the first three in Daniel: the sixth, which is reigning, *i.e.* Rome (the fourth of Dn. 7); the eighth is the same (666), risen, after a seventh which is hard to distinguish (Christendom?). Paganism, dealt a mortal blow by Christ at the time of the Roman Empire, will enjoy an astonishing resurrection before being destroyed (modernism and postmodernism?). Such a hypothesis rests on a bold, speculative reading, as do so many interpretations of the book of Revelation.

67 For this still future interpretation of the antichrist, see J. R. W. Stott, *The Epistles of John* (Leicester: Inter-Varsity Press, 2nd edn. 1988), pp. 108–110.

68 *Le Retour de Dionysos* (Paris: les Bergers et les Mages, 2nd edn. 1976).

69 *Parusia: Hoffnung und Prophetie* (Heidelberg: Verl. Lambert Schneider, 1960), p. 601; the whole of the section pp. 597–617 is relevant to our study, and beyond (p. 624, 'Fleischwerdung des Ewigen Wortes ist Entfesselung . . . des Fleisches').

70 *Ibid.*, pp. 602, 605f., and, on this last point, 609 (p. 608, dialectic destroys dialogue). Schütz's theology suffers, however, from a blind spot: the denial of God's plan for history ('kein Heilsplan', p. 622). Schütz is a victim of humanistic 'freedom', and cannot see that he then has only a God who is finite and stripped of his divinity.

71 '*Mimikri-Kirche*', *CD* IV 3, p. 267. Barth emphasizes the impotence of this evil, despite its danger: the proof is the resurrections of the church from within the false church on more than one occasion, p. 268.

72 *Ibid.*, p. 316.

73 *Ibid.*, pp. 331f.

74 *CD* IV 1, p. 738.

75 *Ibid.*, pp. 735f.

76 *CD* IV 3, p. 333.

77 *Ibid.*, p. 329, then p. 328.

78 *Ibid.*, pp. 329, 360.

79 *Ibid.*, p. 361.

80 *The Return of Christ*, p. 137. Berkouwer gives up trying to find the answer.

81 *CD* IV 1, p. 315.

82 *CD* IV 3, pp. 355f.

83 *CD* IV 1, p. 250; *cf.* II 2, p. 567.

84 *Cf.* Oscar Cullmann's interpretation of the *katechōn*, 'that which still restrains', in 2 Thes. 2:7 – 'there is a reference to the missionary preaching as a sign pointing to the end', *Christ and Time* (ET London: SCM Press, 1951), pp. 164f.; in Rev. 20:3, the devil is bound (and so the final denouement is delayed) in order to allow the evangelization of the nations.

85 Calvin, *Institutes* II 15.4.

Conclusion

1 ' "Tenebrae noctium". Position d'un chrétien de l'eglise orthodoxe russe' in *Le Mal est parmi nous* (Paris: Plon, 1948), pp. 262f.

2 Karl Rahner, *Le Courage du théologien*, dialogues published by Paul Imhof and Hubert Biallowons (Paris: Cerf, 1985), pp. 127f., has stated as his considered opinion that a theology of the death of God (or in God), as found in the writings of Urs von Balthasar, Adrienne Von Speyr and Moltmann, is 'fundamentally gnostic'. (It is Rahner who names them.)

3 Blaise Pascal in 'The Mystery of Jesus', *Pensées* (ET A. J. Krailsheimer, London: Penguin, 1966), no. 919, p. 315.

Islam in the Modern World
A Christian perspective
NORMAN ANDERSON

Sir Norman Anderson explains distinctive aspects of modern Islam – its theology, sacred law, fundamentalism and mysticism. He then considers the historical and contemporary debate about the incarnation and atonement of Christ. The belief systems of Islam and Christianity are thereby thrown into sharp relief. Particularly, he illuminates the astonishing power of Islam as it struggles to confront the conflicting currents of modern culture.

Islamic nations today are becoming increasingly unified by fundamentalism, shaping contemporary events. This book assists in a mutual understanding of the roots of Islam and Christianity, providing a welcome basis for relevant and rewarding dialogue. The author is a Christian and distinguished Islamic scholar. This book represents over half a century of reflection.

256 pages   *Large paperback*

APOLLOS

The Origins of
New Testament Christology
Updated edition
I. HOWARD MARSHALL

A re-issue, with an updated postscript, of a book which first appeared in 1976. In it Dr Marshall is concerned to guide students of the New Testament through the intricacies of the scholarly debate about the person of Christ.

Using the methods of historical and critical study, the author shows how unwarranted is the radical historical scepticism of many scholars. He argues that the origins of New Testament Christology lie firmly in the pre-Easter period and in the resurrection of Jesus.

The postscript briefly traces the course of the continuing debate since 1976 and surveys some of the key contributions to it.

144 pages   *Large paperback*

Apollos

The Faith of Israel
Its expression in the books of the Old Testament
WILLIAM J. DUMBRELL

This book's purpose is twofold. It helps the reader to understand each Old Testament book individually; and it makes plain the message of the Old Testament as a whole.

Following the order of the Hebrew Scriptures rather than the English Bible, William J. Dumbrell outlines the theological intention of the biblical writers, book by book. Throughout he is concerned to relate the message of the Old Testament to the unfolding history of Israel, since he believes that 'Israel's confessional faith came to her progressively and through history'.

288 pages   *Paperback*

APOLLOS BOOKS

Theology of the Reformers
TIMOTHY GEORGE

Here is a book which makes the reformers come alive.

The author is an outstanding younger Reformation scholar who knows how to communicate with the ordinary reader. He lets the reformers – Luther, Zwingli, Calvin and Menno Simons, the great Anabaptist leader – speak for themselves by quoting extensively from their writings.

The carefully selected quotations, together with Dr George's interpretative comments, make you feel that you are with the reformers in their passionate striving for the reformation and renewal of the church.

Because of its exceptional clarity and readability, Dr George's book will appeal not only to students and lecturers, but to the general reader as well.

338 pages   *Hardback*

APOLLOS